"It has been said that suffering is the most common denominator amon~ ' `ans. Whether you are one of the 660 million people our suffering takes another form, you've probably e is a book that addresses the difficult issues surro m- mend Waters and Zuck, and the other contrib ch to provide a biblical response to suffering and

Steve Bundy,
Managing Director, Joni and Friends Christian Institute on Disability

"This is the most comprehensive biblical theology on the mystery of human suffering I have ever read. Illustrated by deeply moving experiences from the lives of many of its authors, it can easily be adopted for effective public teaching."

David C. Cotten, Pastor of Senior Adults, Edmond Faith Bible Church;
Retired Vice President for Student Services,
Professor of Pastoral Ministries, Dallas Theological Seminary

"Sadly, ministry to the disabled within our churches is a much-neglected area. This book rightly identifies it as a priority that demands our thoughtful response. Yet, never before has a single book combined such a rich harmony of insights from scholars across so many disciplines, ranging from biblical studies to the medical field. It reminds us, too, that disabled believers have an important ministry to the nondisabled in the church as bearing witness to the grace of God, who redeems all our sufferings with a loving purpose. This book will serve as a valuable resource in churches, colleges, and seminaries for years to come."

Gary Cook, President, Dallas Baptist University

"Who doesn't ask *why*? It is the question we all consider. I am grateful for this biblical and personal approach to suffering, which will minister love and healing to the body of Christ."

Jack Graham, Pastor, Prestonwood Baptist Church, Plano, Texas

"The question as to why righteous individuals suffer is as old as the days of Job, a contemporary of Abraham. *Why, O God?* first faces the problem biblically, searching the Scriptures to find God's perspective on suffering. Then it faces the problem experientially, as many who have seriously suffered share their stories to show the sufficiency of God's grace and what they learned from their sufferings. A study of the first will provide a foundation for understanding suffering, and a study of the second will be an encouragement to all who suffer, because they bear testimony of the grace of God. This balanced approach provides a work that will answer many questions as to why the righteous suffer, and is highly recommended."

J. Dwight Pentecost, Distinguished Professor of Bible Exposition,
Emeritus, Dallas Theological Seminary

"What a wonderful book! Waters and Zuck have uniquely addressed the problem of suffering through the testimonies of those who have suffered and the lessons God has taught them. The wisdom of these fellow pilgrims is thoroughly buttressed with profound biblical studies by seminary professors, giving us needed insight into the question *why*. Any pastor or counselor will benefit from reading this—most of all, anyone who suffers or who knows someone who does. Highly recommended!"

Joseph Dillow, former President, BEE World

Why, O God?

WHY, O GOD?

SUFFERING AND DISABILITY
in the BIBLE *and the* CHURCH

EDITED BY

LARRY J. WATERS
ROY B. ZUCK

FOREWORD BY RANDY ALCORN

CROSSWAY

WHEATON, ILLINOIS

Why, O God? Suffering and Disability in the Bible and the Church
Copyright © 2011 by Larry J. Waters and Roy B. Zuck
Published by Crossway
        1300 Crescent Street
        Wheaton, Illinois 60187

Cover design: Studio Gearbox
Cover images: Veer and iStock
Interior illustrations: Dawn Waters Baker
Interior design and typesetting: Lakeside Design Plus

First printing 2011
Printed in the United States of America

Unless otherwise indicated, Scripture quotations are from the ESV® Bible (*The Holy Bible, English Standard Version*®), copyright © 2001 by Crossway. Used by permission. All rights reserved.

Scripture quotations marked NASB are from *The New American Standard Bible*®. Copyright © The Lockman Foundation 1960, 1962, 1963, 1968, 1971, 1972, 1973, 1975, 1977, 1995. Used by permission.

Scripture quotations marked NIV from the *Holy Bible, New International Version*®. Copyright © 1973, 1978, 1984 Biblica. Used by permission of Zondervan. All rights reserved. The "NIV" and "New International Version" trademarks are registered in the United States Patent and Trademark Office by Biblica. Use of either trademark requires the permission of Biblica.

Scripture references marked NKJV are from *The New King James Version*. Copyright © 1982, Thomas Nelson, Inc. Used by permission.

All emphases in Scripture quotations have been added by the authors.

Trade paperback ISBN:	978-1-4335-2580-3
PDF ISBN:	978-1-4335-2581-0
Mobipocket ISBN:	978-1-4335-2582-7
ePub ISBN:	978-1-4335-2583-4

Library of Congress Cataloging-in-Publication Data
    Why, O God?: suffering and disability in the Bible and the church / edited by Larry J. Waters and Roy B. Zuck; foreword by Randy Alcorn.
         p. cm.
    Includes bibliographical references and index.
    ISBN 978-1-4335-2580-3 (tp)
        1. Suffering—Biblical teaching. 2. Suffering—Religious aspects—Christianity. 3. People with disabilities—Biblical teaching. 4. Church work with people with disabilities. I. Waters, Larry J. II. Zuck, Roy B.
    BS680.S854W49 2011
    248.8'6—dc22
                                                2011001940

Crossway is a publishing ministry of Good News Publishers.

VP		22	21	20	19	18	17	16	15	14	13	12	11
14	13	12	11	10	9	8	7	6	5	4	3	2	1

CONTENTS

FOREWORD

Randy Alcorn

I have never said yes to endorsing a book, much less to writing its foreword, unless I have believed in it. I anticipated *Why, O God?* would be good, but I am pleased to find it exceptional.

Let me offer some context. Because I've written books about heaven, over the years I've received hundreds of letters from people whose loved ones have died after extended periods of suffering. While researching my recent book *If God Is Good: Faith in the Midst of Suffering and Evil*, I read close to a hundred books on the problem of evil and suffering—books by theologians, pastors, physicians, Holocaust survivors, and atheists. I interviewed many sufferers, some of them victims of abuse, diseases, disabilities, and accidents, others who've lost children and spouses.

This is why I don't appreciate neat, tidy, and superficial references to suffering that seem to say, "Cheer up," and "God will protect his children from suffering," and "It's not so bad if you're a Christian." Actually, it's sometimes *very* bad. As our dear friend Joni Eareckson Tada—one of this book's contributors—told me, "Suffering is a messy business."

Why, O God? addresses issues in the Bible, theology, church and pastoral ministry, counseling, and much more. Each chapter makes a unique contribution, and the whole is greater than the sum of its parts. Rarely have I seen such biblical and theological knowledge integrated with moving and helpful personal stories and extremely practical ministry guidance. And as a bonus, I enjoyed the beautiful art.

There's something in this book for everyone—whether you're looking for biblical perspective on suffering, insights in how to serve those who suffer, hands-on guidance on establishing a disability ministry in your church, or help in dealing with the ethical questions in end-of-life issues.

I particularly appreciate the fact that the writers are not strangers to suffering. After forty plus years in a wheelchair, Joni says, "Disability ministry is not disability ministry unless the disabled are ministering." One of the authors has raised an autistic child, another's wife has multiple sclerosis, one is an insulin-dependent diabetic who's had two kidney transplants and is legally blind. Another—whom I know personally—grew up with a disabled father, stood by his daughter in a long battle with leukemia, then suffered a serious head injury from a biking accident, which has resulted in nine years of nearly constant pain. These are not ivory-tower theologians, out-of-touch academics, or head-in-the-sand clerics. These are real people in touch with real people, daily serving a God who shed real blood on a cross.

One of the things I love about *Why, O God?* is how it demonstrates that there is much more to helping suffering people than wheeling them forward in healing services and then hiding in the back of the church those who aren't healed. My friend John, a church elder, told me of a handicapped woman visiting his church who had been in many other churches over her lifetime. After observing him on the platform in his wheelchair with the other elders, she told him he was the first disabled church leader she had ever seen.

My mind goes to one of the stories in *Why, O God?*, about six men in a church being trained to take care of a disabled man in eight-hour shifts in order to free his wife to attend a weekend women's retreat. Everyone came out ahead—the man, his wife, the men who served, and the Lord who took pleasure in it. This is the church at its best—not denying suffering or ignoring it or cloaking it, but bringing to it the love of our suffering Savior. An uncaring world will never be won to Christ by an uncaring church. But when people see the church behaving like this, they will line up to find out about the Christ we serve.

Finally, I appreciate this book's eternal perspective. Christians are empowered by God's Spirit, covered by his grace, and assured of the resurrection to the happiest life imaginable on a new earth. We should never forget this, and it can sustain us through great heartache. But meanwhile *we are not immune to the fall and the curse.* Only when we fully realize this can we see the loving power of God's sovereign grace. Because even the very bad, in the hands of our Redeemer who turned history's worst Friday into Good Friday, is part of the "all things" God will ultimately work together for our good.

To top it off, the final paragraph of *Why, O God?* is one of the most powerful you'll ever read. You *could* turn to it now, but I recommend reading all the way through to appreciate its significance!

My thanks to each of the authors and also to Larry Waters and Roy Zuck for assembling this excellent book. May it bring honor to the risen Christ and enrichment to his people until the day we see his outstretched hands, marked by the scars of his love for us.

Dawn Waters Baker graduated magna cum laude from Dallas Baptist University. During her college years she became aware that art was her calling. She gives seminars for churches, colleges, and seminaries on how God can be communicated through art. Dawn's work is displayed at the Riverbend Fine Art Gallery, Marble Falls, Texas, and is also collected by many businesses and private owners, including Dallas Theological Seminary and Dallas Baptist University. A list of her awards and commissions can be found at www.dawnsartsite.com.

PART ONE

CHALLENGE AND NEED

Suffering, by Dawn Waters Baker. "I prayed a long time about this painting as I wrestled with how to share suffering to which all could relate," she explains. "At first I had a wheelchair in the picture, but I thought viewers would feel, 'that's them,' instead of seeing themselves. So I had the figure seated as if he is getting up from bed, and the weight of his day is crashing in on him like a storm. The dark sky conveys how suffering feels: there is nothing but darkness. I painted a soft light coming in on the right as God's presence. He is not overtaking the man, and the man has not even noticed the light. Yet God is there."

Joni Eareckson Tada is the founder and chief executive officer of Joni and Friends, an organization that is accelerating Christian ministry in the disability community. A flagship program of Joni and Friends is the Christian Institute on Disability, which offers internships, studies in public policy, curriculum, and coursework in disability ministry. The institute promotes a biblical worldview on key issues related to disability, including stem-cell research, health-care reform, euthanasia, and physician-assisted suicide.

Joni's role as a disability advocate led to a presidential appointment to the National Council on Disability during the passage of the Americans with Disabilities Act. She also served on the State Department's Disability Advisory Committee under Secretary of State Condoleezza Rice.

I

REDEEMING SUFFERING

Joni Eareckson Tada

Greg Barshaw, an elder at the Grace Community Church in Southern California, received a phone call one day from a neighboring pastor. This pastor and Greg often studied the Bible together over coffee in the mornings. The pastor said, "Greg, a friend in my church has a little boy with multiple disabilities, and I'm wondering if your church would want to help this mom and dad and young boy." Greg thought it was a good idea. He would be happy to reach out to this family. But then, when he pressed the pastor further, he realized that additional issues were involved. Then the pastor said, "To be honest, Greg, I'm afraid one day this father will walk into my study, slam his fist on my desk, and say, 'Tell me why God has cursed me with a son with multiple disabilities? How is it that God has done this?' I have no idea how I would answer him."

Greg realized that this pastor had an issue with the theology of suffering and that he was not sure how he would address that family's needs. One can understand that pastor's fear. God's sovereignty is sometimes scary. Sometimes a person wakes up in the middle of the night—even as I do right now with chronic pain that is related to my disability—and he thinks, *Who is this God?*

Does God say, "Into each life a little rain must fall," and then aim a hose in earth's general direction to see who gets the wettest? That's what I thought when

I was first injured. When I took that deep dive into shallow water, I thought that my spinal-cord injury was a flip of the coin. I thought it was a fluke of fate. I thought if God had anything to do with it, he was caught off guard. Perhaps he was off somewhere listening to the prayers of more obedient saints. Or perhaps he was in the Middle East fulfilling prophecy. Or maybe he was listening to the prayers of people with cancer.

I did not know where God was, but I assumed he was not on that raft when I took that dive. I figured that Satan probably was the one who came sneaking up behind me while God had his back turned, and Satan gave a big hard shove with his foot, and off I went. And then God turned around, saw what had happened, and responded, "Oh, my! How will I patch things up for this girl's good and my glory?"

And then I imagined God had to go get his WD-40 and his fix-it glue and come back and scratch his head and try to figure out how he could fix my situation. I assumed God had been caught off guard when Satan threw a monkey wrench into his plans for my life. A view like that may have been the view of a seventeen-year-old girl lying on a Stryker frame, frustrated, frightened, embittered. But a view like that says that God is helpless and is held hostage by my handicap, just as I was.

I realized, though, that God was bigger than that. I had enough sense to know that the Bible probably has answers for my plight somewhere, but I had no idea where to look. I had no idea where to turn.

After I got out of the hospital, a young man knocked on my door. He was a sophomore from the local high school where I had graduated. He knew I had some tough questions about God. He did not have all the answers, but he said he was willing to help me in a Bible study, and he would assist me in tackling the tough questions about why this happened. And when he told me he would be willing to do that, the very first thing I did was ask him straight on, "How can this be God's will?"

Just a year earlier Steve had prayed that God would draw me closer to him. So how could this be an answer to that prayer? If this is the way God treats his believers, especially young believers, he would never be trusted with another prayer again. How could any of this be God's will? That was a good question forty years ago, when I broke my neck, and it is still a good question today.

Many are asking the same question. They may not have broken necks. But some of them have broken hearts, and others have broken homes. Some are experiencing hardships that have ripped into their sanity, leaving them numb and bleeding, and they too ask, "God, how can this be your will?"

Steve said a very wise thing to me. "Look, Joni—think of Jesus Christ. He was the most God-forsaken man who ever lived. And if we can find answers for his life, they should be able to suffice for your life. So, Joni, let me turn your question around. Do you think it was God's will for Jesus to suffer as he did? Do you think it was his will for Jesus to go to the cross?"

"Well," I thought, "that's a stupid question. Of course it was God's will for Jesus to go to the cross."

And then he said something curious. "I want you to look at all the awful things that happened to Jesus on that cross. No doubt it was the Devil who inspired Judas Iscariot to hand over the Savior for a mere thirty pieces of silver. And no doubt Satan prodded Pontius Pilate to hand down mock justice in order to gain political popularity. And no doubt it was the Devil who inspired that mob to scream for Christ's crucifixion. And no doubt it was the Devil who pushed those soldiers to torture Jesus. How can any of that be God's will: treason, injustice, murder, torture?" He had me there, because I could not conceive of those things being part of God's will.

But then Steve did an interesting thing. He turned to and read Acts 4:28. "They"—that is, Herod and Pontius Pilate, the mob in the streets, and the soldiers—"did what [God's] power and will had decided beforehand should happen" (NIV). And the world's worst murder suddenly became the world's only salvation.

God did not violate the will of the people who did those awful things. The sin was in their hearts. God permits all sorts of things he does not approve of. He lets out the rope so that they might fulfill their evil plans and wicked schemes. Perhaps the Devil thought, *I will stop God's Son dead in his tracks. No more of this ridiculous talk about redemption.* But God's motive was to abort that devilish scheme and throw open the floodgates of heaven so that whoever will may come to him. God always aborts devilish schemes to serve his own ends and accomplish his own purposes.

"Joni," my friend Steve said to me, "God permits what he hates in order to accomplish what he loves." Heaven and hell can end up participating in the exact same event but for different reasons. Ephesians 1:11 puts it plainly: God "according to [his] purpose . . . works all things according to the counsel of his will." I found strange comfort in that thought. I believe it was Dorothy Sayers who said, "God wrenches out of evil positive good for us and glory for Himself." In other words, *he redeems it.*

God redeems suffering. The God of life is the only one who can conquer death by embracing it. And so death no longer has the victory, and neither does suffering. Christ has given it meaning, not only for salvation but also for sanctification, and that is the best part. It tells us we are no longer alone in our hardships, our disabilities. Our suffering is not a flip of the coin; it is not a fluke of fate. We are not in the middle of some divine cosmic accident. No, our suffering can be *redeemed*. Oh, the wonder of such a thought that it is all for our sanctification, our relationship with him, and our witness to a world in need of redemption.

God will often permit suffering, just as he is allowing it in my life. After forty years of quadriplegia, with my chronic pain and now shortness of breath, I can say, God will permit that broken heart. God will permit that broken home. God will permit that broken neck. Suffering then is like a sheep dog snapping at my heels, driving me down the road to Calvary, where otherwise I might not naturally be inclined to go.

God is the one who takes suffering like a jackhammer and breaks apart the rocks of resistance. He takes the chisel of the pain and the bite of hardship and chips away at one's pride. And then sufferers are driven to the cross by the overwhelming conviction that they have nowhere else to go. No one is naturally drawn to the cross. Human instincts do not naturally lead people there.

This may well be the most important reason every church needs a disability ministry in its congregation. People with disabilities, unlike others, are driven to the cross by the overwhelming conviction that they have no other place to go. That is eventually what happened to the father of that little boy with multiple disabilities.

The father came to realize that God allowed this in his life. God brought this child into their family so that that family might be united around the cross of Jesus Christ, that they might find help in time of need, that they might find strength in their weakness. People with disabilities may well be God's best audiovisual aids of these powerful truths to the rest of the congregation. Disabled people are audiovisual aids on how suffering should be handled. People who are suffering always have something to say to those who are facing lesser conflicts.

Let me give you an example. If you listen to the *Joni and Friends* radio program or read our materials, you know that we hold retreats all across the country for families affected by disabilities. This year we will hold twenty-two retreats serving almost three thousand disabled children, adults, and other family members. Just before one of these retreats, I was glancing over the registration cards of the people who would be attending. I came across the name Karla Larson, and when I read the description of her disability, I was amazed. She had lost both of her legs. She was legally blind. She had suffered a heart attack, had had a kidney transplant, and had lost three fingers.

I thought, *Oh, my. I'd better meet this woman.* I could not believe that she would be strong enough to make it to our family retreat.

When I wheeled up to Karla Larson, excited to meet her, I said, "Karla, I'm so glad you were able to come. I'm so surprised you're here." She replied, "Well, Joni, I thought I'd better come before I lose any more body parts." Obviously this woman had not lost her sense of humor. And she had such a fabulous time at our family retreat. We had five days of fun, inspiration, Bible studies, wheelchair square dancing, wheelchair zip lines, wheelchair disco—it was such fun.

After the retreat Karla wrote me a thank-you note, tied to the toe of one of her plastic prosthetic legs. She sent me her foot in the mail. And the note read, "Dear Joni, since all of me cannot be with all of you all of the time, part of me will have to do." Observing that woman—a double amputee, missing her fingers, legally blind, with a kidney transplant—I learned something about God.

What I learned is that perhaps the greatest good that suffering can work for a believer is to increase his or her capacity for God. The greater one's need, the greater will be his capacity. And the greater the capacity, the greater will be one's experience of the Savior. Karla is a good example of how people can embrace their sufferings, knowing that God's power will always show up in their weakness.

This is what disability ministry is all about. It is less about helping poor unfortunates. It is less about blessing them. And it is more about them blessing the "nondisabled." It is more about the way people think of what their weaknesses are to do for them. People like Karla should remind believers how suffering "works" in their lives. According to 1 Corinthians 12:22, "The parts of the body that seem to be weaker are *indispensable.*"

In the body of Christ we often admire the hands, feet, eyes, and lips, and all the showy, up-front gifts—the attractive parts. I tend to think Karla Larson would make a good pancreas in the body of Christ. Not very comely, not very attractive to look at. In fact, people do not even talk about the pancreas, but the body cannot survive without it. The body can survive without use of the hands. I can prove that. The body can survive without the use of the feet. I can prove that too. But the body cannot survive without a pancreas.

This is why weaker members are indispensable. People who are weak, people like Karla Larson, showcase Titus 2:7: "Show yourself . . . to be a model of good works." They set an example by doing what is good; they showcase the Lord's ability to others. They sustain those who face lesser conflicts.

If the grace of God can sustain a woman who is a double amputee and half blind, or if God's grace can sustain a quadriplegic who deals with chronic pain, then everyone ought to be boasting in his affliction, delighting in his infirmity. As sufferers rejoice in their weaknesses, they can then boast that Christ's power is made manifest in them.

People's disabilities can be the best embodiment of these marvelous truths from God's Word. Disability ministry is a *ministry of redemption*. If the cross can be seen not as a symbol of torture but as a symbol of hope and life, then a wheelchair can be "redeemed" from a symbol of confinement to a representation of an intimate fellowship with the Lord Jesus Christ.

If someone looks at a person like Karla and thinks, "I could never handle suffering like hers," or if someone looks at me and thinks, "I could never be a quadriplegic like you," then maybe that person needs to read 1 Peter 2:21: "To this you have been called, because Christ also suffered for you, leaving you an example, so that you might follow in his steps."

Karla is now in heaven. Her disabilities finally took over, and she lost a few too many body parts. But I know she's rejoicing in heaven. No more intimate, sweeter fellowship with the Lord Jesus Christ can ever be realized than through suffering. God shares his joy on his terms, and those terms call for believers to suffer in some measure as his precious Son suffered when he was here on earth. And the union and the sweetness of intimacy with the Savior is priceless.

So disability is ministry. It is not an off-to-the-side, nice ministry to pitiable, poor unfortunates who need help. Rather, disability ministry is an up-front, in-your-face demonstration of these valuable lessons. It is a means of showcasing redemption to everyone, helping them learn how to respond to their own afflictions as well as helping them understand God's motives in their suffering.

When my accident happened, maybe the Devil's motive was to shipwreck the faith of that young, seventeen-year-old girl. Maybe he wanted to use her to make a mockery out of God's goodness. Maybe he hoped to defame God's sweet character. But remember, God is in the business of aborting devilish schemes. And God's motive in my accident was to abort that devilish scheme and turn a headstrong, stubborn, rebellious teenager into a woman who can reflect something of his patience, something of his perseverance, something of his endurance, something of his character. And after forty years in a wheelchair, I can say that my own suffering has lifted me out of my spiritual slumber. It has got me seriously thinking about the lordship of Christ in my life. It has helped convince this skeptical, cynical world that my God is worth trusting. It has shown me that we can be loyal to him despite our afflictions and infirmities, that disability ministry should have priority in the church, and that heaven is real.

And my suffering has shown me that there are more important things in life than walking and using your hands. Most of all, it has shown me that Jesus Christ, the Man of Sorrows, saves and sanctifies through suffering. And the wonderful part is that a person does not have to break his or her neck to believe it.

Daniel R. Thomson, a ThM graduate of Dallas Theological Seminary, has practiced physical therapy in both the rehabilitation and home-health settings for twelve years. Because of his clinical and personal experience, he has developed a passion for ministering to and through individuals affected by disability. Daniel and his wife, Kim, a pediatric occupational therapist, share a desire to encourage church leaders to value ministry endeavors that intentionally include the disabled.

2

A BIBLICAL DISABILITY-MINISTRY PERSPECTIVE

Daniel R. Thomson

Disability ministry is not disability ministry until the disabled are ministering.
—JONI EARECKSON TADA

Chuck Jones, a Dallas Theological Seminary graduate of the class of 1984 (MABS) and 1992 (ThM), has recently been diagnosed with amyotrophic lateral sclerosis (Lou Gehrig's disease). This is a degenerative motor neurological disease that results in progressive weakening of the entire body, ending in paralysis and eventual death. It is a brutal, relentless disease with no known cure. When Chuck was first officially diagnosed, his neurologist insisted that he join a local Lou Gehrig's secular support group. Chuck's initial reply was noteworthy, "I don't want to go there right now to learn how to die. I'd rather initially be with fellow Christians who have ALS to learn how to live!" Unfortunately no such group was known to exist.

If there is ever a group of individuals who trust and eagerly anticipate the fulfillment of the eternal promises of God, it is the believing disabled. If there is ever a group of individuals who seek to have God's purposes demonstrated in and through their lives, it is the believing disabled. When Chuck was diagnosed, he did not want to put up the white surrender flag and go home to his deathbed. He wanted to see God work through his life and his disability while coming to know others who had the same goal. Chuck was less concerned about the *why* of his diagnosis. Knowing his sovereign God, he wanted to know the *what*. What did God want to use this disease *for* in and through his life and the lives of others with the precious time he had left?

When encountering individuals affected by disability, believers are often content to "minister" empathetically *to* their needs, if they honestly reach out and minister to this population at all. Rarely do Christians recognize God's potential power when he ministers *through* them. When someone in a wheelchair offers someone a glass of water on a hot sunny day, that speaks volumes. When someone who in the world's perspective has reason to curse God but instead praises him, trusts him, and serves him and others—despite circumstances—there is power! Power that can be felt. Power that can be seen. Power that testifies to the truth of the gospel working intimately in and through their lives. Should believers be surprised to see God work through human weakness? Jesus Christ tells us otherwise: "My grace is sufficient for you, for my power is made perfect in weakness" (2 Cor. 12:9). In weakness his plan unfolds. Through human weakness his purposes are accomplished. When churches as a whole grasp this concept, understanding its full implications, individuals affected with disabilities should be seen as essential in the body of Christ (1 Cor. 12:22).

A Large and Notable Gap

I have worked as a physical therapist for twelve years. Approximately nine of those years have been in home health. Clearly a monumental gap exists between the local churches and the disabled population. All too often individuals and families go through the most difficult trials and circumstances of their lives in isolation from the Christian community. Available support is fleeting. Relationships are few. Stress is high. Caregiver burnout is frequent and inevitable. Marriages fall apart. Abuse sometimes settles in. Financial ruin draws nearer every day. Who will help close this gap while helping to meet real needs? It is the prayer of the authors of this text that the current and future generations of pastors and Christian servant-leaders will lead their congregations to do just that. Typically if the shepherds do not lead, the flock will not follow.

A Growing Population Affected by Disability

Cornell University published its *2007 Disability Status Report* for the United States based on data from the American Community Survey. This study estimated that the approximate number of individuals in the United States with a significant functional disability who are both over the age of five

Table 1.
US prevalence of disability in 2007
Disability Prevalence Rates

6.3 percent for persons ages 5–15
6.8 percent for persons ages 16–20
12.8 percent for persons ages 21–64
29.7 percent for persons ages 65–74
52.9 percent for persons ages 75 and older*

*Erickson and Lee, *2007 Disability
Status Report: United States*, 3.

and noninstitutionalized is 41.3 million. This is approximately one in seven Americans. The study estimated that in southern states, this ratio drops closer to one in five.[1] For example, in the year 2000, Dallas County, Texas, had an estimated population of 392,311 individuals with a disability among 2,014,547 people over the age of five.[2] More realistically the government-funded National Organization on Disability reports that 54 million Americans are affected by disability.[3] This number does not take into account the additional millions of family members who are touched by their loved one's disablement.

The prevalence rates for disability in the United States are striking (see table 1). As age increases, so does the percentage of individuals with a functional disability. Roughly one in sixteen American children between the ages of five and fifteen have a functional disability. The rate skyrockets to approximately one in two for individuals over the age of seventy-five.[4] The US Bureau of the Census predicted that "Americans 65 years old and over will make up 20 percent of the

[1] W. Erickson and C. Lee, *2007 Disability Status Report: United States* (Ithaca, NY: Cornell University Rehabilitation Research and Training Center on Disability Demographics and Statistics, 2008), 3–7. This report uses the American Community Survey definition of disability, which is "based on three questions. (1) Does this person have any of the following long-lasting conditions: (a) blindness, deafness, or a severe vision or hearing impairment [sensory disability]? (b) a condition that substantially limits one or more basic physical activities such as walking, climbing stairs, reaching, lifting, or carrying [physical disability]? (2) Because of a physical, mental, or emotional condition lasting six months or more, does this person have any difficulty in doing any of the following activities: (a) learning, remembering, or concentrating [mental disability]? (b) dressing, bathing, or getting around inside the home [self-care disability]? (3) Because of a physical, mental, or emotional condition lasting six months or more, does this person have any difficulty in doing any of the following activities [asked of persons ages sixteen and older]: (a) going outside the home alone to shop or visit a doctor's office [go-outside-home disability]? (b) working at a job or business [employment disability]? A person is coded as having a disability if he or she or a proxy respondent answers affirmatively for one or more of these six categories" (ibid., 44).
[2] "County Information: Dallas County, Texas," Rural, Research, and Training Center on Disability in Rural Communities: University of Montana, accessed October 15, 2009, http://rtc.ruralinstitute .umt.edu/geography/countydisabilitydetails.asp?county=48113&state=texas.
[3] National Organization on Disability, accessed October 15, 2009, http://nod.org. See Jack McNeil, "Americans with Disabilities: Current Population Reports," *U.S. Census Bureau Demographic Programs* (February 2001): 70–73.
[4] Erickson and Lee, *2007 Disability Status Report*, 3.

total population by the year 2030 compared with about 12 percent currently."[5] The brief concluded that the prevalence of disability in most communities is expected to accelerate notably in the coming decades.

Key Observations from Disability Statistics and Prevalence

Observation 1: Suffering and Disability Are Normal in This Life

Often one of the first things my patients say while processing their long-term prognosis from a functionally limiting disability is, "I just want to be *normal* again." Are they experiencing a "normal" experience on this side of eternity? Should Christians be surprised by disability? Considering its prevalence, is it normal or abnormal to have a disability in this life? Taking this question a step further, is it normal or abnormal to suffer even if one is a Christian?

In her insightful book, *Same Lake, Different Boat*, Stephanie Hubach asks these same questions. While processing a biblical theology of suffering and disability when her child was born with Down syndrome, Hubach wrote:

> On every level of every dimension of the human experience there is a mixture of both the blessedness of creation and the brokenness of the fall. Disability is essentially a more noticeable form of the brokenness that is common to the human experience—a normal part of life in an abnormal world. It is just a *difference of degree* along a spectrum that contains difficulty all along its length.[6]

The prevalence numbers suggest that having a disability is actually a normality in this present world. Unfortunately the prosperity gospel suggests that since Jesus Christ suffered and died for the world, people need not suffer in this life. With this view, many people of faith see disability as an abnormality. When we suffer personally or encounter individuals who are suffering, it is vitally important to maintain a biblical perspective toward God's goodness and his sovereignty while also recognizing the reality of evil and suffering in this world that impacts *both* Christians and non-Christians. Several chapters in this book discuss a biblical theology of suffering and disability, but here it is important to capture a glimpse of God's overarching plan for suffering and disability as it relates to the timeline of human history.

---

[5]John M. McNeil, "Disabilities Affect One-Fifth of All Americans: Proportion Could Increase in Coming Decades," *U.S. Census Bureau Census Brief* (December 1997): 1–2.
[6]Stephanie O. Hubach, *Same Lake, Different Boat: Coming alongside People Touched by Disability* (Phillipsburg, NJ: P&R, 2006), 29 (italics hers).

Living between the Trees

Trees maintain a prominent place as representative markers in God's plan for human history (see fig. 1).[7] Specifically the "tree of life" is the focus here. Twice this tree is found in Scripture. In Genesis 2:9 it is at the heart of the garden of Eden. In Revelation 22:2 the tree of life is found bordering the "river of the water of life" (v. 1) in God's eternal kingdom. People today are living in a time "between the trees." In both contexts the tree of life flourishes in a place unblemished by the effects of sin, without the presence of suffering and death. Suffering and disability are literally nonexistent in these worlds of perfection.

Figure 1.
Living between the trees: a biblical perspective on suffering and disability

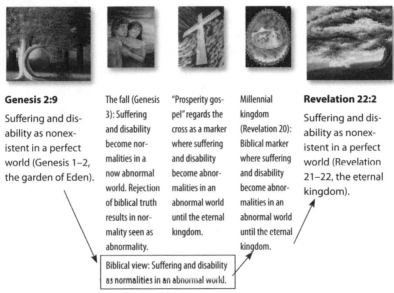

Genesis 2:9

Suffering and disability as nonexistent in a perfect world (Genesis 1–2, the garden of Eden).

The fall (Genesis 3): Suffering and disability become normalities in a now abnormal world. Rejection of biblical truth results in normality seen as abnormality.

"Prosperity gospel" regards the cross as a marker where suffering and disability become abnormalities in an abnormal world until the eternal kingdom.

Millennial kingdom (Revelation 20): Biblical marker where suffering and disability become abnormalities in an abnormal world until the eternal kingdom.

Revelation 22:2

Suffering and disability as nonexistent in a perfect world (Revelation 21–22, the eternal kingdom).

Biblical view: Suffering and disability as normalities in an abnormal world.

Adam and Eve were the only human beings to dwell in the perfect world of the garden of Eden. Something drastic changed the everyday reality that every human being after them would face, including Adam and Eve later in their own lives. When sin entered, suffering and disability become a normality in what is now a cursed, abnormal world (Gen. 3:14–19). After the fall, suffering and disability now exist as a normality in that they are common and expected. This is now a cursed, abnormal world for it is tainted by the effects of human sin, now outside of God's perfect environment of the garden of Eden. This reality of suffering and death from its onset persists for both believers and nonbelievers to this very day.

---

[7] Artwork by Dawn Waters Baker (Dawn@dawnsartsite.com) and Tom Banker (www.faithartists.com).

If one holds a prosperity-gospel perspective toward life, suffering and disability in a sense have become an abnormality in this abnormal world until the eternal kingdom begins. After all, if a believer is not supposed to suffer ("God wants you to have health and wealth in this life"), then suffering and disability do not fit the paradigm. With this viewpoint suffering and disability historically become an abnormality at the cross of Jesus Christ. He suffered and died so that people do not have to. With this belief, faith in him and his sacrifice provides access to his extended grace (including physical and material blessings).

Biblically speaking, believers should expect hardships, sufferings, and even disability in this life (e.g., John 15:18; 16:33; Rom. 8:23, 35–39; 2 Cor. 4:16–18; 2 Tim. 2:3; 3:12; 1 Pet. 1:6–7). Suffering and disability are a normality in an abnormal world, as Hubach observes, even beyond the cross of Jesus Christ. Long-term earthly prosperity with the absence of suffering is not the norm. However, in the future—in the millennial kingdom (Revelation 20)—suffering and disability will become an abnormality in an abnormal world. With Jesus reigning on the throne with resurrected saints (vv. 4–6), death and suffering will not have a hold on those who have been resurrected. Disability and suffering will be abnormal (actually nonexistent) among those who have been raised. Even with Christ on the earthly throne of David, suffering and death will still exist during this future time in history, especially against the deceived (vv. 7–9), which makes this time period abnormal, not yet a part of God's perfect plan to be revealed with the eternal kingdom.

One day as promised, the Devil, suffering, and death will finally be done away with forever (vv. 10, 14). But until then they still have a presence among and against humanity. Today faith in Christ does not exempt one from suffering, hardship, and eventual death before the return of Jesus Christ. The beauty of it all is seen in what God ultimately accomplishes through suffering as part of his sovereignty and plan (Rom. 8:28), with the sacrifice of Jesus on the cross being the ultimate example. God works redemptively through suffering and death—even if people do not understand or see all the reasons *why*. Believers, however, do know the *Who*, which makes it possible to endure temporary hardships as one maintains an eternal hope and biblical perspective toward the realities of life.

Observation 2: Something Needs to Change!
How many church rosters reflect the prevalence rates for disability in the United States? Are local churches honestly inviting to those affected by disability? Does the children's ministry have one child with a disability for every sixteen

who are present? Herein lies the gap. Research shows that the disabled are out there—often behind closed doors where few go.

As a home-health physical therapist, I have witnessed what suffering and disability in isolation can do to families in the home. Something needs to change. Outcomes from the 2000 US census suggest that two in every seven American families have a family member with a disability.[8] Think of the ramifications! The impact of disability goes far beyond the individual with the disablement. If a church does not intentionally minister to the needs of individuals with functionally limiting disablements, the family as a whole is not being ministered to adequately. The whole family may avoid church if there is no place for their disabled loved one. Considering the millions of families who in turn suffer in isolation, it is not surprising that families who have children with a disability have significantly higher rates of divorce or separation, as well as lower average household incomes, when compared to families with children without a disability.[9] What is being done to minister to these families? Through their research and satellite offices around the country, Joni and Friends (a leading global disability ministry organization, joniandfriends.org) estimates that only 15 percent of churches have an organized disability ministry. Something major needs to change.

Observation 3: Disability Ministry Needs to Reach across the Whole Spectrum
Bonnie Banker, director of Joni and Friends, Dallas, recently compiled a list of known church-based disability ministries in the Dallas–Fort Worth metroplex. Her search revealed fifty-three churches in the metroplex with an "official" disability ministry. However, in the Dallas yellow pages alone (not including Fort Worth) there are fifteen pages of churches listed in small print! Of the fifty-three ministries, thirty-five minister only to *children* with disabilities (66 percent). As stated earlier, in the year 2000 Dallas County had an estimated 392,311 individuals with a disability among 2,014,547 people over the age of five.

Several conclusions can be drawn from these facts. First, disability ministries are relatively few in light of the overwhelming number of churches in the metroplex. Second, the ratio of disabled to nondisabled in most churches is probably much wider than the ratio in the community (one in five). Third, the focus of the majority of disability ministries in the metroplex is with children, the segment of the population with the fewest disabled. This final point is not

---

[8]Qi Wang, "Disability and American Families: 2000," *U.S. Census Bureau Demographic Programs* (July 2005): 1–3.
[9]Robert M. Hodapp and Diane V. Krasner, "Families of Children with Disabilities: Findings from a National Sample of Eighth-Grade Students," *Exceptionality* 5, no. 2 (1994–1995): 71–81.

meant to downgrade the importance of "special-needs" ministries to children and their parents. These ministries are doing a great job. However, a children's "special-needs" disability ministry is just the starting point. True disability ministry needs to go much further since the majority of the disabled population is over the age of eighteen. If a disability ministry is led by a children's pastor, this may be more of a hindrance than a help, for over time this can stunt growth of the ministry to other age-groups.

The First Church of the Nazarene in Pasadena, California (paznaz.org), has a disability ministry called In His Image that more adequately covers the age spectrum. The keys to the whole ministry are an involved, accepting church led by a senior pastor who enthusiastically supports the ministry, and the disability pastor assigned to lead it.

A person with a disability does not necessarily have a cognitive impairment. Take, for example, Henry, who recently suffered a stroke that paralyzed the right side of his body and impaired his ability to speak. He can clearly understand everything stated to him, but he is not able to respond verbally. This condition is known as expressive aphasia, which commonly follows a stroke that affects the left side of the brain. Henry decided he wanted to visit a local church one Sunday morning. He entered the building in his wheelchair, and an usher greeted him. When Henry was unable to respond, the usher instinctively directed him to the adult special-needs ministry class, which teaches a fourth-grade level curriculum. Insulted, Henry did not return to the church, nor had he any desire to pursue any church relationship following this incident.

A true disability ministry must reach across the age spectrum and the cognitive spectrum. A disability ministry that is geared only toward those who are cognitively dependent can cast a degrading shadow within the church culture on those disabled who are cognitively independent. This observation is not meant to place cognitively independent disabled individuals in a corner. However, having an intentional aspect of the disability ministry that serves them is essential. This aspect of the ministry can be a key available resource to reach out and meet real needs while promoting healthy integration within the church and its ministries. Often the ministry needs first to reach "in" to the nondisabled congregation and church staff to educate them about common disablements and appropriate etiquette rooted in unconditional love, a nonjudgmental approach, and mutual respect.

Observation 4: Disability Ministry Is Not Just a Ministry "Out There"
It is easy for someone to read the statistics, consider the conclusions, and gain a glimpse into the needs of the disabled, yet not *feel* a connection to disability

ministry. After all, this is a portion of church culture that has been mostly out of sight and out of mind. However, disability is closer than many realize.

The words *disability, abnormality,* and *special needs* often have strong mental images and perceptions associated with them. Yet no one desires to be labeled, especially when the label conveys the idea that one is not able to perform a task or that he is special, abnormal, or needy. For a moment, let us turn the table. A label that everyone without a disability wears, whether knowingly or not, is *temporarily able-bodied.* It describes people who are not disabled but live one accident, disease, or event away from disability. The truth is that we are closer to the possibility of disability than we may realize. The prevalence rates confirm this. As age goes up, so does the prevalence—from one in sixteen among children to one in two among senior adults. Much time, money, and effort can be invested in creating and leading a disability ministry that serves "others." One day, however, this ministry may in fact serve you! What would it mean then to you personally? What would it mean to your family?

Closing the Gap While Promoting God's Ministry

Disability ministry does not have to begin in a church with a fully devoted salaried staff and an itemized budget. It can begin with one individual seeking to meet the needs of another. It can be as simple as reaching out to the child in the corner in a wheelchair or offering to babysit for a church member who has a child with a disablement. It can be opening the doors of the church and allowing a secular Alzheimer's support group to use the church facilities for free. Or some church members can volunteer to help a local assisted-living facility or nursing home. However it begins, the principle is to start small and build well. Eventually the ministry can grow to a point where a more structured disability ministry is needed.

Figure 2 offers a general guide to organizing and developing a more official disability ministry.[10] It is by no means exhaustive or inclusive of all possible church contexts. It does, however, provide insight into a few key items needed for the ministry to succeed over the long haul.

A Word about Church Culture

As shown in item number 1 on the diagram, the key to a successful, well-integrated disability ministry is to first assess and then take steps to further develop a healthy, accepting church culture. A disability ministry will not flourish in an environment where the church is uninviting and not open to change. Scott Daniels and Steve

---

[10]Adapted from James Rene, "How to Start a Disability Ministry in the Church," in *Foundations: Christian Perspective on Disability Ministry* (Agoura Hills, CA: Joni and Friends, 2009).

Figure 2. A suggested method of development

1. Assess Culture	2. Approach Leadership	3. Develop a Unified Team	4. Survey Church and Community
a. Conviction	a. Success depends on it	a. No "lone rangers"	a. Needs assessment
b. Value	b. Battle the view, "high cost, little return"	b. Involve medical, educational special- ists, and disabled	b. Interviews
c. Ownership			c. Community research
d. Action			

5. Plan	6. Vision Cast	7. Train Volunteers	8. Launch
a. Short/long-term goals	a. Church leaders	a. Policies and procedures	Remember, start small, build well!
b. Policies and procedures	b. Congregation	b. Behavior tips	
c. Training manuals	c. Community	c. Safety	
d. Curriculum	d. Website	d. Disability overview and etiquette	
e. Room prep	e. Awareness events		

Green have developed an Action Assessment Chart that attempts to identify how receptive a church is to those with disabilities. Their four cultural stages have been expanded and described below by Joni and Friends:[11]

- *Stage 1: Conviction*—"A belief that something should be done by someone, but not necessarily by your church. At this stage, churches are content to let the church across town offer a disability ministry."
- *Stage 2: Value*—"The next step toward action. Churches begin to value a ministry when they recognize that it is in line with their church's mission statement. Leaders begin to consider how a disability ministry could help them accomplish their vision and reach their community."
- *Stage 3: Ownership*—"Happens when one or more people volunteer to take responsibility for the ministry with the approval of church leaders. Until someone says, 'I'll do it!' ownership may be only a mirage."
- *Stage 4: Action*—"Occurs when church leaders give their blessing to a plan and the plan is implemented. Goals are set and reported on. Families affected by disability feel welcome and included at church."

Senior pastors can encourage their churches to minister to individuals affected by disability, thus creating avenues where disability ministry flows as

---

[11]Ibid. See also Pat Verbal, *Special Needs, Special Ministry* (Loveland, CO: Group Publishing, 2004), 34–35.

a normal aspect of church life. Having a servant-minded, respectful, and loving church is essential for an integrated disability ministry to succeed.

A Suggested Ideal

A fully developed and mature disability ministry should minister to individuals of all ages and all cognitive abilities across the entire disability spectrum. This may require having a disability pastor who is over the entire program. One possible model includes four primary components: children's "special-friends" ministry, teen/young-adult disability ministry, adult disability ministry, and inreach/outreach disability ministry.

Children's Special-Friends Ministry

Integrating children with special needs in regular church classrooms is a meaningful goal when it is in line with parents' wishes. Often an older trained "buddy" assigned to a child with a disability can promote and assist with successful integration. Other times having a "special-friends room" geared toward the child's needs is the best option. Working with the parents is key when making this determination. Jessica Baldridge, former director of disability ministry at Prestonwood Baptist Church in Plano, Texas, further elaborates in her chapter on such a special-friends room and on serving those who benefit from such a setting.

Service directed specifically to the child with a disability also ministers profoundly to the parents. Knowing their child is included, loved, and cared for by the church creates a sense of belonging that is often absent in the community at large. Having a special-friends ministry allows parents to reconnect with each other and God. It also promotes relationships with others in the church community, which is desperately needed in this population. Often parents with a disabled child go it alone. They need Christian families without disabled children to walk alongside them and their difficulties, actively assisting when needed. Some churches can and should develop care groups that adopt a special-needs family. Having genuine (not superficial) friendships grounded in a common faith is essential while living out the Christian life. Having friendships with other families affected by disability is also comforting. Creating a parent support group that regularly meets at the church is essential when constructing a special-friends ministry. It is wise to have trained volunteers care for the children at the church during these meetings, which creates a "safe place" for parents to relax and relate.

Another aspect common to many special-friends ministries is to have "respite night" at least one night per month. The idea is to have trained one-on-one volunteers take care of and play with children with disabilities while parents go on a date or spend time with their nondisabled children. Many churches have had success with such programming. Since divorce is common in families affected by disabilities, it is essential to minister to the whole family. Helping provide such a ministry can and does save marriages, and it is a healthy outlet for church members and volunteers to serve and be blessed by serving.

Teen/Young-Adult Disability Ministry

Integrating children with disabilities in a group is a noteworthy goal with children's disability ministry. But this can become more complicated when working with teens and young adults, especially if a cognitive deficit is present. Peer pressure and image become an issue. Teens want to be with those with whom they can identify. They do not necessarily view it as "cool" to hang out first with people who have disabilities. Unfortunately, some teen disability ministries have disabled teens and buddies sit in the back row with little or no connection to the main group.

A determined, gifted, sensitive, and involved youth pastor can model and lead teens to understand that it is in fact "cool" to reach out to teens with disabilities. Teens can minister to fellow teens with disabilities in impactful ways. After all, teens with disabilities want to belong too. Teens who reach out first to people with disabilities are being Christlike by connecting with those on the margins and bringing them in intentionally (Luke 14). What's "cool" is when the teens *with* disabilities minister to the teens *without* disabilities. This is the big surprise with this ministry. Teens with disabilities can model and often demonstrate unconditional love and acceptance that other teens need to see and experience. An effective teen or young-adult disability ministry can help build Christlike character in young people. Having a disability pastor who works intimately with the youth pastor can yield positive fruit if successful integration is a goal.

In some circumstances (and especially if it is the parents' preference), reverse integration can be an option. This occurs when a group of teenagers without disabilities integrates into a class designed for teens with disabilities. In this venue the teens with disabilities have fellowship and interaction with their peers in an environment that can be more inviting and interactive. It also spares teens with disabilities from having to listen to a thirty-minute talk from the youth pastor in the mainstream class if attention span is an issue.

Church leaders should make every effort to include teens with disabilities in mass outings that the youth ministry holds. Using buddies can be helpful, but incorporating groups of teens to help can also aid in promoting unity within the youth group. Also, service projects should not be reserved just for the able-bodied. When the disabled serve, no matter how small or how large the task, they are given opportunity to use their spiritual gifts for God's glory.

Adult Disability Ministry
Integration, reverse integration, group outings, and service-by-disabled principles can apply also to adult disability ministry. Having groups just for adults with disablements can also be considered (and may be preferred by some with a disablement), but unity in the body of Christ is the goal. It is too easy to develop a Bible fellowship just for adults with disabilities as a separate entity or place where these individuals are expected to go. Having an adult disability ministry does not mean that *all* disabled have to be cornered into this ministry, including the cognitively independent individuals affected by disability. But the ministry should exist and have options that reach across the entire spectrum.

As alluded to earlier, church staff and ushers in particular need to be educated on how some physical disabilities can mask an individual's true cognitive ability. The lesson can be summed up by the old cliché, "Don't judge a book by its cover." Beneath the disability may indeed be a treasure hidden in a jar of clay. It may also be helpful to educate the congregation at large on being "disability friendly." Perhaps even devoting a series in Sunday school or an adult Bible fellowship on disability education is something to consider. Joni Eareckson Tada's *Barrier Free Friendships: Bridging the Distance between You and Friends with Disabilities*[12] is an excellent resource that can be used in a small-group setting for such a purpose.

Disability Ministry Inreach and Outreach
Individuals with disabilities who are served in the church may in turn serve best with the church's disability outreach. Ministry *to* can become ministry *through*. After all, the disabled can empathize with other disabled individuals as no one else can. This does not, however, exclude the congregation at large from actively participating. There may be some in the congregation with various specialties to serve in unique ways. This could include those in construction, doctors, physical therapists, occupational therapists, speech therapists, behavioral specialists, and teachers, to name a few. Utilize their gifts as the Lord guides. Below are a few suggestions for disability ministry outreach:

---

[12]Grand Rapids: Zondervan, 1997.

- Network with doctors, schools, and community services that serve individuals affected by disability. This should include home-health agencies.
- Reach out to local secular disability support groups. Offer services and assistance. Attend meetings. Develop relationships with attendees. Involve the congregation.
- Host a free church-wellness clinic.
- Offer a free, well-advertised, well-organized wheelchair repair clinic.
- Create "adoption groups" that adopt a family with a disabled loved one in the church or in the community. Groups of at least eight or nine will help prevent burnout.
- Have church members volunteer at local schools, targeting teachers, parents, and children affected by disability.
- Host a Young Life Capernaum group.
- Be involved in your local Special Olympics program.
- Have construction teams available in your church to build ramps or assist with home remodeling issues.
- Create care bags that can be taken to homebound disabled persons. Be sure to follow up with these individuals. The key here is relationships, not just a one-time service. Joni and Friends has a Special Delivery ministry (joniandfriends.org) that can assist with this ministry in particular.

Remember Chuck?

Chuck Jones now attends a secular Lou Gehrig's disease support group. He has learned the value of suffering alongside those in similar circumstances—choosing community over isolation. Chuck's focus, however, has not changed. He is focused not so much on a cure or the disease itself, but on living out the Christian life with trust in God's sovereignty and plan. Through his faith God is ministering in Chuck's disablement. Chuck is reaching those he would not have reached in other ways, many through his ALS support group. He is an encouragement to others in the group. He comforts them "with the comfort with which we ourselves are comforted by God" (2 Cor. 1:4). God's work through Chuck's disablement goes much further than the walls of where the group meets.

Speaking at a recent ALS fundraising meeting, Chuck stated, "There are three things I thank God for: (1) my current struggle for what I can still do, (2) the emotional and spiritual support I get from Christian friends, and (3) the fact that I face death with confidence because of my faith in Jesus Christ. In Christ, 'Death is swallowed up in victory. O death, where is your victory? O death, where is your sting?'" (1 Cor. 15:54–55). Afterward both Christians and non-Christians approached Chuck. One individual responded, "You have a great attitude, and your faithfulness to our Savior in the face of this terminal disease has encouraged me to examine my commitment to Christ. Thank you." Another said, "Your speech had an impact on me. I am now looking at life, death, and eternity in a startling different light and considering the Christian faith more than ever before."

A Look at Jesus Christ

Disability ministry was a daily, normal component of Christ's ministry while he walked on earth. He routinely ministered to and through those with disability of all ages, of all types of disabilities, and at all levels of cognitive understanding. Twenty-three of Jesus's thirty-five miracles recorded in the Gospels involve individuals affected by disabilities. He regularly lived and worked around those in the margins—bringing them into the community at large. Jesus spoke to them. Touched them. Healed them. Loved them. When the God of the universe so clearly values those who are suffering, should not believers do the same?

The name *Christian* carries with it the charge to live and walk like Christ. To represent him well by ministering to and through those who suffer and those who are disabled. To be like the men in Matthew 9 and Mark 2 who brought their paralytic friend to Jesus by whatever means necessary (in their case, through the roof) because they believed that Jesus would help their friend. Jesus still helps those who are suffering. However, physical healing is not the norm today. After all, physical healing is temporary. Spiritual healing, however, is available in abundance and is eternal. Jesus used physical healing in his ministry in part to validate his identity while he walked the earth. Jesus still validates his identity today in and through the lives of individuals affected by disability. As with Chuck, that is often through their praise and testimonies.

The Closing Charge

Believers should create supportive environments in their churches where God's purposes can be optimally fulfilled to and through disabilities. Christians need to remember that God powerfully works through weakness. In fact, "the parts of the body that seem to be weaker are indispensable" (1 Cor. 12:22). As Joni puts it, "Individuals affected by disability are your best visual aides to the truths of God."[13] A local church cannot be fully representative and fully functioning as part of the body of Christ if the most vital part of the body is missing! Work to bring them in!

---

[13]Joni E. Tada, "A Theology of Suffering," Dallas Theological Seminary chapel message, February 11, 2009, accessed November 5, 2009, http://www.dts.edu/media/play/?MediaItem ID=099ea001-bcbf-48e3-8546-9d84ffcbb402.

Jessica James Baldridge received her MEd degree from the University of North Texas and has taught in the Texas independent school district for ten years. A board certified behavior analyst, she served as director of the special-needs ministry at Prestonwood Baptist Church, Plano, Texas. Jessica and her husband, Morris, have three grown sons, one with autism. This and her professional specialization in autism have fueled her passion to equip leaders to teach the Word of God confidently to persons of all levels of learning ability.

3

CHURCH-BASED DISABILITY MINISTRIES

Jessica James Baldridge

Exceptional Ministry Creed: "To equip church leadership to teach the Word of God confidently to all persons, believing that all can learn in spite of differing abilities and thus can significantly improve their lives."
—JESSICA JAMES BALDRIDGE

Since the inception of the government bill known as the Individuals with Disabilities Education Act (IDEA) in 1975, educators have been developing programs in public schools for students with disabilities. Fifteen years later, in 1990, Congress passed and President George H. W. Bush signed one of the most significant civil rights laws since the Civil Rights Act of 1964—the Americans with Disabilities Act (ADA). He referred to "the unjustified segregation and exclusion of persons with disabilities from the mainstream of American life." The ADA's primary goal is to promote access for disabled persons to all aspects of social interaction, including education, employment, commerce, recreation, government, and transportation. The ADA provides the means for full implementation of the act and legal recourse to redress discrimination on the basis of physical disability. In most cases religious entities are exempt from the ADA requirements.

A total of fifty-six million disabled citizens reside in the United States. Prejudice and discrimination based on unjustified stereotypes continue and place many individuals with disabilities in a position of helplessness and hope-lessness. The inability to contribute fully deprives people with disabilities of a sense of independence. These unique individuals and their families did not ask to become disabled, but for the most part they accept the limitation graciously.

Stress exponentially multiplies when a lifelong disability involves one's child. Developmental milestones are missed and mourned, repeatedly. Finan-cial strain is present. Emotional depletion results from long-term stress. The divorce rate is between 85 and 90 percent and the unchurched rate between 90 and 95 percent among these families. They face something bigger than they are. Yet churches have been reluctant to reach out to the disabled in desperate need of good news!

According to "Access to Religious Services," a report of the National Orga-nization on Disabilities, July 24, 2001, people with disabilities are much less likely to attend religious services. Yet more than eight out of ten people with and without disabilities consider their faith to be important to them, and approxi-mately 65 percent say their religious faith is very important. Pastors should urge their congregations to implement and enforce the provisions of the ADA by developing integrated programs in their churches.

People are looking for answers. Churches should therefore seek to build bridges to meet these individuals at their point of need and connect with them on their terms. Christ brings compassion. Love and compassion view inconve-nient obstacles as opportunities.

Focus on the Spiritual Growth of the Entire Family
Churches should do the following for the disabled. Enable families of the disabled to build relationships with other families and focus on the entire family's spiritual growth. Be available and offer assistance. Be compassionate and listen. Be encouraging. Pray with and for them. Be their informant and pave the way before them by providing helpful information. Make it easy for families to be active in church. Welcome all to be safe and feel safe, valued, respected, understood, appreciated, and accepted as God's creation. Demonstrate Christ's unconditional love, be courteous, ensure dignity and respect, maintain confidentiality, and establish trust and expectancy.

If no one in a church has disabilities, this should be cause for concern because disabilities *are* in every community. Many individuals with disabilities live in group homes, in apartments, or with their families. If no one with special needs is attending your church, then determine if the church has unknowingly put up barriers. Persons with disablements will not continue attending a church where they do not feel welcome.

For Families of the Disabled, Life Is Forever Changed

When the genetic makeup reveals abnormalities, additions, and deletions of chromosomes, the information is abrupt and shocking. When medical tests reveal lifelong trauma, the information is suffocating. Following the impact of trauma (injury-caused disabilities or disease-caused disabilities) life is forever changed. Grief begins and progresses and regresses in no particular order: denial and isolation, anger, bargaining, depression, and acceptance. Envisioned dreams fade away, and yet they are replaced by a sense of immediacy and action.

Families of the disabled are not given an alternative; they have been thrown immediately and abruptly into a whole new way of life. These families try to make sense of the news that has been delivered to them. Desperate pleas, questions, and bargains to God are initiated. Families are uncertain God is there. And if he is, they may sense he does not care. They often ask, "Why, O God?" This problem was definitely not what they expected.

Emily Perl Kingsley, in her poem "Welcome to Holland," relays her experience following a diagnosis. She likens her experience to planning a fabulous vacation trip to Italy. After the tedious preparation and eager anticipation to study the language, history, and spectacular sites, the bags are packed. But upon arrival, the flight attendant announces the surprising news: "Welcome to Holland." The culture shock of ending up at a different destination is overwhelming. Not that Holland is a horrible place; it is just a different place. It is slower paced and a little less flashy than Italy. After a while one begins to notice and appreciate the windmills and tulips. But on the return trip home, it seems that everyone else is coming from Italy.

When friends hear the news about her unexpected destination, they flounder on what to say or not say. Apologies are issued rather than words of encouragement and hope. So she feels isolated, alone, and helpless.

Bearing One Another's Burdens

The following suggestions can help sufferers neutralize this season of suffering:

1. *Suffering disables.* Help those who suffer gather information, or assist them with the early intervention process.
2. *Suffering overwhelms.* With a disability new special needs are constantly being identified. Encourage those in need. Ask how you can help them.

3. *Suffering paralyzes.* Help the newly suffering to gain confidence in meeting this challenge.

4. *Suffering is personal.* Remember that their problem is not about you and your feelings of how you could not handle this. Cast a vision for them to see the obstacles as opportunities.

5. *Suffering excludes.* Be available. Continue to call, visit, and encourage. Love unconditionally through the awkwardness or discomfort.

6. *Suffering suffocates.* Encourage sufferers by means of God's Word. Fill up their empty vessel with encouragement and hope. Help them transition back to God's house.

In general, talk less; listen more. Offer hopeful statements and helpful actions. Empathize; do not pity. Show love and concern rather than sadness and shame. Avoid saying, "God only gives special challenges to special, strong people." Avoid questioning what the future holds. The present is scary enough! Do not ask, "Will he be able to achieve developmental milestones?" or "Will he be able to live independently some day?"

Many people feel uncomfortable around those with disabilities. Much of this may stem from lack of previous contact with these individuals or fear of a socially awkward moment. Church members need to learn how to act around persons with disabilities and how to make them feel welcome and a part of the church. Equip believers to authentically greet and welcome all.

God Weaves Beauty out of Similarity and Diversity
A person is not defined simply by physical or mental attributes. Every human has some limitations. Churches should accept uniqueness with grace. Building a bridge to attitudinal access is more critical than physical access. Individuals with disablities, who need God, are taking a huge step to come to church. Therefore they ought not be met with physical and attitudinal obstacles.

Churches should minister in the following ways:

1. Lift the hopeless and soften the hardness of indifference.
2. Teach the love of Christ and meet others where they are.
3. Share the love of Christ by leading them through the Bible.
4. Listen with discernment.
5. Teach the Word in specific ways that people will clearly understand.
6. Encourage spiritual growth within the entire family.

Pastors should embrace the ministry to exceptional persons and encourage congregations to give priority to those with differing abilities. Pastors should provide the tools and resources to equip their congregations for ministry.

Churches should do ministry *responsibly*!
Do what needs to be done.

Churches need to do ministry *timely*!
Do it when it needs to be done.

Churches need to do ministry with *excellence*!
Do it the best it can be done.

Churches need to do ministry *consistently*!
Do it that way every time.

Churches need to do ministry *inclusively*!
Do it how it needs to be done.

Rather than seeing the disabled as victims, see them as victors. Include and honor the diversity of each person in the church. Be sure they are not isolated socially (e.g., include individuals with disabilities in conversations). A church is called to touch each person with the love of Jesus, to nurture individuals in their relationship with Christ. Therefore focus on people, not programs. Integrate people with disabilities into various church activities.

Language Reflects and Influences Perceptions

When someone refers to an "autistic boy," people form an image of what it means to be autistic. The subject of the sentence, "boy," does not have a chance to be thought of as a regular person. Conversely, if he is referred to as a "boy with autism," the reverse tends to occur. The focus is then on the individual, as it should be, and not on the limitation.

In conversing with a person who has a disability, do not make the disability the focus. View the complexity of the total individual. Labels only describe a fraction of that person. Perhaps we have simplified and dehumanized people by using labels. All humans have limitations. Labels simply *magnify* one facet of a complex person. If one's very being is identified by disability, other facets of his personality tend to disappear, leaving only embodied disablement.

In other words, see the person rather than the disability. Avoid negative words like "suffers from," "afflicted with," "struck by," "a victim of," or "crippled with." These produce pity and devalue the individual. Various groups have claimed euphemistic terms such as "impaired," "physically challenged," "differently abled." Of the main noneuphemistic terms, "disabled" has come to be preferred over "handicapped." "Disability" implies a functional limitation that is experienced as a result of impairment, whereas "handicap" refers to the social consequences of the disability. Students with pervasive developmental disorders (e.g., autism and Asperger's syndrome) tend to avoid the term "disabilities" and tolerate the term "special needs."

The following section offers more suggestions for interacting with individuals with various disabilities. First are broader guidelines, then suggestions related to specific disabilities are given.

Suggestions for Positive Interaction

General
1. Think of each individual as being made in God's image.
2. Ask the person if he or she requires assistance.
3. Although impairment is apparent, assume that cognitive abilities are intact.
4. Utilize as many senses as possible through a multisensory approach.
5. Face the person directly, and do not look away to do something else.
6. Speak clearly at a normal volume.
7. Encourage cooperative rather than competitive activities.
8. Empathize and modify activities accordingly.

Deafness or Other Hearing Impairments
1. Always ascertain which communication medium the deaf or partially hearing person intends to use (e.g., lip reading, texting, signing).
2. Rephrase sentences rather than repeating them.
3. Communicate in writing, if necessary.
4. When a sign-language interpreter is present, he should face the person and speak normally.
5. Address the person directly while the interpreter signs. Omit phrases such as "Please tell him that . . ."
6. Learn and then use survival words in American Sign Language (ASL).

Physical Disabilities

1. Follow ADA requirements.
2. Use special materials (e.g., pencil grips, loop scissors); tape material to a work surface; use Velcro to attach objects to a tray.
3. Do not remove a person's mobility aid (i.e., crutches, cane, walker, wheelchair) without his consent.
4. When talking to someone who is in a wheelchair, if the conversation continues for more than a few minutes, sit down or kneel to be on an eye level with him. This averts neck strain and is much more positive.
5. Do not lean on a person's wheelchair unless you have his permission; it is his personal space.

Speech or Other Language Impairments

1. Listen patiently and avoid completing sentences for the person unless he looks for help.
2. Talk normally to the individual; he is not deaf.
3. Do not pretend to understand what a person with a speech disability says just to be polite. Ask if he will change the rate of his speech or communicate in writing.
4. Ask close-ended questions that require a yes or no answer.
5. For him to respond, replace verbal opportunities with alternate response opportunities (e.g., picture cards, word cards).
6. Learn and then use survival words in sign language.

Blindness or Other Visual Impairments

1. Orient the person to the area, explaining where major furniture items are located. If the person has been there before, inform him of any changes or new obstacles.
2. Keep doors fully open or, where necessary, closed to prevent accidents.
3. Offer to read written information for a person with a visual impairment, when appropriate.
4. If you are guiding someone, let him take your arm just above the elbow, and guide rather than lead or propel the person. Give him clear instructions, such as "This is a step up," as opposed to "This is a step."
5. When giving directions, use specific words such as "straight ahead" or "forward." Refer to positions in terms of clock hands: "The chair is at your 2:00." Avoid vague terms such as "over there."

6. Don't assume the person will recognize you by your voice even though you have met before. Identify yourself by name, maintain normal voice volume, speak directly to the person, and maintain eye contact.

Autism and Other Pervasive Developmental Disorders
Persons with autism are primarily visual learners. So use concrete terms and simple language; repeat them if necessary.

1. Focus on strengths and keep expectations reasonable.
2. Allow time for responses.
3. Allow frequent breaks.
4. Give lots of praise.
5. Do not attempt to physically block self-stimulating behavior, such as pacing, rocking, or hand flapping.
6. Remember that each person is unique and may act differently from others.

Families are looking for congregations that will welcome them and accept them. Proactively seek out these families who have stopped looking for a church. Integrate and include others without partiality. View disability as a "different ability." Some individuals may walk or talk differently. Change your attitude of expectancy, and learn from this new disciple.

Autism
Research indicates that parents of children with autism experience greater and more unique stress than parents of children with intellectual disabilities. This may be because of diagnostic confusion and professional "turfism," the child's uneven and unusual course of development, excesses and deficits in one's behavior, expensive therapy choices, or social isolation and exclusion.

Autism occurs in about one in ninety-one births and is four times as prevalent among males as among females. Autism is not the result of bad parenting, nor is it a mental illness caused by psychological factors. Autism is a lifelong complex neurological disorder, affecting individuals in social interaction and communication. The characteristics can occur in varying degrees of severity.

Neurological impairment in persons with autism prevents normal learning and results in severe behavioral deficits. People with autism lack imitation skills; therefore they are less likely to imitate the models in their everyday environment. Behavioral approaches are especially useful in teaching appropriate behaviors to those with autism who may not otherwise pick up these behaviors by watching. Other approaches that work with neurotypical students and other types of disabilities will not work with this population.

An understanding of the neurological processes is necessary to comprehend how the brain perceives, encodes, and decodes information through the sensory channels. People with autism may be overresponsive and try to escape or avoid stimulation, or may be underresponsive and seek out stimulation. This population processes information and responds differently because of several regions of the brain that are affected, including the cerebrum, corpus callosum, cerebellum, and amygdala. Understanding these cerebral abnormalities can help us understand autism or trauma brain injury:

1. *Cerebrum*: Controls thinking, memory, reasoning, and action, including voluntary muscles. The left hemisphere is known for logic, and the right hemisphere for abstract thinking.
2. *Corpus callosum*: Connects and communicates between the two hemispheres (logic and abstract) of the brain.
3. *Cerebellum* ("little brain"): Regulates balance, movement, and coordination and affects sensory processing.
4. *Amygdala* ("emotional brain"): Regulates emotions.

All behavior is functional, communicative, and contextual. Behavior is related to the environment, so it is critical that churches provide a stable supportive environment for individuals with autism. Positive reinforcement must be contingent on appropriate behavior and then delivered moderately and immediately. Based on these behavioral assumptions, teachers can use applied behavior analysis to increase desired behaviors, decrease inappropriate behaviors, and teach new appropriate, alternative replacement behaviors.

Individuals with autism have unique differences of behavioral excesses, such as aggressive behavior, meltdowns, or panic attacks. Not so obvious are behavioral deficits, that is, appropriate behaviors that are lacking. These differences need to be understood (e.g., "I won't" usually means "I can't without your support"). Be caring but firm. Be demanding but patient. Be respectful, consistent, energetic, but calming. Display integrity and sensitivity, and honor confidentiality.

Common Characteristics of Autism
Autism differs uniquely among almost two million individuals. But the following common characteristics set these unique individuals apart from others:

1. An inability to relate to others in an ordinary manner and with little or no eye contact
2. An extreme aloneness that seemingly isolates the individual
3. An apparent oversensitivity and resistance to being touched or held
4. An apparent high pain tolerance, an insensitivity to pain
5. An apparent deafness, although hearing is fine; possible misunderstanding of what is said or lack of response to verbal cues
6. No real typical fears of danger, yet extreme fear or reactions to loud noises
7. Deficits in expressive language including mutism and echolalia
8. Laughing for no apparent reason or showing distress for reasons not apparent to others
9. An appearance of anxiety or nervousness; peculiar actions; darting away from others unexpectedly
10. An obsessive desire for repetition and insistence on sameness
11. A resistance to change; difficulty in making transitions
12. Few spontaneous activities such as typical play behavior
13. Sustained odd play; obsessive attachment to certain objects
14. Bizarre and repetitive self-stimulating behaviors such as hand flapping, spinning, perpetual rocking, pacing, and others
15. Being unresponsive to normal teaching methods

Many parents and teachers experience frustration in trying to understand and respond to the behaviors of a person with autism. Discipline strategies that work for others do not work with those who have autism. Therefore parents and teachers should focus on simplified instructional steps and consistent reinforcement. They should be aware of the differences between teaching appropriate behavior and punishing inappropriate behavior (see table 2).

Avoiding Breakdown and Meltdown
Individuals with autism face many frustrations because of communication and socialization breakdowns. That is why many people on the autistic spectrum often have tantrums and tend to have meltdowns. A meltdown is a loss of composure, coherence, rationality, or awareness of reality. Parents and teachers

Table 2.
Differences between teaching and punishment

Teaching	Punishment
Teaches what a child should do	Punishes what a child should not do
Ongoing process	One-time occurrence
Sets an example to follow	Insists on obedience
Leads to self-control	Undermines independence
Positive	Negative
Accepts child's need to assert	Makes children behave
Fosters ability to think	Thinks for the child
Bolsters self-esteem	Defeats self-esteem
Shapes behavior	Condemns misbehavior

should watch undesirable behaviors closely to see what triggers those behaviors and what happens immediately after the behaviors to reinforce them. These inadvertent reinforcers should be removed from the environment. Behavior problems often occur when an individual does not know how to communicate or express basic needs.

The following are hints for helping individuals with autism avoid breakdowns that may result in meltdowns.

Avoid Setting the Individual Up for a Meltdown
1. Provide a structured environment and a predictable routine (e g , use visual schedules and timing devices).
2. Be aware of when he needs some calming support.
3. Give him plenty of space.
4. Respect his ownership of his favorite toys.
5. Be sensitive to transitions.
6. End each activity on a happy note.
7. Positively reinforce appropriate behavior.
8. Model calmness and think clearly.

Stop the Meltdown at the Beginning
Look for factors that warn of the onset of a meltdown (e.g., complaining loudly or pounding on a table or wall).

1. This is *not* the time to escalate. Do not match negative behavior with negative behavior. That would only increase tension.
2. Keep words to a minimum and keep emotions intact. Use a firm tone of voice and simple language. (E.g., "Sit down. Look at me.")

3. Quickly divert attention to a more acceptable activity.

4. Prompt the person to use appropriate, alternative behavior.

5. Be flexible. Focus on teaching alternative behavior.

6. Be prepared to remove him from the situation, no matter how inconvenient it may be.

7. Ignore the inappropriate behavior, *not* the child.

8. Do not try to discuss or pray with the individual, for this will escalate his behavior.

9. Offer sensory input through (a) deep-pressure touch (the type of pressue that is exerted in firm touch or holding; deep-pressure touch is relaxing and calming) or (b) deep-pressure activity (e.g., rolling up in a gym mat, hanging in a hammock-type swing).

10. After things have calmed down, this may provide a teachable moment.

Exceptional Ministry Is Dynamic and Multifaceted

Different environmental variables make this exceptional ministry dynamic and multifaceted. These variables include students, parents, and leaders who have different abilities, temperaments, behaviors, expectations, experiences, knowledge skills, and codes of conduct. Respect and understanding are the cornerstones to developing trust among these groups.

There is no room for apathy and pity when discipling students. Leaders must see beyond the disability; have empathy; be teachable, flexible, and patient; be team players; and have a love for all students. When a student walks into the room, he will ask himself, *Am I wanted? Will I fit in? Am I safe?* So see the individual as a person capable of improving and taking an active part. Provide support to make this happen. Focus on the student as a valuable and responsible person.

Setting Up a Successful Special-Needs Ministry

Welcoming of Students

1. Greet and meet students where they are without touching or entering into their personal space. Use the student's name and comment on an item he has or clothes he is wearing.

2. In the classroom immediately begin establishing rapport and gain his trust. Follow him to discover his preferences. When he picks up an item, interact with him even if it is one-sided interaction.

Arranging the Environment

1. Arrange the environment to increase motivation and present ample opportunities.
2. Have a highly structured environment with consistent, predictable routines supported by appropriate accommodations tailored to the individuals.
3. Capitalize on structure, routines, schedules, and predictability.
4. Make transitions smoother by using timers and referring back to a visual schedule (i.e., written or picture) to see how many tasks the student needs to complete.
5. Be aware of levels of sound. Keep earphones on hand for listening to music. Sounds that are too noisy and rooms that are overcrowded may precipitate sensory overload and produce disruptive behavior.
6. Remember that play is work and work is play. Assist students in interacting socially with peers.

Teaching

1. Keep the teacher-to-student ratio low.
2. Assume all students can learn (even those who are nonverbal).
3. Look for teachable moments.
4. Focus on student's interests, strengths, and motivation.
5. Maintain attention through energetic teaching and using multisensory methods.
6. Meet individual needs by adapting and modifying activities as needed.
7. Encourage active engagement throughout the day with repeated learning opportunities and frequent response opportunities to practice new skills.
8. Assess the assigned task level. If needed, break a task into smaller components and a proper sequence. A person avoids a task when it is perceived as too laborious. If he is allowed to escape a task by exhibiting disruptive or maladaptive behavior, he will communicate this through his behavior repeatedly.

Assisting Communication

1. Even if they are verbal, these individuals are often unable to express their needs adequately. So provide assistance; prompt or use a communication system (e.g., written or by pictures).

2. Communicate simply and directly, giving clear, brief directions in close proximity to the person.
3. Provide continuous feedback.

Using Movement
1. Incorporate motor activities to help enhance motor skills.
2. If the student is expected to sit quietly without any movement, disruptive behavior will follow.

Vicariously Representing Jesus to the World
Parents and professionals need to work together. Professionals should have some understanding of the student's behavior and communication skills at home, and parents should let professionals know about their expectations as well as what techniques work at home. Appropriate behavior (at home) does not always carry over to new or different settings. The structure will be easier on the students if they are consistent in attendance, are on time, and eat a good breakfast. Urge parents to treat church attendance with the same priority as school attendance.

Focus on the student's perspective. Thank the parents for entrusting their loved one to your care. Be sensitive in comments you make to the parents. All comments must be made from the vantage point of the best interest of the student. Say, "How can I communicate better?" rather than being critical of the student. Share positive comments first. When there is a concern to share, balance one concern with five positive comments. Let the student know that you are looking forward to spending the next time with him.

Ministry to exceptional individuals means being like Jesus—loving unconditionally as he would love, seeing what he would see, responding as he would respond. His love is all-encompassing and includes everyone. What a privilege to be his hands and feet and to have a heart like his to welcome opportunities to minister to those in need![1]

My Life
by John Bannister Tabb[2]

My life is but a weaving between my Lord and me.
I may not choose the colors; He knows what they should be.

---

[1]For more information on exceptional ministry, see www.jessicajamesbaldridge.com.
[2]Adapted.

For He can view the pattern upon the upper side,
Which, from beneath, a tangle of mysteries may hide.
Sometimes He weaves my sorrow far as the eye can see,
But I will trust His judgment and work on faithfully.
'Tis He who fills the shuttle; He knows just what is best;
So I shall weave in earnest and leave with Him the rest.
Not till the loom is silent and shuttles cease to fly,
Shall God unroll the canvas, disclosing reasons why
The dark threads are as needful in Weaver's skillful hand
As threads of gold and silver to patterns He has planned.
He knows. He cares. He loves me. Nothing this truth can dim.
He gives His best to those who entrust designs to Him.

Michael A. Justice served in music ministry at several churches before losing his sight because of diabetic retinopathy. Nearly blind, he enrolled at Dallas Theological Seminary, where he completed the ThM program. Since then, he has served as a hospital chaplain in an acute-care unit and in three physical rehabilitation hospitals. He also served as an associate pastor at Rowlett (TX) Bible Fellowship.

A type-one diabetic for forty-four years, Michael is totally blind in one eye and severely legally blind in the other. He also suffered kidney failure and the rigors of dialysis before receiving a kidney transplant. That transplant lasted over seven years before he received a second kidney transplant, donated by his wife, Terri.

4

DISABILITIES AND THE CHURCH

Michael A. Justice

God ministers to and through individuals affected by disabilities. This is apparent in both the Old and New Testaments. Issues like crippled feet, blindness, withered hands, speech impairments, deafness, paralysis, and disabling diseases color the stories of the various characters whom God used to accomplish his plans. Isaac, Moses, Mephibosheth, Zacharias, Bartimaeus, the man born blind, the man with withered hands, the demon possessed, the many who were lame and paralyzed, and the mute—these all demonstrate that God works mightily through their challenges and weaknesses.

Some were healed of their disabling conditions, while others were not. Some were in their conditions because of a sinful lifestyle, while others were born disabled. Some had faith and were made whole, whereas others who did not have any faith in God were healed. Some were used as object lessons to teach the people that they were spiritually blind or to lead them to knowledge that the Lord Jesus is the promised Messiah. And in some cases we simply do not know what God's plan was. Yet a large part of Jesus's recorded ministry was to the sick and the disabled.

Today churches face the challenge of ministering to an ever-growing population of people with disabilities. The extent of such ministry efforts may range from doing nothing at all to integrating those individuals into every aspect of church life. The dilemma of how to minister to them and how to involve them in ministry creates some unique circumstances. Awkwardness, fear, ignorance, and rejection are a few responses one might feel when someone who is disabled comes into a local church. The following examples demonstrate this dilemma, although these are only a few of the problems.

Moses was a man who could not speak well, yet God commanded him to be the deliverer of the Israelites out of Egyptian bondage. In Exodus 3–4, Moses raised three objections to God and his choice of deliverer. Basically Moses felt that he was not worthy of such a call, and he wondered who would believe him anyway. The third objection, however, went to the root of his problem, for he told God that he was not a man who could speak well. He was "slow of speech and of tongue" (Ex. 4:10).

Interestingly, God did not say to Moses, "If you had enough faith, you would be healed of your speech problem"! Nor did the Lord argue with Moses about his speech impairment. Instead God asked his servant three questions and then told Moses that he, God, would give him the words to say and would send Aaron along with him to help. "Who has made man's mouth? Who makes him mute, or deaf, or seeing, or blind? Is it not I, the LORD?" (Ex. 4:11).

Lori was born with spina bifida, a condition in which the spinal column is partially exposed, resulting in various neurological issues. Lori also had kidney failure and some deformation of her facial features and left shoulder. In spite of her physical flaws she said that Jesus made her pretty on the inside.

After she accepted the Lord as her Savior, she joined a local church in the Dallas area. There she loved the preaching and teaching of the Bible. Someone invited her to come to the women's ministry one evening for more Bible study, so she eagerly went, fully expecting to grow in her knowledge. After the program was over, she sat in her wheelchair waiting for her transportation van to take her home. While she waited, three ladies stood nearby, and one kept looking at Lori, then quickly glancing away. Repeatedly this occurred till the lady said in a loud whisper that Lori was ugly. The inhabitants of the room heard the comment, including Lori, resulting in snickers throughout the room. Lori was heartbroken that her new Christian friends would see her only in that light. She never returned to the church. Lori said, "I don't have nice clothes, I don't have the money to buy makeup, I don't have nice hair like those other ladies, but Jesus made me pretty on the inside!"

At the local dialysis clinic she boldly witnessed that Jesus made her pretty on the inside. To the doctors, nurses, therapists, and others who dialyzed, she proclaimed that Jesus died on the cross to pay for our sins, was buried, and rose again the third day. Then she invited anyone who would believe in him to do so.

Anna was born blind because of a lack of oxygen to her optic nerves. She became a Christian early in life and attended the same church for many years. Though she used a white cane well, she decided to seek training in the use of a guide dog. After a month of training, she and her new golden retriever, Patricia, came back to attend the church. Two ushers met her in the foyer and welcomed her, but told her that the dog would have to stay in the foyer because new carpet had recently been laid in the auditorium. She told the men that it was the law that the dog could go anywhere with her, but they refused her and Patricia.

So Anna used her cell phone to call the police. She was not about to go in without Patricia, whose eyes she used to help her with mobility. In minutes two officers came and informed the leaders that legally, they would have to allow Anna and Patricia to go inside. The leaders did so grudgingly. But after a few weeks Anna knew that people were angry at her since no one wanted to sit with her. Several told her she should not have called the police. But she told them that they should not have rejected the dog. To reject the guide dog was the same as rejecting her.

She eventually left that church, and fifteen years went by before she attended another. At the new church, however, she and her guide dog are an integral part of the women's ministry. Her former church rejected the dog, thus rejecting Anna. But her new church accepted and enjoyed Patricia as if she too were a member.

Dennis lived with the scourge of multiple sclerosis for over twenty-eight years. As a 1975 ThM graduate of Dallas Seminary, he was once invited to preach at a local church. When he arrived, he was met with resistance over the fact that the pastor felt that the stage was "sanctified" along with the furniture on it. The pastor told Dennis that if he was to preach while sitting in a wheelchair, he would defile the stage and the sanctified furniture.

Dennis did not let that keep him from preaching God's Word. He chose to locate his chair in front of the stage during his sermon.

These testimonies are typical of many who live with the daily grind of a disability. They also demonstrate how fear and ignorance often guide well-meaning Christians in forming their perceptions of disabilities, accessibility issues, and assimilation into local-church ministries. One might think that inreach and outreach to the disabled is futile if one faces such fear and ignorance. But answering some basic questions puts the matter in a better light, especially since God was never thwarted by disabilities and suffering. The following questions and answers can help lead local churches into a better understanding of God's plan for the disabled.

Why Is Church-Based Disability Ministry Needed?

To Raise Awareness

First, a church-based disability ministry is needed to raise awareness in three crucial areas: (1) the challenges of facing differing disabilities, (2) accessibility, and (3) assimilating those with physical challenges into vibrant Christian service.

(1) It may seem obvious that the deaf need sign-language interpretation to benefit from the preaching and teaching in a service or Bible study, whereas a lady with muscular dystrophy does not need that type of communication at all. Someone with dyslexia may use a specific method to engage a Sunday school lesson, but a man who limps from polio would not. Someone who is blind may or may not read Braille, whereas a lady with cerebral palsy would never use Braille at all. The challenges are different, though there are some adaptive means that these people share. One example is that the wheelchair helps those with quadriplegia, paraplegia, amputation, rheumatoid arthritis, and muscular dystrophy, to name a few conditions. Many blind and visually impaired individuals now have access to voice-synthesis software that can enable their computers to read files, books, web pages, and e-mails. Even people with dyslexia can use this same software if they are trained to do so.

Differences and similarities between disabilities are many. Not knowing them, however, limits one's understanding of how a disabled person can function effectively. Knowing that the blind and visually impaired use audio formats can help church leaders understand how the impaired can read, learn, and teach the Bible within the church. Adaptive resources enable those who need them to both embrace and serve within most settings.

(2) Regarding accessibility, a great gulf, so to speak, is fixed between those who need special access and those who do not. One's awareness is raised when an individual suddenly cannot climb stairs and no wheelchair ramp is available, cannot get to a particular office for a meeting when door plaques are not marked in a manner that is comprehensible, cannot get to a restroom because the hallway or door to that room is too narrow for a walker or wheelchair, or cannot attend a Bible class because it is located on the second floor of a building that has no elevator, or the door handles are simply unreachable or unusable

by those with weak or nonfunctioning hands. These are just a few examples of what some disabled individuals might face when they visit a local church facility.

Awareness of inaccessibility usually comes when one is personally faced with the challenges. In other words, if a person does not need special access, he or she will probably never think that anyone else does either. On the Joni and Friends ministry website, a free accessibility checklist can be downloaded to help Christian workers assess whether their church buildings are accessible.

The notion that a church does not need a wheelchair ramp because no one in attendance would use it shows a lack of awareness. The fact that no one attends who uses a wheelchair may be because there are no ramps. Individuals with rheumatoid arthritis may have periods of remission. One month a lady uses a wheelchair, and six months later she walks through the door as if she has never been disabled at all. Even this, however, does not preclude the need for the ramp.

If lack of funds is the barrier to pursuing accessibility, perhaps the awareness that Jesus ministered to so many who were disabled should rule, particularly when one realizes that the disabled too need the gospel and good Bible teaching and preaching. The value of someone's soul is greater than the cost of cement, wood, railings, door plaques, and any other means of adaptation that promote easy access. Amazingly, many people who quickly embrace the fact of the Lord's suffering balk at reaching out to those around them who suffer.

(3) Assimilation into the various ministries of the church is crucial in reaching the disabled. A blind or visually impaired man who can get into the building and enters the auditorium may fit in fine until he is faced with the matter of not being able to read a hymnal, a song sheet, or a PowerPoint presentation. Perhaps he will recognize the song when the introduction is played, but not having the words excludes him from worshiping fully, as others so easily can do. Braille hymnals are available for purchase through organizations like Bridge Christian Education for the Blind (7205 Church Park Rd., Fort Worth, TX 76133; phone 817-920 0444). These hymnals cost only thirty-five dollars each, and a hymnal includes over two hundred well-known hymns in Braille. This organization also sells a large-print hymnal of the same songs.

Another option for those who can read large print is to enlist several in the congregation to type the words each week into a document format, then enlarge the print according to each individual's need. With this, the church can make their own hymns or books of choruses.[1] This allows better assimilation

---

[1] This may be done only for works in the public domain or with express permission for works covered by copyright.

as those individuals can then worship as others do. Sunday school materials are also available in various formats, such as large print and audio. Various disabling conditions may demand different adaptations, but usually this is a small problem, and once a solution is offered, those who can engage it feel much more a part of the church.

With every disability the issues are different, but the answers are almost always within reach. Rearranging furniture to make it easier for someone who does not walk well to get to a place of safety in a Sunday school room should be an easy task. Or a class might switch locations with another class. Materials in different formats are usually available for adults and children with learning disabilities. The Internet is an excellent place to research for those materials. A church's Christian education department, along with the church-based disability ministry team, can easily solve these problems of assimilation.

To Overcome Fear and Ignorance

Second, a church-based disability ministry can help break down barriers of fear and ignorance. Unless a person spends a lot of time with someone who is disabled, it is doubtful that any great level of understanding will exist. The notion that blind and visually impaired people are illiterate because they cannot read is easily challenged as one learns how they use adaptive means such as Braille, large print, and audio formats to study the Bible or read a commentary.

On a side note, 2009 was the two-hundredth anniversary of the birth of Louis Braille, a man who went blind at a very early age. When he was twelve, he developed a system of raised dots to aid the blind and visually impaired to read printed materials such as books and articles. Though his teachers thought it somewhat promising, they eventually concluded that it would never be widely used. For over one hundred years, however, Braille has been used in virtually every country as a means of helping the blind read effectively.

A common assumption is that all people who use a wheelchair for mobility must be cognitively challenged, but most of the time that is not true. The Holy Spirit has gifted them to serve in teaching, organizing, or evangelizing, for example.

When the disciples were walking along with Jesus, they came across a man who had been born blind. They asked the Lord whether the man or his parents had sinned to cause his blindness (John 9:2). In their ignorance they asked Jesus a multiple-choice question and gave him only two possible answers. But when Jesus spoke, he gave them a third answer: the man's blindness happened "that the works of God might be displayed in him" (v. 3).

People then, as now, believed that anyone who was disabled was being judged for his sin. Jesus, however, raised the disciples' awareness by revealing the true reason—that God would do a mighty work through the man's disability and healing. In this man's suffering, as he begged each day on the streets for his daily sustenance, God demonstrated how desperately he needed physical sight. God also demonstrated that the blind man, the townspeople, and the religious rulers desperately needed spiritual sight. Only Jesus, "the light of the world" (John 9:5), could accomplish that work. In doing so, Jesus demonstrated again that he is the promised Messiah spoken of in Isaiah 61:1–2 (cf. Luke 4:18).

To Manifest Strength through Weakness

Third, church-based disability ministry provides an arena in which God's strength is manifested through weakness. In 2 Corinthians 12:7–9 Paul wrote to the believers at Corinth that he asked God to remove a "thorn" in his "flesh." But he wrote that though God did not remove the "thorn," he did give Paul grace to live with it. No one knows what this "thorn" was, but some believe that Paul had a visual impairment, since he had to write in large letters to the churches at Galatia (Gal. 6:11). Whatever it was, God did not take it away. Instead he left the apostle weak "so that the power of Christ" could be manifest through him (2 Cor. 12:9).

Many people in the New Testament were healed, but many were not. In the Old Testament, Isaac was not healed of his old age blindness, Moses's speech impairment remained, and so did the crippled feet of Jonathan's son, Mephibosheth. Perhaps God left them as they were to demonstrate a different purpose. The same could be true of the people who were left sick and disabled around the Pool of Bethesda (John 5:1–5). If the Lord were more interested in wellness than weakness, he surely would have healed all who had a need.

The notion that those in the Bible who were not healed must be lacking in faith does not make sense when one examines passages such as John 5:1–5. Jesus offered the opportunity for healing to only one person, and the one whom he did heal had faith only in the angel coming to stir up the waters. If someone had told the apostle Paul he simply needed enough faith that his thorn would be removed, that person would have been in direct violation of God's plan to work through Paul's weakness. Many disabled believers today have great faith, but the Lord has left them to cope with severe disabilities or illnesses. Who is to say what God will or will not do through any kind of suffering?

To Provide Respite Care

Fourth, church-based disability ministry provides opportunities for respite care. Paul admonished the Galatian believers to "bear one another's burdens," thus fulfilling Christ's law (Gal. 6:2). Those who are caregivers for children, adults, or disabled spouses often need respite care since the daily responsibilities are exhausting. Offering them a night off or a weekend away while church members take care of that loved one gives the caregivers time to refuel and rest. Some training might be needed, but if several work together to help, this can be an enormous blessing to that family.

One lady wanted to attend a weekend women's retreat, but she could not leave her husband unattended with his daily routines because of his multiple sclerosis. Six men from the church trained to take care of him and then worked in eight-hour shifts to cover the care until the man's wife came home on Sunday afternoon. It was wonderful for her to spend the time away without the daily responsibilities for her husband and also to be with her women's group.

To Affirm the Dignity of the Disabled

Fifth, church-based disability ministry can show that the disabled have value and dignity. According to Genesis 1:27 all people, including the disabled, are made in the image of God because they are humans. Likewise the psalmist speaks of man's value in Psalm 8:4–5. People who live with disabilities, however, tend to struggle with the feeling that they are of no value. They may even feel absolutely worthless, particularly if they sense there is no need for them at their local church.

Value and dignity are often felt through usefulness. The blind man whom Jesus healed in two stages in Mark 8:23–25 served as a wonderful object lesson to the disciples that their view of Jesus was distorted, needing eventually to become clear (as in Peter's confession that Jesus is the Christ, the Son of the living God, Matt. 16:16). Even through Moses's inadequacies and doubt, God used him to demonstrate grace, power, and provision to the people of Israel.

Tom wanted to be on the greeting team of his church, but he was mute. He could see and hear well, but he could not speak. How could he even think of greeting people as they entered the building? Since the leaders of that ministry turned him down, Tom went home and made a sign that he would wear around his neck each Sunday. On it were three well-printed lines.

> My name is Tom.
> I cannot speak.
> Welcome to our church!

When Tom walked throughout the foyer and noticed new visitors, he would show them his sign, then give a big smile, and shake their hands as a welcome to the church. Tom's proposal was rejected at first because the leaders feared what visitors might think. But the more Tom showed people his sign, the more favorably people responded to his being on the team. Now he is second in command of the greeting ministry, thus using his gift of hospitality. Tom feels useful, and he certainly provides a unique service to help his church. No one has left that church because of Tom's speech impairment, nor because of the disabling issues of any others.

A church-based disability ministry is more than a ministry *to* those with disabilities; it is also a ministry *through* them. But what can be done to accomplish outreach, not only to the disabled but also to anyone who is suffering? Perhaps the best idea is to consider what can be learned from those who are disabled and suffering.

What Can Be Learned from the Disabled about Ministering to the Suffering?

Sufferers Are Vulnerable

First, we learn that sufferers are vulnerable. This is seen in physical, emotional, and spiritual ways. One example is found in Genesis 27, which states that Isaac went blind in his old age. Then his wife, Rebecca, and son Jacob conspired together to deceive Isaac into giving the blessing of the firstborn to Jacob, not Esau.

Jacob told his father several lies, including the lie that he, Jacob, was Esau. Isaac reacted as any blind person would when he told his son that he sounded like Jacob but felt like Esau. To a blind person, the senses of hearing and touch are the best ways to connect with the world. Isaac was deceived by his own family, which must have been shocking and painful to discover later. In addition, knowing that God could have kept this from happening introduced a deeper level of vulnerability.

With disability always comes vulnerability, and the same is true for any kind of suffering. Statements such as, "If you just had enough faith, you would be healed," or "That suffering is all about you," often come across as arrogant and insensitive to the one who is suffering. The fact that the only legitimate person to make such statements would be God ought to discourage people from saying things like that to anyone, especially to those who are already hurting. After all, how can anyone possibly read the amount of faith in someone else's heart? To say that something is "all about" that individual is a cheap shot. Perhaps God is giving grace to that sufferer by not removing his or her "thorn," and God is thereby demonstrating his strength through the very weakness that person is experiencing.

Hearing either of those statements can be frustrating and even hurtful to those who struggle with their faith. In fact, it may be more discouraging than challenging. For some reason, ministering to anyone who is suffering carries the risk of being condescending, which is no doubt felt by the sufferer. Unfortunately people often take advantage of others emotionally, physically, and financially.

Sufferers Can Relate to Sufferers

Second, we learn that sufferers often relate well to fellow strugglers. Many sufferers look for someone who can identify with them in that part of their lives. The best example from Scripture is when the writer of Hebrews 12:3 encourages believers to consider the Lord Jesus Christ, the perfect example of walking the life of a sufferer.

Early in my visual impairment, I needed someone to understand. I had gone through the typical grief responses of shock, anger, enormous terror, and depression, mainly because I thought there was no way out. I begged God to heal me, and I asked him why he would allow such a horrible thing to happen to me. One afternoon I was so angry, I told my heavenly Father that I would like to crawl up in his lap and gouge out his eyes. I foolishly thought that in all the things that he had suffered, he did not know what it was like to be blind. I expected to be severely rebuked, but after getting all of my anger out, I felt deeply loved by the Lord.

Many years later a friend showed me Luke 22:63–64, which reports that in Jesus's trial the soldiers blindfolded Jesus and then told him to tell them who struck him. When I listened to that verse, I felt so sorry that I had ever railed against God, for I knew then that Jesus had indeed been blind for a time. Though I had never been beaten for my faith, he was beaten for my sin. I knew that God could understand, for he identified with me in my suffering.

Compassion Is Better Than Talk

Third, compassion, comfort, understanding, and empathy are more beneficial than advice. God's servant Job certainly had a large dose of advice as his friends Eliphaz, Bildad, and Zophar came to him to offer comfort. At first they kept their mouths shut (Job 2:11–13), but eventually they began to unload a torrent of verbal advice, all of which God rebuked toward the end of the book. People ought not be too hard on these men, however, for few have learned to listen or offer comfort well. Perhaps the notion that Christians should always have an answer to pain and suffering stems from the desire to know the Word of God and to explain theologically the meaning of suffering.

The writer of Proverbs 20:12 says it best.

> The hearing ear and the seeing eye,
>   the LORD has made them both.

Why did the Lord not refer in that verse to "the flapping jaw"? Because to observe, to listen, and to understand are far more beneficial to the sufferer than theological explanations. Paul told his readers that they should give comfort as they are comforted by the God of all compassion and comfort (2 Cor. 1:3–4). Sufferers desperately need people with compassionate hearts that comfort them rather than preach to them. Ironically, many people who live with disability rarely if ever give advice. Usually there is a lot of understanding simply because they remember what it was like to hear numerous answers but with little or no sympathy.

One of my most memorable experiences of advice occurred when a young man at seminary told me a story about his grandmother. He knew I was frustrated by the rigors of school in light of my blindness and diabetes. Since I said that I was ready to quit, he evidently felt that it was time to deal with my real problem. His words of advice were so unbelievable that I frankly did not know what to say.

His grandmother, he said, was totally blind. She started to drink two gallons of carrot juice each day, and after thirty days she had 20/20 vision. My brow furrowed as he shared the miracle. I could not imagine how long I would spend in the emergency room from what that amount of carrot juice would do to my diabetic blood sugar. I found the advice nothing less than absurd, although I am convinced that the young man meant well.

After he finished, I asked him if I might contact his grandmother to hear this story from her perspective. He said, "Oh! She died about a year ago." Now, I do not know how you would have responded, but this was not the advice I was looking for, because it was not relevant at all to my problems.

I also recall that after my first kidney transplant was rejected, a lady called me to share the good news of her most recent business venture. She was sure this would be exactly what I needed or what my transplanted kidney needed. She was selling a particular regimen of vitamins that were advertised as being the most authentic form of vitamins ever on the market. I told her I was not interested since I already took some vitamins, but she insisted that I at least listen to her five-minute spiel.

Five minutes later she completed the talk and asked what I thought. She said she knew that I would certainly want to do the best thing for my kidney transplant. I thought for a moment and then asked, "So would these vitamins boost my immune system?" Excitedly she told me that they would. In fact she also told me that there were recorded testimonies on that issue that she could send me if I wanted to hear them.

Her heart was in the right place, but I had to explain that the key to any kind of transplant is the immuno-suppressive drugs that compromise the immune system, thus lowering it to keep it from rejecting the transplanted organ. If her products did what she said they would do, then they would certainly put me back into kidney rejection. After just coming out of one such rejection, I never wanted to experience that again. She could not understand why I would not buy the products. I finally gave up and ended the call.

That evening I called a friend who had multiple sclerosis and described the kidney rejection episode. He listened for a long time, let me get it all out, and then he prayed in tears over the phone for me and my wife. As a man who knew well the ups and downs of disability, he prayed that our Great Physician would personally be in charge of my medical care, especially the recovery of my transplant.

Suffering Builds Character

Fourth, we learn that enduring in suffering builds character. In God's process of maturing his children, he is much like a blacksmith in his shop. He uses the anvil, hammer, and fire of suffering to forge a tool that is fit for his purposes. The apostle Peter speaks of this process, stating that believers must go through the trials of suffering much as the Lord did (1 Pet. 4:12–16). After all, why should believers not fellowship with Christ in his sufferings? God brings growth to believers through the things they endure. And in that daily grind of struggle and endurance they become strong.

The tendency of many people is to want to deliver the sufferer from the blacksmith's fire into a life of peace, even though God's plan may be to leave the person there for a time or even a lifetime to accomplish a much higher goal. People with disabilities who know the Lord often settle into a quiet calm of acceptance and faith after a time, for they come to realize that their sufferings are for a much higher purpose. Others, however, never understand it, and they resort to illegal drugs, alcohol, and even suicide. This is true of even caregivers, for the divorce rate is extremely high when one partner suddenly has a stroke or debilitating illness that throws a wrench into their retirement plans. But for those who endure, their faith grows strong as they learn to trust God.

What Does It Mean to "Witness by Suffering Well"?

To "witness by suffering well" means to embrace and endure one's suffering as a part of God's plan to bring glory to himself. The best example of this is the perfect sufferer, the Lord Jesus Christ. He walked the path of intense suffering, leading up to his death, burial, and resurrection. He has already gone through every kind of suffering people experience today.

Even in the garden of Gethsemane, Jesus embraced the challenge of the cross as he surrendered his will to the heavenly Father's will. Jesus did this because something greater lay ahead (Heb. 12:2). Therefore he endured the cross of shame and then ultimately took his rightful place at the right hand of God.

In the incarnation Jesus left heaven, took on flesh, and became obedient to the death of the cross (Phil. 2:5–8). But "God has highly exalted him" and given him the name above all names, and every knee will bow and every tongue will "confess that Jesus Christ is Lord, to the glory of God the Father" (vv. 9–11).

To witness by suffering well means that a person who suffers must embrace his or her suffering and accept it fully, because it is very much a part of that individual's walk with Christ. By viewing it that way the aspect of endurance is much more plausible, because Jesus identifies with the sufferer, and the sufferer with him. The believer is not alone in his suffering, no matter what that suffering may be.

Moses did not think himself worthy or adequate to do what God commanded him to do, especially since he had a speech problem. But he suffered well as he obeyed God's call. People like Lori, who are not pretty, beautiful, or acceptable by today's standards of beauty, may be effective evangelists as they share their beautiful testimony of Christ's love and care for them. People like Anna, who have felt the deep pain of rejection, know well what Christ suffered and are determined not to reject others. People like Dennis keep serving faithfully when life's challenges and perceptions might cause some to give up in despair.

With Dennis, however, the challenge to continue in his service to Christ drove him to share his faith, no matter what the doctors said. He would share God's Word so long as he had a voice left, and when that was gone, he prayed for others to know Christ. He was definitely a man who suffered well in spite of his physical challenges.

For all who suffer and are serious about their calling by God and yet feel unworthy, as Moses felt, the challenge of embracing and enduring what God brings their way is a gift from the Almighty. In this way they also suffer with Christ, even though they may never understand the reasons for the suffering or understand how God is carrying them through times of confusion and frustration.

Suffering is inevitable, but the manner in which believers handle it is up to them. Hopefully as one learns to view his or her trials and pains as a necessary part of spiritual growth, he or she will move forward in faith, enduring all that comes. Suffering must be accepted obediently, for this was the example Jesus left for believers to follow. Whatever one's problems, God will be glorified.

Gregory A. Hatteberg graduated from Moody Bible Institute and received the ThM degree from Dallas Theological Seminary. He worked in admissions at Moody and at Dallas Seminary before becoming director of alumni and placement for the seminary. He is an instructor for Walk Thru the Bible Ministries, a licensed tour guide for Israel, and coauthor of *The New Christian Traveler's Guide to the Holy Land*. Greg and his wife, Lisa, who suffers from multiple sclerosis, are a model of abiding love and of care for a disabled spouse.

5

THE ROLLING THRONE

Gregory A. Hatteberg

One day the routine of driving into downtown Dallas to pick up my wife, Lisa, at work became the beginning of anything but routine. She worked as an executive secretary at a major bank. I asked her how her day went, and she said fine, except that her eyes were bothering her. She was seeing double and a little fuzzy. She shrugged it off as being a little tired.

As the symptoms continued for the next few days, we decided to get her eyes checked. After a few brief tests, the doctor gave a sigh of concern and said that it could be a tumor, the onset of a potential aneurism, or multiple sclerosis (MS). He said we needed to have additional testing because the symptoms were classic for MS. Unfortunately, in 1984 the MRIs to detect MS were not well developed. The neurologist who examined Lisa concluded it was MS. She preferred not to do the scans, to avoid putting it on our insurance record. MS is something that people can have without major incident. After a few steroid shots the symptoms went away and we hoped it was over.

The Disappointment
This was the first time in my spiritual life I began to grapple seriously with the question of suffering and God's goodness. Through my tears I began to recall all that I had done for God. This was my first semester at seminary. We had committed our lives to serving him. We had left our families. Most of my

relatives lived in a small farming community, almost 90 percent of them within ten miles of my home. I was now a thousand miles from home and feeling alone. I left a farm that had been in the family for over 185 years. My degree was in agriculture, and I was the last son to take over the farm.

I was upset at God as I reviewed all the things I had done for him. My heart screamed, "Hey, God! I left my family, my friends, the farm—all for you, God. Where are the ministry perks?" The fact that God's Son had left his home, left his Father, gone to a foreign place, and *died* had totally escaped me.

Unfortunately we were wrong about the steroid shots eliminating Lisa's problem. The flare-ups continued, along with numbness in her fingers and legs. Then we were excited when the symptom subsided. But later it was replaced with a kind of sickness that she had not encountered before.

After another visit to the doctor it was determined that Lisa did have another condition—pregnancy! Interestingly for the next five years, while Lisa was having our four babies, she did not have one incident of MS. We thought we had found the cure! Each pregnancy became more high risk, as delivery dates were two, five, six, and ten weeks early. As recommended by our OB-GYN, for her safety and the baby's we decided that we were done having kids.

Six months later the MS we thought we had escaped came back with a vengeance. As we were touring Israel, Lisa started having symptoms of a paralysis on one side of her body. And with the eventual loss of bladder control, we knew something more was developing. By the end of the trip Lisa needed a wheelchair to get around.

One incident in Israel pictured our experience for the next twenty-five years. I remember it clearly. While going through the old city of Jerusalem with its many steps and varying levels, I and three other tour members had to carry Lisa's wheelchair up the Via Dolorosa, the "Way of Suffering."

Our years have been peppered with sacrificial servants who have come alongside Lisa and me to help us carry the load on our "Via Dolorosa." Repeatedly our life is a reflection of the passage in Luke 5. A paralytic was brought to the place where Jesus was teaching, but because of the crowds the lame man could not get close (v. 19). The ones carrying him went to the roof and lowered the paralytic down in front of Jesus. Verse 20 indicates that Jesus, seeing *their* faith, forgave the paralytic of his sin and healed his legs. When Lisa and I have been too weak physically and spiritually to keep going, the faith and effort of those near us have carried us through. It is amazing how God continually comforts us through his people and his church. How do we keep going when we are at the end of our rope? The truth of Luke 5 becomes reality.

Who are the ones who have lowered us into the Lord's presence as we have traveled life's path? Prayers and support from family? Absolutely. Friends sensitive to everyday needs? Essential. Our church? Critical.

I do not know what I would have done without our church family. I know churches have benevolence and meal programs to help someone temporarily. But for the last twenty-five years our church has been a picture of enduring love. Church members have stood with us and helped us with meals and even financial burdens because of extra medical bills or needs for Lisa.

One Sunday a friend at church saw me picking up Lisa from her wheelchair and putting her into the car, and he offered to help. Lisa does not weigh much more than one hundred pounds, so lifting her is not an issue. But when we consider the lifting for just one trip to church, it becomes wearing on her and me. The steps involved are several: lift her (1) from the bed to the wheelchair; (2) from the wheelchair into the car; (3) out of the car at church and back into the wheelchair; (4) after church, out of the wheelchair into the car; (5) at home, out of the car into the wheelchair; and (6) out of the wheelchair to the bed. And that does not include additional lifts if we want to go to lunch with friends after church. By the end of the day both of us are exhausted.

I can never fully express my deep appreciation for the sensitivity the leaders at the church had when they wanted to get together to talk about a "group of concerned friends" who wanted to get us a van to replace our "ailing" car and reduce the times of lifting Lisa from six to two by just rolling her into the van, from the bed to the wheelchair at home, and back into bed at home. It does not take much thought to encourage someone who is dealing with those who are disabled, but once you enter into their pain (empathy), a little kindness can go a long way.

The Doctor

After we returned from Israel, tests were done to confirm that Lisa had MS. This would help rule out any other potential causes and give us direction regarding the best treatment. After the tests, while the nurses were helping Lisa get dressed, the doctor called me into his office. He confirmed what they suspected all along. Then, in a comment that I did not know how to process, he indicated that this is when the spouse usually leaves. I sat there stunned. Was he implying I should leave? The thought was horrifying. How could I leave my wife at this time? What would she do? Who would help her? Why would someone leave a spouse in her greatest time of need? Ringing in my head were the words from our wedding vows "in sickness and in health." This is my vow to her and to God. I stayed.

The Decline

During the ensuing years we experienced the gradual decline of Lisa's health. Shortly after returning from Israel, she lost the use of her legs. Now we had to plow through the emotional barrier of confinement to a wheelchair. Along with the general numbness, she would no longer have use of her hands, which had cross-stitched so many beautiful patterns.

This left me with most of the day-to-day responsibilities. Let me set the stage. We were adjusting to new situations daily with the development of Lisa's limitations. She was feeling the deep sadness at the loss of her arms and legs. She was frustrated at not being able to function in the home as a young mom. I was trying to handle the normal duties of the home. Our children, who were ages five years, three years, one year, and two months, presented challenges that were starting to overwhelm us.

There is a reason God wired moms to nurture and dads to repair. Unfortunately when those wires get crossed, sparks fly. I recall one day at "changing time" (remember, three were still in diapers) I laid all the kids down on the floor in the living room, one next to the other. Beholding diapers off, legs up, and powder flying everywhere, Lisa commented from her chair, "Remember, Greg, these are your children, not an assembly line!"

After many suggestions and attempts of alternative methods of treatment by well-meaning friends and family, one of the final blows to Lisa's world would be the loss of most of her eyesight. Commenting on this portion of her journey, Lisa said, "I can use my wheelchair when I lose the use of my legs. I can even make it with someone else's help without my arms. But without my eyes, my world feels like it's closing in."

God at Work

One weekend when I was teaching a seminar, I mentioned Lisa's struggle with MS. A man came up to me at the break and said, "God has told me, when you go home tonight, Lisa will run to the door proclaiming she has been healed to the glory of God. I would like to tell you more over lunch." As we were eating, he continued to describe more of the details of how God revealed Lisa's healing in his vision. He probably read the look on my face and asked, "Don't you believe God can do it? Don't you believe in miracles?"

I nodded and said, "I believe with all my heart that God can do that. I pray that when I go home, Lisa runs out to greet me. And if she does, you will be the first one I'll call so we can praise God. But if when I go home and walk through the door, Lisa is sitting in her chair where she usually sits and looks up at me to give me a kiss and say hello, and asks, 'Did your *Walk Thru* seminar go well?'

I just want you to know another miracle happened that day . . . the miracle of God's sustaining grace keeping her close to him another day."

Many times we want God to do something miraculous to take away what causes us distress. If he does, we can glory in his power. If he chooses not to, we can still glory in his presence. God never promised us the absence of tough times. He did promise us his presence.

To Focus on Him

Suffering has a way of showing us things. The positive and the negative. Both enlightening. Psalm 119:71 says,

> It is good for me that I was afflicted,
> that I might learn your statutes.

This has been Lisa's life verse and a continual source of strength. When asked why it is her favorite, she responded that her suffering has been the most strategic thing God has used to get her attention off herself and drawn to him. As Lisa grew up, she was a gymnast and sprinter in high school before going to college to prepare for a discipleship ministry to girls. She was proud of her abilities. She enjoyed it when people applauded her performance. But that ability drew her away from God, limiting her understanding of who he is and keeping her attention from being in the right place.

I commented to her that it seems to make God mean. Why would a good God take something that could be used by him as a platform for ministry, like the prowess of an NFL football player, an Olympic gymnast, or some other high-profile individual?

Her response was reflective of someone who has lived and learned from God. She said, "No, not when it's something that will hurt or destroy you." She continued, explaining that it is only a loving father who will take away a knife from a three-year-old child for protection. "Yes, the child may fuss when you take it away and he may think you're mean, but he doesn't realize that what he's holding could hurt or kill him."

Ultimately this attitude comes from an understanding of God's goodness. Six times Psalm 119:65–72 expresses how God is good or is the source of good. The Hebrew text begins with the word for "good" in five of the eight verses, emphasizing God's goodness. It states that he is good in the way he deals with us (v. 65), that good discernment and knowledge come from him (v. 66), that God is good and does good (v. 68), that even affliction is good (v. 71), and that his law is better than any gold or silver (v. 72).

The progression of the psalmist's commitment to and affirmation of God's word grows with each statement as he understands God's work and God's ways. First, he understands God's commandments and "believes" them (v. 66). Next, he moves to action when he "keeps" God's word (v. 67). With all his heart he "observes" God's precepts (v. 69). And he then moves to enjoyment by his "delight" in God's law (v. 70). And he esteems it more than anything else this world can provide by stating that it is better than gold and silver (v. 72).

Chuck Swindoll, in his devotional *Bedside Blessings*, shares the following truth: "When you persevere through a trial, God gives you a special measure of insight. You become the recipient of the favor of God as He gives to you, and those who suffer with you, something that would not be learned otherwise."[1]

What Is Normal?

Circumstances around our home are not what you would consider *normal*. I don't know how "normal" things would be even if Lisa did not have MS, but our daily situation is especially out of the ordinary now. I have tried to allow the kids to maintain normal activities and schedules. Though confined to a bed, Lisa still desires to do the things a mother usually does.

We make every effort to be at basketball and soccer games, concerts, and special events. Lisa always says, "I may not be able to go as fast as I used to, but getting there is the goal." Even though there are times when she is too tired to go, the kids know she wants to be there. The phrase, "Oh, we can't do that because our mom has MS," is one that I have tried to keep to a minimum. The *modus operandi* we live by is, "If Mom feels good, let's roll!"

The dinner table (or supper table, for those of us with a Midwest farming background) usually represents the place where conversation, communication, and relationships happen. With the difficulty and sometimes discomfort of Lisa getting to the table, our center for gathering and eating has migrated to our bedroom. When the pizza is delivered, it has gone straight back to our bedroom. Some kids are on the floor. Another is sitting in Lisa's wheelchair. Others are lying on the bed. I think this has helped all of us "normalize" Lisa's situation. Often when I come home, one of the kids is lying on the bed talking to Lisa.

We have tried to keep from thinking of the medical equipment and wheelchair as part of an "abnormal" life. This attitude has allowed the kids to be sensitive to the needs around them and yet not look at those who have disabilities with strangeness. We have to accept the fact that everyone has some type of "handicap," whether it is physical, emotional, or mental. I love the story of the

---

[1]Chuck Swindoll, *Bedside Blessings* (Nashville: Countryman, 2002), 322.

little guy with Down syndrome who rode in the car pool with his mom, brothers, and sisters. His mom had done a great job of instilling in him self-confidence and an understanding of his limitations. One day as they went to school, they picked up a neighbor boy he did not know. As the boy jumped into the back seat, the little guy with Down's looked him over and said, "Hi. I'm retarded. What's wrong with you?"

I have asked the kids if seeing Mom confined to a bed bothers them. "Oh, no. We miss not being able to jump in the car and go to the mall. But we always know where Mom is. She is not gone all the time like some of our friends' moms. We know she is there and will listen."

In addition to developing sensitivity to those with disabilities, it has also caused the kids to understand that everyone needs to pitch in and help. I have had my share of "chore programs" that bombed. But for the most part what we expect from the kids has been within reasonable limits.

We have to keep a sense of humor too. Yes, we have the tears of loss and frustration, but God also provides joy. Lisa's eyes water and need to be wiped. I will come into the room and she will have one eye closed. It looks like she is winking at me, so I will say, "Are you trying to seduce me?" She replies, "Sure, if it works!"

Yet the fact that "normal" is not going to be the "norm" has to be a settled understanding. Lisa will apologize, often saying, "I am so sorry that I can't do the things I used to. I am so sorry that I don't look the way I used to." I tell her I understand. I feel the same way, and I don't even have MS! She is experiencing the same things I will one day be experiencing, only doing it twenty years earlier.

A Different Type of Ministry

It took many years for Lisa to work through her inability and to see what God could do through her. One of the most significant ministries Lisa has is prayer. At first it felt to her like a ministry by default. She would say, "It's all I can do. I can't do anything else for anybody, so I guess I will pray for them." She has no idea of the impact she makes through her intercessory praying. Often I will bring home prayer requests from friends, students at the seminary, and people at church. Lisa's ministry has the same goal as the BASF Chemical commercial. Their tagline is, "We don't make the products you use; we just make them better." Lisa can't do things, but she helps others do them better—through prayer!

A lifeline for Lisa has been Moody Broadcasting Network that we can hear through the Internet. Until I get home to feed and take care of her at lunch, she listens to MBN programming. Chris Fabry, Chip Ingram, Erwin Lutzer, David Jeremiah, James McDonald, Dennis Rainey, Chuck Swindoll, and *Midday Con-*

nection are her radio companions. Most days when I come home, she will ask me to write to various broadcasts, to people she has been praying for, wanting to be an encouragement to them.

Lisa's disability affects not just her ministry; it also affects ours. People have asked me if it bothered me not to be involved in ministry the way I had envisioned. Will I be able to use my Bible-college and seminary training?

Sure, there is loss. Yes, there has been grief from the death of a dream or vision of a ministry I thought God was leading me into. But what I came to realize is that our *vision* may not be his *version* of ministry. It may not be my training that the Lord wants to shape. Instead it might be me.

I appreciate what Dr. Lanier Burns, former department chair of systematic theology at Dallas Theological Seminary, says regarding his study of the Word. Echoing his wife, Kathy, he states, "She says my study of the Scriptures has made me more holy. And that's the greatest compliment I could ever receive." It is through God's Word that we see him.

It is not what we do for him that determines blessing, but rather what he does in us. It has been the tough stuff that has caused me to look to God in a way I never would have otherwise.

Don't Take My Spot

I have been asked many times, "What is it like living with someone who is handicapped?" I respond, "That might be a question better asked of Lisa. She is the one who has to live with the one who is handicapped!" When you think about it, we all are handicapped in some way or other. When I say this to Lisa, she says, "Yes, but make sure they know it doesn't mean they can take my handicapped parking spot!" What are some of my handicaps that keep me from loving deeply?

When My Love Is Conditional, Not Unconditional

The commitment I made to Lisa on our wedding day was to love her from that day forward. It was not only to love her as she was on that day but always to love her. Dr. Renald Showers, who did one of our six marriage counseling programs (God knows we needed more than just one), said, "If you are not ready to tear the 'D' words (divorce and desertion) out of your dictionary, you're not ready to get married."

We were standing at the altar. Lisa was absolutely gorgeous in her beautiful gown, handmade by her mom. We were overflowing with dreams and health. I know I did not completely comprehend at the time what the commitment to love someone "till death do us part" entailed. It is God's wisdom that I did not know. When we were standing at the altar, we heard "for better," "for richer," and "in health." Then when we walked out of the church, the words "for worse," "for poorer," and "in sickness," were soon to become reality.

The value of a personal example is powerful. I think of my dad, who recently laid his bride of sixty years in the arms of the Lord. I picture them walking hand in hand through the mall, wallpapering a friend's bathroom together, tenderly holding hands in church, or my dad even popping her on the bottom as they walked up a flight of stairs. (He did not realize I was watching.) They endured many difficulties but were committed to holding on to each other and the Lord through each trial.

The man I am privileged to call my teacher, Dr. J. Dwight Pentecost, spoke to me about his dear departed wife, Dorothy. He said, "I loved her. It's no mystery. If she had needs, I was committed to do everything possible to meet them." This reflects his lifelong study of the life of Christ. In John 13:34 Jesus stated, "A new commandment I give to you, that you love one another, even as I have loved you, that you also love one another."

I admit there are days when the responsibility of Lisa's care takes a toll. Going home at lunch every day to care for her and then quickly returning to work for meetings; being a nutritionist, calculating her food and feeding her through the tube; being a health-care nurse and dealing with medications, catheterizations, and feminine needs; and doing this four or five times a day, every day, is difficult. Anticipating three or four steps ahead on every trip. Making sure we can get there. Figuring out how to get there. Trying to avoid situations that are not handicapped accessible so as to not make her feel like an inconvenience.

Lisa apologizes all the time for her situation, either for not being able to help me around the house or for her disability. It frustrates her each time I am cleaning the bedroom and bathroom. She tells me she wishes she could do the vacuuming so I could do other things. She realizes her situation causes more work for the kids. I console her that I know she wants to do it but that it's not all it's cracked up to be. She's not missing anything, but I understand her desire to contribute.

The other thing she apologizes for is being disabled. She says she knows I did not bargain for this. At various times she has said she wished I had a wife that could do things and be the wife I wanted. I tell her that I feel bad for her because I was not what she bargained for either. Would she have even given me a second look if she had known I was going to turn out bald and fat? (One is not my fault; the other, I'm working on!) We have to remember our vow to God is not just a preference but a promise to each other and to him. We will struggle until we realize that God never intends for us to do this on our own or in our own strength. Our love has to reflect and be drawn from his love for us. Unconditional. Eternal. Personal.

When My Love Is Selfish, Not Sacrificial

"What about my needs?" I hear this phrase all the time. If you are in a relationship, a marriage, and even a friendship for what you are going to get out of it, you are in it for the wrong reason. It is not about me, no matter what the country song says.

> I wanna talk about me
> Wanna talk about I
> Wanna talk about number one
> Oh my me my
> What I think, what I like, what I know, what I want, what I see[2]

Unfortunately this perspective is all too common, and we fight it daily. Paul wrote in 1 Corinthians 15:31, "I die every day." I realize that we all need personal time for refreshment and rejuvenation. But our focus is what will lift us up or weigh us down. Do we have personal time to establish a connection with the Source of our power, or do we try to disconnect from everything to focus on ourselves? Paul continues this theme of sacrificial love in Ephesians 5:25–27:

> Husbands, love your wives, as Christ loved the church and gave himself up for her, that he might sanctify her, having cleansed her by the washing of water with the word, so that he might present the church to himself in splendor, without spot or wrinkle or any such thing, that she might be holy and without blemish.

What Christ gave for his bride was total, and that is what he calls for me to do as I serve Lisa. The best part is that he provides the power.

An excellent example of love that moves from duty to opportunity is the story of Muriel. In March 1990, Robertson McQuilken announced his resignation as president of Columbia Bible College. He did so in order to care for his beloved wife, Muriel, who was suffering from advanced stages of Alzheimer's. In a letter presented to the university he wrote:

> Perhaps it would help you to understand if I shared with you what I shared at the time of the announcement of my resignation in chapel. The decision was

---

[2]Toby Keith, "I Wanna Talk about Me," from the album, *Pull My Chain*, August 28, 2001, Dream-Works Nashville.

made, in a way, forty-two years ago when I promised to care for Muriel "in sickness and in health . . . till death do us part." So, as I told the students and faculty, as a man of my word, integrity has something to do with it. But so does fairness. She has cared for me fully and sacrificially all these years; if I cared for her for the next forty years, I would not be out of debt. Duty, however, can be grim and stoic. But there is more; I love Muriel. She is a delight to me— her happy spirit and tough resilience in the face of her continual distressing frustration. I do not have to care for her. *I get to!* It is a high honor to care for so wonderful a person.[3]

In Matthew 19 Jesus recounts the principle of Genesis 2:24, "Therefore a man shall leave his father and his mother and hold fast to his wife, and they shall become one flesh." I have always connected that principle of marriage with Ephesians 5:28–29, "In the same way husbands should love their wives as their own bodies. He who loves his wife loves himself. For no one ever hated his own flesh, but nourishes and cherishes it, just as Christ does the church." We are joined as one flesh when we take the commitment of marriage. I view Lisa's body as if it were my own, and meeting her needs as the care I would want if I were in her place.

This is reflected in the way we get ready for church on Sunday mornings. We get up and I brush her teeth and then brush mine. As I get her ready for a shower, it's just easier to take one also since I'm going to get wet anyway. I dry and do her hair. I shave (that's one she does not have to worry about). When it comes to putting clothes on for church, I pick out a nice outfit for her and then find something for me that matches. It takes less creativity and effort on my part to match her color. Treating her the way I would want to be treated is the basic principle of being one flesh, and I love her as I love myself. For Lisa it is care and concern. For me it is connection.

A comment I often get relates to how I take care of Lisa. It does take extra effort and planning. But then how many moms get thanks for doing the same thing for their kids? Not as many as should! Yet day after day, Sunday after Sunday, they get them ready, help them look nice, and hardly ever get a positive comment or compliment. How about our aging parents? We take care of them, yet hardly anyone even acknowledges those who are faithful in that responsibility. I guess the reason for the expression of appreciation is that Lisa is an adult, and she is "supposed" to be able to take care of herself. Are we not to help those in need? First Timothy 5:8 says, "But if anyone does not provide

---

[3]Robertson McQuilken, *A Promise Kept: The Story of an Unforgettable Love* (Wheaton, IL: Tyndale House Publishers, 1998), 22 (italics his).

for his relatives, and especially for members of his household, he has denied the faith and is worse than an unbeliever."

My heart breaks when I hear of the spouses who have left their disabled mates because of irreconcilable differences, or parents who have abandoned their children because they could not stand the pressure of taking care of a child with a disability.

We prefer the passages about rewards, but we are often unwilling to persevere through the verses on obedience. We read the verses on character but not the ones on testing. We come across passages like Philippians 3:10 and read, "that I may know him" (and we feel, "Oh, the sweetness of knowing him!") "and the power of his resurrection" (and we say, "Oh, what power!"), and then we read the rest, "and may share his sufferings, becoming like him in his death" (and we slam on the brakes, "Oh, time out!"). We want his presence and power, but we hesitate when it comes to the process. A friend, Walter Baker, states, "Love is never really manifested until it is tested." The strength of a beam is not proven until it is bent.

When My Love Is Natural, Not Supernatural

One of the questions many people ask is, "How do you do it?" My first response is, "Some days not very well." I have to pray each day that the Lord will allow me to love Lisa and the kids in his strength, not mine, and with his love, not mine.

Some days I have come to the end of *my* rope, but that is where I think God wants me to start. Too often I focus on *what* I need to do, not *how* I need to do it. I get concerned with the right actions, not the right attitude. Paul writes in 1 Corinthians 13 about *agapē* love, the type of love that is the source of strength. It has been explained this way:

> This word, *agapē*, describes a love that is based on the deliberate choice of the one who loves rather than the worthiness of the one who is loved. This kind of love goes against natural human inclination. It is giving, selfless, expect-nothing-in-return kind of love.
>
> Our modern "throw-away" society encourages us to get rid of people in our lives who are difficult to get along with, whether they are friends, family, or acquaintances. Yet this attitude runs in complete contrast to the love described by Paul. True love puts up with people who would be easier to give up on.[4]

---

[4]Earl D. Radmacher, Ronald Barclay Allen, and H. Wayne House, eds., *The Nelson Study Bible: New King James Version* (Nashville: Nelson, 1997), 1933.

My natural inclination is to try to live by the old Nike motto, "Just Do It." The problem is my sin nature wars against doing anything like the *agapē* love described. In addition to that, I do not even have the capacity to do it. I have to depend on God's love to hang in there. *Agapē* love is the kind of love Christ had for the church. Love gives and does not expect anything in return. But when Christ does receive back love, he rejoices all the more. That is not a love that comes from me; it comes from God.

Our Hope

Promises are a funny thing—you tend to depend on them. One night as I was tucking my daughter, Sara Beth, into bed, the reality of Lisa's situation was starting to work on her little mind. She eventually asked, "Daddy, will Mommy walk in heaven?"

"Oh, sweetie, probably not," I said. As I saw the disappointment in her eyes, I followed it up with, "You see, Sara Beth, Mommy was a runner in high school. When she gets to heaven, she won't walk; she will run. And you won't even begin to catch her!"

I saw the smile of peaceful contentment break across her face, as she said, "That's good." That hope keeps me going, knowing that someday Lisa will have a new, transformed body, unhindered and totally free. That hope gives me the joy of the Lord during difficult days, strength in knowing all things will be made right.

What If?

One day I asked Lisa what would be the first thing she would do if she woke up and discovered the Lord had totally given back her health. I thought she would say something like call her mom and dad, run around the house, or jump up and down in the backyard, but her gentle response was, "I would take your hand and walk around our block with you. I miss our walks."

With a love like that, how can I *not* want to do everything possible to make her life a little more enjoyable? There are times when I come home and a commercial on TV has prompted her request for something like a McDonald's Double Cheeseburger, a Butterfinger Blast from Sonic, or a York Peppermint Pattie. Because the MS has weakened her throat muscles, she is on a feeding tube, and the possibility of aspiration rules out her eating or drinking anything. But we have agreed that "tastes" are okay. She says, "If it causes me to 'go earlier,' it will be worth it!"

No, we are not going to do anything stupid, but we are not to live in fear. A few years ago Lisa had an episode with infections that eventually led to pneumonia. After a couple of weeks in the ICU, the doctors sent her home, indicating that she may not live more than two months or six at the most. The doctor also indicated that if the pneumonia did not get her, the blood clots from inactivity would. Talk about living in fear. Every day as I came home at lunch to feed and take care of her, I walked in wondering whether she was asleep or gone. Two years later Lisa and I decided that we are not going to live like she is going to die at any moment. So within reason we have been traveling. People ask me, "Doesn't the travel make her tired?" I respond that traveling makes *me* tired. Even though it is something that takes a little more planning and preparation, we have always enjoyed it, and it is worth it.

Her Eyes

I have always told my kids that when you marry, it is not based on how a person looks, or what the person says, but rather who that person is. The heart is reflected through the eyes. Eyes are indicators. You can know much about people if they have "soft eyes" or "hard eyes."

What first caught my attention when I met Lisa were her eyes and smile. (I am being honest! It was an added bonus that God happened to put them in a beautiful wrapping!) The Lord gave her beautiful blue eyes and a gentle smile. They reflected a pure heart committed to her Lord.

I remember asking her while we were students at Moody Bible Institute in Chicago why she came to Moody. Her response was, "If I wanted to be a good wife and mother, then I needed to know the Bible." I can remember the light post I nearly walk into on LaSalle Boulevard when the thought hit me, "Now that's the type of woman I want to marry and with whom I want to raise my kids!"

I am thankful for those same eyes and heart for the Lord that I see each day. When she gets discouraged about what she cannot do because of the loss of her arms and legs, I tell her that I did not marry her for what she could do, but for who she is. I assure her that eventually every one of us will be limited in what he can do, and it will be at that time that we impact people based on who we are. The beautiful wrapping does not last long, but a good gift does. The best gift Lisa has given me is her good heart.

Even though MS has taken most of Lisa's vision, it does not mean she cannot see. Her eyes still reflect her heart and her hope. Lisa's favorite song is *Blessed Assurance*. Fanny Crosby's second and third verses of hope are especially meaningful since she too was visually impaired.

> Perfect submission, perfect delight,
> Visions of rapture now burst on my sight;

Angels descending bring from above
Echoes of mercy, whispers of love.

Perfect submission, all is at rest
I in my Savior am happy and blest,
Watching and waiting, looking above,
Filled with His goodness, lost in His love.

His Work, His Glory

We have not had Job's three friends in our living room, but I think we have had his relatives. Many of these people are well meaning. But a greater point of stress for us has come from within as reflected by the question asked by Jesus's disciples in John 9 regarding the blind man: "And his disciples asked him, 'Rabbi, who sinned, this man or his parents, that he was born blind?'" (v. 2).

This thought has crossed our minds many times. *What did we do? Is there some sin we have not confessed? Is there something God is punishing us for?* We have searched our hearts.

Jesus's answer is comforting. "It was not that this man sinned, or his parents, but that the works of God might be displayed in him" (v. 3).

Sometimes we sound like Job asking the questions God never intends to answer this side of heaven. But we are thankful that while we may not have the answers, he does give us a purpose. His glory.

Until then, if you have never seen a picture of a peace that passes all understanding, I encourage you to come visit my Lisa. She will be riding, and I will be pushing her in her wheelchair, her "Rolling Throne" of glory.

PART TWO

BIBLICAL FOUNDATIONS

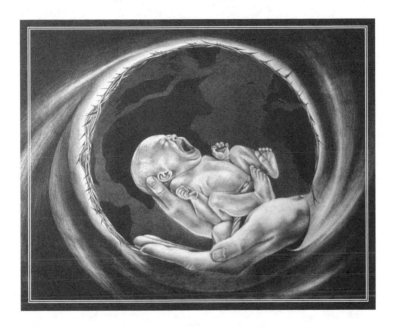

Immanuel, God with Us, by Dawn Waters Baker. The hand holding the newborn Jesus is that of Joseph, who courageously took this baby as his own after helping his wife give birth. The second, larger hand is that of God the Father, who cups the dark earth into which he releases his precious Son. A lamb silhouette behind baby Jesus's head depicts the role he will play, and the thorns in which the world is ensnared will form the "crown" the Son will wear at his death.

Often Jesus is pictured in quiet repose as a well-groomed Mary tenderly holds him, both looking freshly bathed. Sleeping newborns do look peaceful and sweet, but newborns also cry, sometimes with screams as they adjust to their new world. When Jesus became one of us, he felt the cold and hurts that we feel. Though sinless, he was fully human. And though fully human, he was undiminished deity—God with us.

Stephen J. Bramer (MDiv, Ontario Theological Seminary; ThM, Trinity Evangelical Divinity School; PhD, Dallas Theological Seminary) is the department chair and professor of Bible exposition for Dallas Seminary. He taught for sixteen years at Briercrest Bible College and Biblical Seminary in Saskatchewan, Canada, before joining the faculty at Dallas. Dr. Bramer serves as an adjunct professor for Word of Life Bible Institute, Hungary, and the Jordan Evangelical Theological Society in Amman, Jordan. He also is a teaching elder at Waterbrook Bible Fellowship, Wylie, Texas.

6

Suffering in the Pentateuch

Stephen J. Bramer

The first five books of the Bible, also called the Pentateuch and the Torah, establish the foundation of many themes of Scripture, including suffering. These books reveal what Moses, the great prophet, leader, and spokesman for God to the nation of Israel, said about suffering.

Genesis

When God created everything (Genesis 1–2), there was no emotional distress, no suffering, and no death, though the possibility of death is mentioned as a consequence of disobedience. God created a perfect creation. If there was anything that we might call pain, it was a beneficial discomfort that would alert humankind to limitations of the human body. This pain was something short of suffering associated with a fallen humanity. Throughout the initial creation story the author continually states, "And God saw that it was good" (1:4, 10, 12, 18, 21, 25). At the conclusion of the account God summarized all of this wonderful creation by saying, "It was very good" (v. 31).

Often the question is asked, "Why did God create suffering in the world?" However, this is an invalid question because God created a perfect world without suffering and death. Evolutionists face a problem here because they say that in the fossil record death existed even before the creation of man! God created humans as male and female, as the pinnacle of his creation, both in his image. He gave them dominion over what he had created. This was not an absolute dominion or authority that enabled them to do whatever they wanted. They were created to rule, but they were under God's ultimate rule, for they were given restrictions about the tree of the knowledge of good and evil (Gen. 2:16–17). Man was not created equal to God, nor was he created independent of God. The fall of humankind into sin (Genesis 3) introduced much of the pain and suffering people experience today. This is because man rejected God's word over him.

The serpent, one of the animals the Lord made (Gen. 3:1), spoke out as more than an animal. Was this animal also Satan? All the animals God had created were good (1:25), but this one questioned God's word. Revelation 20:2–3 refers to this adversary of God as a deceiver of the nations, one who led the world astray—"the dragon, that ancient serpent, who is the devil, or Satan" (v. 2; cf. Rev. 12:9). Thus a spiritual power (Satan) behind the serpent introduced evil into the world through the man and woman whom God created. God did not create evil. Evil stemmed from the desire of one of the angels, Satan, also called Lucifer, to be like God (Isa. 14:13–14).

As a result of the serpent's suggestion, Eve was deceived (1 Tim. 2:14), and she ate from the tree of which she had been warned not to eat (Gen. 3:3). Adam willingly chose to eat from it as well. As the head of the whole human race—Adam (and Eve who was taken from Adam)—disobeyed, and thus everyone who has come from Adam is sinful (Rom. 1:18–32; 3:23; 5:12).

The consequences of this original sin are many and varied. God pronounced curses on the serpent, the woman, the man, and the earth. He had previously stated, "For in the day that you eat of it [the tree of the knowledge of good and evil] you shall surely die" (Gen. 2:17).

But man is far more than just a physical being, and death is far more than the cessation of a heartbeat. God breathed into man the breath of life (v. 7), so he is both a physical and a spiritual being. The moment Adam and Eve ate from the forbidden fruit, they died, though they still breathed. Obviously death can occur over time and in different ways. They felt shame (3:7)—a form of spiritual death. They attempted to cover their nakedness by their own means. No one had told them they were naked. They had seen each other before. But suddenly they realized that their bodies could be misused, abused, lusted after.

Also Adam and Eve felt guilt, for when they heard "the sound of the LORD God walking in the garden . . . the man and his wife hid themselves from the presence of the LORD God among the trees of the garden" (3:8). They previously had fellowship with God. But now they did not want to be with God, and so they hid behind some bushes or trees in the garden. The Lord called out to them, "Why are you there?" He did not say, "Where are you?" because he knew. Nor was his question for the purpose of obtaining information, for he knew what they had done. Instead Adam responded, "I heard the sound of you in the garden, and I was afraid, because I was naked, and I hid myself" (v. 9). First, there was shame, then guilt, and now fear—he disobeyed God. He had died spiritually.

When God asked, "Who told you that you were naked?" Adam responded, "The woman whom you gave to be with me, she gave me fruit of the tree, and I ate" (vv. 11–12). Adam was blaming God indirectly and Eve directly. Then the Lord said to the woman, "What is this that you have done?" and the woman responded, "The serpent deceived me, and I ate" (v. 13). One of the consequences of sin is that people tend to blame others for their actions. Part of the pain and suffering that comes in people's lives is because they blame each other rather than taking personal responsibility.

The fall also resulted in physical death. Genesis 3:19b makes this clear.

> . . . till you return to the ground,
>> for out of it you were taken;
> for you are dust,
>> and to dust you shall return.

Sin resulted in physical death.

In Genesis 3:15 God said to the serpent,

> I will put enmity between you and the woman,
>> and between your offspring and her offspring;
> he shall bruise your head,
>> and you shall bruise his heel.

Some people think this is only saying that women will abhor snakes! However, this statement is known as the *protevangelium*, the first glimpse of the gospel and how Satan would be dealt with and how death would be overcome. From both the woman and the serpent there would be offspring, literally "seed." Someday a descendant from the woman—Jesus Christ—would crush the head of this Evil One (Rom. 16:20; Rev. 20:2–3, 10). But throughout human history a great battle between good and evil is being waged. While Genesis 3 does not say it in so many words, one of the ways people suffer is in spiritual battles between the forces of good and evil (Eph. 6:12). For believers who resist evil, much pain will result.

To the woman he said,

> "I will surely multiply your pain in childbearing;
>> in pain you shall bring forth children.
> Your desire shall be for your husband,
>> and he shall rule over you." (Gen. 3:16)

The bearing of children was to be a blessing. It was designated as part of the woman's role before the fall. Now greater physical pain would be part of the experience. The Hebrew word translated "childbearing" could refer to all that is part of conceiving, including the menstrual cycle, so that even women who do not give birth to children experience physical discomfort and some pain because of this judgment.

The expression "Your desire shall be for your husband, and he shall rule over you" (v. 16) is difficult to interpret. Some say this "desire" is a positive longing for one's husband, even though a pregnancy may result with its accompanying pain. The word "desire" is used in this way in Song of Songs 7:10. However, in Genesis 4:7 it is used for sin's attitude toward a person. Sin's "desire" is for the woman, that is, "Sin wants to dominate you." Possibly the woman's desire for her husband could mean that because of the fall, the female would desire to rule. Thus one of the consequences of sin is that marital relationships do not always work the way they were originally designed to work. Friction in relationships leads to misery, both in unbiblical, abusive male domination and in unbiblical female usurpation.

And to Adam he said,

> "Because you have listened to the voice of your wife
>> and have eaten of the tree
> of which I commanded you,
>> 'You shall not eat of it,'
> cursed is the ground because of you;
>> in pain you shall eat of it all the days of your life;
> thorns and thistles it shall bring forth for you;
>> and you will eat the plants of the field.
> By the sweat of your face
>> you will eat bread,
> till you return to the ground,
>> for out of it you were taken;
> for you are dust,
>> and to dust you shall return." (3:17–19)

No longer would the earth respond properly to man's care and tending. Now that man has fallen, all that man ruled over is also fallen. Specifically people have a difficult time eking out an existence from what they are able to draw from the earth. This world is fallen.

Though Genesis does not state that earthquakes, volcanoes, and hurricanes will occur, the implication is that these happen because the earth has been cursed. This is substantiated in Romans 8:22: "For we know that the whole creation has been groaning together in the pains of childbirth until now." Human suffering does not mean God does not love human beings.

Some people ask, "How can God be good when there is so much evil and suffering in the world?" The answer is that God made a perfect world and man messed it up! The entire earth is fallen, and yet there is grace. Someday the seed of the woman, Christ, would crush the serpent's (Satan's) head! Because Adam and Eve ate from the tree of the knowledge of good and evil, man has become like God in a certain respect (Gen. 3:22). Before the fall, God decided what was good and what was evil. Now that man has disobeyed, he seeks to decide what is good and what is evil.

Genesis 4 gives a glimpse of how sin affects human society. When Cain and Abel, Adam and Eve's sons, brought offerings to God, he rejected what Cain brought (fruit) and accepted Abel's sacrifice (an animal). Cain was frustrated and angry. "The Lord said to Cain, 'Why are you angry, and why has your face fallen? If you do well, will you not be accepted? And if you do not do well, sin is crouching at the door. Its desire is for you, but you must rule over it'" (vv. 6–7). Suffering can be brought on a person if he refuses to do what is right according to God's Word. Not all suffering results directly from what Adam and Eve did. Abel did nothing wrong; he worshiped God properly, and yet he was murdered.

The fact that Abel, who brought the right kind of sacrifice, died shows that some suffering comes because of the sinfulness of fellow human beings, some of them even close relatives. Many times suffering comes because a person, though knowing the right thing to do, decides in pride or anger to do the opposite. Pride makes it difficult for people to accept God's Word on any matter. This results in a lot of pain.

Because of the length of the book of Genesis it is not possible to deal with every story that touches on suffering. So the following are selected incidents that might lead to further reflection on the causes and consequences of suffering.

The flood, recorded in Genesis 6–9, came about because of mixed marriages (6:1–3), evil thinking and corrupt living (v. 5), and violence (v. 13). Because of sin, God said, "My Spirit shall not abide in man forever, for he is flesh: his days shall be 120 years" (v. 3). God's judgment included limiting the length of man's life on earth. "Then the LORD saw that the wickedness of man was great in the earth, and that every intention of the thoughts of his heart was only evil continually" (v. 5). People were thinking evil thoughts, so judgment would come on the entire human race; people would be taken away in the flood. Some suffering comes from God's judgment on a society that walks away from him.

After the flood, God started human society over again with Noah and his sons. But God emphasized that if man is to receive his blessing, man must respect human life, treating people properly.

> Whoever sheds the blood of man,
>   by man shall his blood be shed,
>   for God made man in his own image. (Gen. 9:6)

Human society is responsible to see that people are treated with the respect they deserve and that required punishment is carried out. This first biblical reference to human government is in the context of maintaining justice. God holds nations responsible for how they treat people, even those whom they conquer.

In Genesis 10–11, the genealogies of Noah's sons (table of nations) are given, and in the midst of the genealogies is the account of the tower of Babel. People had begun to multiply and were building a tower so they could "make a name for [them]selves, lest [they] be dispersed over the face of the whole earth" (Gen. 11:4). They were not building a tower to reach to God. Rather they were defying his command to fill the earth. God had said, "Be fruitful and multiply and fill the earth" (Gen. 1:28). So here was a group of people who were defying the Word of God. Because of that, God came down and scattered them by the multiplication of languages so that they were not able to work together.

In Genesis 12 God made a covenant with Abram, promising him a land, a seed, and a blessing. Then God "cut" the covenant, making it unilateral because God was the only one to walk between the halves of the animals (15:17). God declared, "I will bless those who bless you, and him who dishonors you I will curse" (12:3).

Why is there suffering in the world? One answer is that some people and nations have chosen not to bless Abraham and his descendants. God said he would curse those who curse them, and he would bless those who bless them. Throughout the Old Testament God is saying, in essence, "If you don't treat Abraham and his descendants properly, you won't be treated properly." Whenever God "curses" someone, it involves pain and suffering to some extent. The choosing of Abraham and his descendants has implications for all other humans in relation to the way they treat God's choice and the benefits they can derive from that choice.

But even this chosen man, Abraham, faced consequences for both himself and his family when he sinned. For example, Sarah had to live a lie or else disobey her husband (Genesis 20). She was placed in a terrible position. Abraham's sin also affected Abimelech and his family. None of the women in his household could become pregnant. Abraham's lie probably affected Isaac, who followed his father's sinful example. This is just one example of many in Genesis where one person's sin resulted in others' suffering. The stories of Isaac, Jacob, and Esau all give proof to the principle that sin inevitably affects others.

Genesis ends with the story of Joseph, a great example in the Old Testament of trusting the sovereignty of God (50:20). Despite Joseph's great suffering after being sold into slavery, being unfairly jailed, and enduring separation from his family, God worked all things together for good.

Exodus

In the book of Exodus the theme of suffering is seen in four main instances: first, in the suffering of the Israelites as slaves in Egypt; second, in the Egyptians' suffering from the plagues; third, in the suffering of Israel in the desert journey from Egypt to Mount Sinai; and fourth, in the great suffering following the incident of the golden calf.

The suffering of Abraham's descendants in Egypt (Exodus 1) was not a direct result of any sin. God described to Abraham that his family would be mistreated for four hundred years in a foreign land (Gen. 15:13), but also one of the blessings to Abraham would be fulfilled because they would leave with "great possessions" (v. 14; cf. 12:2; Ex. 12:35–36). God used Egypt to preserve the Israelites, and later he used their return to the Land of Promise to judge the Amorites (15:16). Suffering in Egypt caused God's people to call out to him, to remain a distinct people, and to understand how to treat people properly once they were in their own land (Ex. 22:21). Another blessing to Abraham's descendants that occurred even while they were suffering as slaves was their increase in numbers (1:12; cf. Gen. 12:2). Not all suffering should be seen as God's displeasure, and there is the possibility of blessing in the midst of suffering as part of God's plan.

The suffering of the Egyptians in the plagues was part of God's attempt to get Pharaoh's attention and to teach him and the Egyptians that Yahweh is Lord (Ex. 6:1; 12:12; 14:4). Some of the plagues apparently affected even the Israelites—though not all—since they were living in the land of Egypt. In the plague of the death of the firstborn, if the Israelites had not sacrificed the lamb and put the blood on the lintel doorposts, they too would have suffered. Suffering may have multiple purposes and sometimes multiple recipients, depending on the circumstances. Believers need to be careful about stating that they know the purpose of others' suffering, especially to those who are enduring the suffering.

In 15:26 God said to Israel, "If you will diligently listen to the voice of the LORD your God, and do that which is right in his eyes, and give ear to his commandments and keep all his statutes, I will put none of the diseases on you that I put on the Egyptians, for I am the LORD, your healer." Some people have taken this verse and developed the principle that if you are obedient, you'll never have any illness. But the context and the content suggest a different reason. What were the diseases brought on the Egyptians? The ten plagues. Why? Because they did not know the Lord. It was as though Pharaoh said, "God, who?" and God answered, "Let me introduce myself." God was saying to his people that it might be necessary to bring plagues and diseases on people because they did not understand who God is. But if they would understand and obey him (unlike the Egyptians), then they could avoid certain suffering.

The suffering of Israel in the wilderness is recorded in Exodus 14–18. The purposes of the wilderness suffering—and this was before they reached Mount Sinai—varied. God wanted to test them to see if they would trust him (15:25b–26). And he wanted to challenge them to be his people and to live differently than all the other nations so that all peoples would know he is the Lord God (19:5–6). He wanted to teach them how to worship him in a manner different from that of other nations (Exodus 25–40). All of this occurs in the God-planned circumstances of suffering and subsequent necessary trusting.

In the middle of Exodus 19–40—the section containing the Mosaic covenant, the giving of the Law, and the instructions for the tabernacle—an event is recorded that brought suffering. The people disobeyed God by creating and worshiping a golden calf (chap. 32). This is the first general act of disobedience on the part of Israel, the nation that had committed itself to being God's people and obeying him (Ex. 19:8). Often the first act of disobedience receives full judgment so that everyone can know God's view of the matter (e.g., Achan in Joshua 7, and Ananias and Sapphira in Acts 5). Many were killed, and in Exodus 32:34 God refers to a "day" when he will punish wrongdoers. God is a just Judge who does not ignore sin, even among his people.

Some think that the Mosaic Law should be treated as a cause for suffering since the Bible often refers to the Law in negative terms. But there was much good benefit from the Mosaic covenant and the Law that was part of it. It was given to God's people not to bring them into a relationship with the Lord, for they had already believed in the Lord (14:31). Because they were God's people, he said that they would be blessed if they obeyed the many stipulations in the Law. This was not a matter of legalism, though later it became such for some people. It was a matter of how one's relationship with God could flourish. By obeying, the nation would be distinct from all other nations.

The giving of the Law was an act of grace, for it details how God's people could serve and worship him acceptably. But if the people did not obey the Lord, the Law was a gracious reminder to come back to the Lord and his standards.

Leviticus

The overall message of Leviticus might be stated as follows: "Proper fellowship—and when necessary, restoration of fellowship with God—by God's covenant people should reflect the holiness of God and should recognize the means by which his people can enjoy fellowship with him." While Leviticus is not primarily about suffering, suffering will occur when God's people sin or when they refuse to recognize the means by which their sins can be covered.

The book of Leviticus outlines God's expectations of Israel and the consequences of not meeting those expectations. The consequences of disobedience are summarized in Leviticus 26. When people suffer, they need to acknowledge their disobedience to the Lord (vv. 16–17). Refusal to learn from God's discipline may result in increased discipline so that learning might take place (vv. 18, 21, 24, 28). Leviticus 26:27–43 describes the possibility of exile, even indicating the length of that exile based on the nation's refusal to celebrate the sabbatical year. Yet in the middle of this significant chapter on possible future suffering because of disobedience, God's mercy and forgiveness are stressed (vv. 40–45).

Leviticus has two historical incidents that illustrate a refusal to obey and the suffering that results. The first incident is the suffering and death of Nadab and Abihu—sons of the high priest Aaron—who offered unauthorized fire before the Lord (Lev. 10:1). This stemmed from a conscious, belligerent attitude on the part of those who knew better. So God sent fire on them, which resulted in their death (v. 2). Some suffering results from disobedient actions and must be recognized as such.

The second incident involved a blasphemer (24:10–16). When the Lord was consulted regarding just judgment of the blasphemer, the Lord demanded the punishment of death by stoning. In God's community, punishment must sometimes occur in order to protect the health of the society. The blasphemer's suffering, brought on by the person himself, had ramifications for his family and the greater society who had to carry out the death sentence. Seldom is self-inflicted suffering limited only to the guilty person.

Numbers

The book of Numbers records how the first generation of Israelites insisted on being disobedient and what resulted from it. After a wonderful prologue detailing obedience (the refrain "as the LORD commanded" occurs often), the nation as a whole complained against the Lord (Num. 11:1–3; 14:1–4; 21:4–9). Also Moses (11:10–15; 20:1–13), Aaron, and Miriam (12:1–2) complained. That first generation suffered for forty years in the wilderness because of constant grumbling, complaining, disobedience, and unbelief.

During those years of wilderness wanderings, God was seeking to show his people that they could not make it on their own and that faith is required. Having a relationship with God has always been and will always be by faith and never by mere ritualistic obedience. In Numbers, disobedience often results from disbelief (cf. Heb. 3:7–19). God used suffering to alert his people to their lack of faith, as seen in their disobedience. Some suffering allows time for God's people to repent.

Deuteronomy

The book of Deuteronomy gives the second version of the history of Israel, with a new generation in mind. In Deuteronomy God is seen as gracious. He promises to give Israel the land, and all the nation had to do was to go in and take it! The history of the nation is recorded in chapters 1–4 so that the new generation might learn from past suffering and thus not repeat the mistakes of the older generation.

Much of the "updating" of the laws pertains to the new generation and questions that were not directly dealt with earlier (e.g., rules about a king, Deut. 17:14–20). Otherwise the content and perspective of Deuteronomy are consistent with that of Exodus, Leviticus, and Numbers. This is true for the topic of suffering as well. One helpful aspect of Deuteronomy is the extensive summary of God's curses on disobedience in chapter 28.

The importance of Deuteronomy 28 (and the parallel in Leviticus 26) for the understanding of the rest of Old Testament history cannot be overstated. Possibly more than a thousand references in the prophets allude back to this material. Much of the suffering God's people experienced came as a fulfillment of the curses recorded in this chapter in God's response to their disobedience.

However, Deuteronomy 30 focuses on God's promise of blessing.

> And when all these things come upon you, the blessing and the curse, which
> I have set before you, and you call them to mind among all the nations where
> the LORD your God has driven you, and return to the LORD your God, you

and your children, and obey his voice in all that I command you today, with all your heart and with all your soul, then the LORD your God will restore your fortunes and have compassion on you, and he will gather you again from all the peoples where the LORD your God has scattered you. (vv. 1–3)

The prophets of Israel often spoke of the hope of restoration based on this promise of God.

Deuteronomy helps us understand God's purpose and plan behind some of the suffering Israel experienced in the next thousand years. The book also helps us understand God's plan to bring this type of suffering to an end. It gives hope that even though God's people experience his curses, his promises to Abraham are true. Someday, God will bring his people back to himself.

Conclusion

Suffering is now a part of life in this fallen world! And it began with the very first couple, Adam and Eve. Sometimes suffering results from our purposefully disobeying God, as they did. Other times suffering stems from the conduct of others. Even entire nations, like Israel, may suffer because of failing to follow God's ways. The Pentateuch reveals some startling facts about the dilemma of suffering. And yet in it all, God gives hope in the midst of heaviness, confidence in the face of conflict.

7

SUFFERING IN
THE HISTORICAL BOOKS

Stephen J. Bramer

A few years ago I received this anonymous illustration attached to an e-mail:

The Maker of all human beings is recalling all units manufactured, regardless of make or year, due to a serious defect in the primary and central component of the heart. This is due to a malfunction in the original prototype, code named Adam and Eve, resulting in the reproduction of the same defect in all subsequent units.

This defect has been technically termed subsequent internal non-morality, or commonly known as S.I.N. Other symptoms are the loss of direction, foul vocal emissions, amnesia of origin, lack of peace and joy, selfish or violent behavior, depression or confusion in the mental component, fearfulness, idolatry, and rebellion. The manufacturer, who is neither liable nor at fault for this defect, is providing factory-authorized repair and service free of charge to correct this sin defect.

The repair technician, Jesus, has most generously offered to bear the entire burden of the staggering cost of these repairs. The number to call for repairs in all areas is PRAYER. Once connected, please upload your burden of sin through the repentance procedure. Next, download atonement from the repair technician, Jesus, into the heart component. No matter how big or small the sin defect is, Jesus will replace it with love, joy, peace, patience, kindness, goodness, faithfulness, gentleness, self-control.

Please see the operating manual, Holy Bible, for further details on the uses of these fixtures. As an added upgrade, the manufacturer has made available to all repaired units a facility enabling direct monitoring and assistance from a resident maintenance technician, the Holy Spirit. Repaired units need only to make him welcome, and he will take up permanent residence on the premises.

This humorously illustrates that sin has affected everyone. The experience of the nations and individuals in the Old Testament demonstrates the universality of sin and the consequences for the many who refuse to repent from such actions.

The Historical Books (the Jews call them the Former Prophets) include Joshua, Judges, Ruth, 1 and 2 Samuel, 1 and 2 Kings, 1 and 2 Chronicles, Ezra, Nehemiah, and Esther. These books graphically show what suffering fallen individuals can inflict on themselves and others, even on a nation. These books demonstrate that much suffering results from humans not treating other people properly. People suffer because they do not obey the instructions of their Creator. Suffering comes on both the individual and, often, those around him as divine consequences.

Because of the length and number of books in this division of the Scriptures (twelve of the sixty-six books in the Bible, approximately 25 percent of the biblical text), this chapter will state some broad principles developed in these books and selectively illustrate general truths from specific instances. These books are primarily the historical record of those whose ancestors committed their descendants to live under the Mosaic covenant (Ex. 19:8). No doubt not everyone in the land during the period reflected in these books desired to live under the Mosaic Law. Their dilemma was that their ancestors, on behalf of all subsequent generations, had agreed that they and their descendants would participate in the Mosaic covenant.

This corporate identity and responsibility is difficult for people in Western cultures to understand. Faith is often very individualistic and personal: "Have you personally received the Lord Jesus Christ as your Savior?" This is a decision that a person must make for himself. Yet the personal nature of salvation has been so often emphasized—and, of course, that element is crucial—that it is easy to forget the element of corporate responsibility, which was especially emphasized in a covenant nation. Each individual still had to express faith in the promises of God—faith has always been involved—but there is corporate responsibility as well.

Most of this section of Scripture is *descriptive* historical material. There is limited *prescriptive* material, for much of this has already been revealed and recorded in the Pentateuch. In addition, theological interpretations and applications are often assumed. The historical books do not say, "You suffer because of this or because of that." Moral criteria are implied in the context and understood from the rest of Scripture. Also, personal reflections of some of the people involved in these books (especially David and Solomon) can be found in the poetic books of Psalms, Proverbs, and Ecclesiastes. Some psalms are highly theological in their interpretation of historical events.

Joshua

Joshua is a book about how God's people under the Mosaic covenant were prosperous and successful. Joshua 1:8 says, "This Book of the Law shall not depart from your mouth, but you shall meditate on it day and night, so that you may be careful to do according to all that is written in it. For then you will make your way prosperous, and then you will have good success." As Israel was coming into the Promised Land, they may have wondered how to avoid discipline and suffering. The Lord said, in essence, through Joshua, "Meditate on my word and obey it. That is the way you will be blessed."

The book of Joshua is a book about historical success. Living under God's blessings, without the discipline of self-generated suffering, is possible when obedience is present. The crossing of the Jordan, the setting up of the stones of remembrance, the celebration of circumcision and the Passover, and the conquering of Jericho form a continual story of obedience to God's word and success (Joshua 1–6). Joshua is an encouraging book. But in a few instances recorded in Joshua, there was suffering.

Chapter 7 records the incident with Achan. He took goods that had been declared *korban* or dedicated to the Lord (6:17). Because of that one sin, the Israelites as a nation were defeated in their first attempt to conquer the city of Ai (7:7). Many families lost sons and husbands in the battle because Achan had acted unfaithfully in taking what was to be devoted to the Lord. The result of this sin was the death of thirty-six men and the suffering of grief by Achan's wife and children. This incident clearly illustrates that an individual sin can have corporate consequences. However, a specific incident is not sufficient to develop a universal principle.

The incident in Joshua 9 with the Gibeonites reminds God's people that he must be consulted in decision making. Joshua as leader was deceived into thinking that these Gibeonites had come from a far distance. Joshua at first seemed apprehensive, but then, 9:14 states, "So the men [of Israel] took some of their provisions, but did not ask counsel from the Lord." This decision violated God's standards (Deut. 20:16–18). It was based on what the Israelites' ears heard and their eyes saw, not on their consulting the Lord. Joshua was a godly man, but Numbers 27:21 had a provision for such a case as this, when the limited information available was insufficient for making a firm decision. If Joshua didn't know what to do, then he should go to the high priest, who would consult the Urim. Joshua should have said, in essence, "You know what, everything *looks* good, but there's something here that's not quite right. Let me go consult the Lord through the high priest." This incident illustrates that suffering can come because one assumes he knows what is right while he unintentionally disobeys God's Word.

This also illustrates that some decisions can cause long-term suffering. The Gibeonites were now going to be living among God's people because Israel promised to protect them. When the Gibeonites were attacked by other Canaanites, they appealed to Joshua for help (Joshua 10). Joshua had to gather his army, march all night from Gilgal (seven hundred feet below sea level), up over mountains (almost three thousand feet high), to attack in the morning. This was not an effortless task. Joshua could have delayed his arrival, and the Gibeonites would have been wiped out. But Joshua kept his word. Afterward, the Gibeonites were required to work as woodcutters for the tabernacle (9:23). Later on, things were not good around the tabernacle (1 Samuel 2–3). Might part of the problem have been that unqualified people were working there, people who were not committed to the Lord God? Wrong decisions have their consequences, sometimes for a long time.

Joshua 21:45 (and similarly 23:14) declares, "Not one word of all the good promises that the Lord had made to the house of Israel had failed; all came to pass." All God's promises were fulfilled at least in kind, though not in extent because of the lack of complete commitment on the part of God's people. Canaanites were still in the land. God's word came true, but it still needed to be fulfilled in greater ways.

God's people in each generation need to continue to choose for God. This is clearly seen when Joshua stood and said, "Choose this day whom you will serve, whether the gods your fathers served in the region beyond the River, or the gods of the Amorites in whose land you dwell. But as for me and my house, we will serve the Lord" (24:15). Why were the Israelites considering other gods? After all that time in the wilderness and in the Promised Land, they were still prone to wander, in part because a new generation had not experienced what Joshua's generation had.

So the book of Joshua is a wonderful book of success, with little record of suffering by God's people, because they were obeying the Lord. However, the few incidents of lack of complete obedience mentioned above show that full blessing by all requires full obedience by all.

Judges

The book of Judges covers a period of several hundred years subsequent to Joshua, and Judges stands in contrast to Joshua. Judges is a book of failure—failure to keep God's word and the subsequent suffering that results from it. Much of this suffering came through foreign domination, as Moses had warned (Deut. 28:25). A cycle in the narratives of the major judges consists of the following: (1) God sends a foreign power (e.g., the Midianites); (2) these people oppress the Israelites; (3) God's people cry out to God; (4) God sends them a judge, and the judge delivers them. As long as the judge is alive, they overtly follow the Lord. Then as soon as the judge dies, they are back to their evil ways, and God has to send in another foreign nation to oppress the Israelites.

Besides the tribal or national judgment that occurred, suffering also came because of individuals such as Gideon who disobeyed the Lord (Judges 6–8). When I was in Sunday school, I always thought that Gideon was a wonderful man, but apparently my teachers always stopped the story a little too soon! The Israelites asked Gideon to be king and he essentially said, "No, no, the Lord your God is king" (8:22–23). But he then named his son, Abimelech, which means "My father is king" (v. 31). Gideon took the gold they had given him as a reward and made it into a pagan object. After Gideon died, people worshiped this idol (v. 27).

The last judge before Samuel was Samson. He had everything going for him (Judges 13–16). He had physical strength. He had a promise from God before he was ever born. He had a godly mother and father. People around him were prepared to help him. Yet he rejected all this and turned to gambling, illicit sex, and otherwise spending time doing what God had not commanded him to do. Though he had great potential, Samson did not relieve much of the suffering by the Philistines. He killed more in his death than he did in his entire lifetime. But he died humiliated and alone. Men like Gideon and Samson served as examples for Israel and for subsequent generations. Some suffering occurs and continues because of a lack of consistent obedience on the part of leaders whom God has raised up.

Ruth

The book of Ruth shows how the righteous should act under God's discipline as a nation. The book begins, "In the days when the judges ruled there was a famine in the land" (Ruth 1:1). The famine was in response to Israel's disobedience (see Lev. 26:18–20; Deut. 28:22–24, 38–40). When famine came, the Israelites should have repented. But Elimelech left the Land of Promise. He tried to get away, but of course God disciplined him for his action (Ruth 1:3).

In the book of Ruth the man who followed the Lord was Boaz. He stayed in the Promised Land that God had given him. The grace of God was at work as the Moabitess Ruth was included among God's people. Though pagan Moabites were not allowed to be part of the assembly of God (Deut. 23:3), Ruth had decided that Naomi's God would be her God. "Your people shall be my people, and your God my God" (Ruth 1:16). Ruth's statement was not a commitment at a wedding ceremony, although today her words are often used that way. Her statement was the commitment of a daughter-in-law to her mother-in-law.

Naomi said, "Do not call me Naomi; call me Mara, for the Almighty has dealt very bitterly with me. I went away full, and the Lord has brought me back empty. Why call me Naomi, when the LORD has testified against me and the Almighty has brought calamity upon me?" (vv. 20–21). She had lost her husband and her two sons. God's discipline had been on them. Nevertheless, God was gracious to Naomi through the committed obedience of her daughter-in-law Ruth, and Ruth's husband, Boaz. In reference to suffering, the book of Ruth shows how a righteous man (Boaz) can be blessed even in difficult times. God's gracious mercy is also seen in his relieving suffering from both the committed follower (Ruth) and the complaining mother-in-law (Naomi).

1 and 2 Samuel

The message of 1 and 2 Samuel is that national and individual security rests primarily not with human kings, but with the nation and the individuals whose hearts turn to God. Some evaluation and reflection of this period is found in the poetic sections of the Old Testament. In the Psalms, David reflects on some events recorded in 1 and 2 Samuel.

First Samuel begins with the birth narrative of Samuel and the emotional suffering that his mother, Hannah, endured before his birth. Hannah's suffering of being childless was not caused by her sin. God used it to prepare her for the sacrificial giving of her son into the Lord's service. One would think that not being able to have children for a number of years would make her cling to her child even more. But Hannah's suffering seems to have prepared her heart spiritually. God can and does use suffering to change a person's spiritual heart.

Eli and the nation suffered because of his own sins and the sins of his sons (1 Sam. 2:12, 17, 22, 25). But the word of God (chap. 3) and the power of God were still available to the nation. The sin of God's people does not mean God is any less powerful, although he may not choose to act on Israel's behalf. This principle can be seen in the ark of the covenant narratives (chaps. 4–7). The ark was taken by the Philistines, but they experienced great suffering because of its presence in their midst (5:6–12). The men of Beth Shemesh also suffered because they did not treat God's ark with the respect God demanded (6:19–20).

Chapter 8 prophesies the suffering that would come to the nation because they were not willing to be patient in God's provision of a king. In Genesis 17:16 God promised that kings would come from Abraham, and in Genesis 49:10 he promised that kings would come through the line of Judah. According to Numbers 24:17–19 and Deuteronomy 17:14–20, God's plan involved a king. Israel was to wait for God's timing, but they were not patient (1 Sam. 8:19). They insisted on their own timing and their own purposes: "that we also may be like all the nations, and that our king may judge us and go out before us and fight our battles" (v. 20). They had completely misunderstood that God was their king and that he was willing to fight their battles. God had proven that he is able to conquer (e.g., Jericho), and in the ark narratives it is clear that he was powerful even over the gods of the Philistines. Yet Israel did not want God as king. Why? Because if he was their king, they would need to submit to his kingship. They would rather have a king of their choosing, whom they could control or manipulate. God warned them of the physical, financial, and spiritual suffering such a king would cause them (vv. 10–18). Some suffering comes about because of unwise decisions.

Saul became king in accord with God's permissive will (chaps. 9–10). Saul started well, but in the end he caused the nation all sorts of trouble, including resisting God's choice of David. In David, God had a blessing for the people, for he was a man after God's own heart (13:14; 16:7). However, Saul would not give up being king. He knew that the Spirit had departed from him. An evil spirit had come on him and caused him great suffering (16:14). Saul suffered, David suffered, and the nation suffered.

Saul became fearful, angry, and jealous. This was a terrible situation. God had communicated to his people through the prophet Samuel, and he had given David to the nation. Yet God's people repeatedly suffered because they were unwilling to trust God or turn to him and his provisions. They wanted to have it their own way.

Second Samuel depicts David as a true-though-imperfect representative of God, the ideal theocratic king. David was a man after God's own heart. God had chosen him, and David, as seen in the Psalms, showed in return that he had a heart for the things that matter to God. Yet he was imperfect. So 2 Samuel demonstrates how God in his justice had to judge David for his sin. His sin with Bathsheba resulted in the prophet Nathan bringing a message of judgment to David (2 Samuel 12). While it is true, as seen in Psalm 51:3–4, that David repented of his sin, there were consequences for him personally, as well as for those around him.

David's four sons died, conspiracy developed against him, and violence never departed from his family because of this sin (2 Sam. 12:6, 10–11). David, who was supposed to bring blessings to the nation, had to run for his life because of a coup in his own family. God's blessings are always available, but suffering often comes as a consequence of sin in God's people, even the chosen king.

1 and 2 Kings

The consistent message of 1 and 2 Kings is that God's covenant people experienced exile by God's judgment in spite of his merciful delays and sustaining promise to David. God's people in both the northern and the southern kingdoms suffered by going into exile. Judah experienced God's merciful delays in judgment as part of God's sustaining promise to David. God promised that David's line would be an everlasting line (2 Sam. 7:11–13). The northern kingdom fell in 722 BC (2 Kings 17:7–23). But in his mercy, God kept David's line going longer. Finally it too ceased to exist (2 Kings 25:21).

First Kings 1–11 is about Solomon, who wrote much of the book of Proverbs and all of Ecclesiastes and the Song of Songs. Proverbs has wonderful maxims about suffering. One should read these in context and in light of the genre. A proverb is a general statement of truth to which there may be exceptions.

Solomon brought great blessing to the nation as he followed the Lord, but he also set the nation up for great suffering because of his sinful lifestyle, especially as he grew older (chap. 11). Much of the nation's suffering occurred after his death. But his excessive spending, lack of preparation for transition, poor modeling in many areas—all these affected the next generation. Some suffering seems delayed in the normal course of events, and natural consequences sometimes take time to develop.

In 1 Kings 12—2 Kings 17, the history of the divided kingdom is detailed. In terms of theological assessment, in addition to the comments within the historical records (e.g., the statements of whether the king was good or evil), the prophets Elijah, Elisha, Amos, and Hosea evaluated and warned the northern kingdom of Israel. Elijah and Elisha prophesied in the ninth century BC. They and others warned about the nation's spiritual decline into Baalism. A century later little had changed when Amos and Hosea appeared on the scene. The rebellious, abusing, spiritually unfaithful people would suffer at the hands of the dreaded Assyrians. In the southern kingdom of Judah the prophets Isaiah and Micah prophesied, even while the northern kingdom existed until its exile. Isaiah and Micah spoke of the near collapse of the northern kingdom as a warning to those in the south. In addition, during this time, Jonah prophesied to the Assyrians in Nineveh (ca. 750 BC). The very ones who would cause so much suffering in Israel had at least a brief turning to God, and judgment was postponed. This incident would serve as a reminder to God's chosen people of the need for repentance.

Second Kings 18–25 includes material mostly about the activities of the Judean kings during the last 135 years of the southern kingdom. Again, in addition to the theological comments in this historical record, prophets spoke and wrote during this period. Nahum prophesied about Nineveh, telling the Assyrians that they were finished (though they had responded in repentance during the time of Jonah). Zephaniah, Habakkuk, and Jeremiah prophesied to Judah during the period covered by 2 Kings 18–25. The northern kingdom had gone into exile, and the prophets warned the southern kingdom that the same experience awaited them.

The northern kingdom had sinned terribly. The Israelites engaged in Baal worship with King Ahab and his wife, Jezebel, and even before that they had erected golden calves at Dan and Bethel. The southern kingdom was always about one step behind them. Whatever happened in the northern kingdom seemed to occur later in the southern kingdom. God was gracious and merciful to them, but they were deserving of certain judgment too.

Second Kings 17:2–23 gives God's reasons why the northern kingdom had to go into exile. They had sinned against the Lord their God (v. 7). This is an inspired theological interpretation of what was happening. Though it is not necessarily what people would have said if they were asked, it is what God said, and that settled the question. They might have described how their king had not made proper military preparation, how they had not put enough money into research for metallurgy, and that they did not have the latest iron swords or spears!

People often miss the hand of God in why certain things happen, since the broader context is often misunderstood. The same could be said of how prayer works. The only way one can know a specific event to be an answer to prayer is by understanding and believing the biblical theology of prayer, including who God is and how he works; otherwise apparent answers are just coincidence. The unbelieving world might tell Christians not to worry about the reason for suffering. "What will be will be." But the Scriptures indicate that at least sometimes there are knowable reasons why a person or nation does or does not suffer. Discerning those reasons may not be simple, but what is clear from most of Israel's history is that defiant, consistent rejection of God's standards leads to judgment by suffering.

1 and 2 Chronicles

What do 1 and 2 Chronicles contribute to the topic of suffering? These books were probably written after the exile. They seek to encourage faithful temple worship out of a loyal heart for Yahweh by chronicling the blessings enjoyed by the Davidic line in faithful worship. These books actually chronicle the *blessings* enjoyed by the Davidic line. Sin and suffering are seldom mentioned in Chronicles. Even David's and Solomon's major sins are understated, if not ignored completely. The northern kingdom is not mentioned, except in brief references to its connection to the southern kingdom.

The books of 1 and 2 Chronicles are about the southern kingdom, the temple, the offerings, and doing things right. This is an inspired theological view of what caused the blessings that Judah experienced before the exile. The question facing the returned remnant was, how can we avoid the suffering of exile all over again?

These two books do not explain why the people suffered and then went into exile. Instead they emphasize how the people should live, based on what pleases God. First and 2 Chronicles answer the question of how a worshiping remnant should respond to God.

Ezra

Ezra is similar in theme to 1 and 2 Chronicles because it narrates the restoration of the covenant worship of the Lord by the returned remnant. How could the remnant worship properly? They needed a temple (Ezra 1–3; 6). How should they be separate from those around them who defile Israel? The returning remnant should separate themselves in their lifestyle, including whom they marry, so they could more faithfully obey their covenant God (Ezra 9–10).

The worshiping remnant was still living in a fallen world. They would still encounter sinful individuals, but some suffering would be avoided. Today some people question the idea that things sometimes happen because of sinful actions. Through their suffering, believers can learn the kind of people God delights to bless and use.

Nehemiah

The book of Nehemiah highlights the Lord's faithfulness to postexilic Israel. He instilled hope in them by demonstrating his providential working among kings and governments. God willingly blessed his people, as is seen in the amazing events that transpired (Neh. 6:16). When Nehemiah insisted by his actions that the city of Jerusalem is holy, the place where God chose his name to dwell, and that it ought to reflect the Lord, God blessed the people. Nehemiah and the people who followed him put in effort, time, and money to back up this theology. God blessed them, and in fifty-two days the task of rebuilding the wall was completed. This demonstrates that people can live for God and that God can be pleased with them. The suffering involved in their sacrifices rectified their pattern of abuse and neglect. However, in chapters 8–13 the necessity of individual reformation is seen. Some suffering did occur because of unbiblical intermarriage (13:25) and a further neglect of God's temple (v. 8). Many of God's blessings in this world are not unconditionally guaranteed; they are conditioned on the obedience of his people.

Esther

Does the book of Esther have anything to say about suffering? The message of Esther is about God's sovereignty even when evil men seek to bring suffering into the lives of the exiled Jews. The story of Esther is not about luck or coincidence. Many events in the narrative benefit the Jews, and the timing of these events is more than coincidence. The book is one way of God's saying, "Although I might not be mentioned, I am behind everything, and I can preserve my people even in the midst of those who would have them dead." God's preservation of his people and their deliverance from unjust suffering came because of the availability of a young Jewess, Esther. Mordecai said to his relative, "For if you keep silent at this time, relief and deliverance will rise for the Jews from another place, but you and your father's house will perish. And who knows whether you have not come to the kingdom for such a time as this?" (Est. 4:14). These words declare God's sovereignty and Esther's responsibility. Her willingness to take a risk delivered many from suffering.

Summary

The Old Testament historical books include both negative and positive examples, recording what has caused suffering and blessing in the life of God's people during this period of time. These books graphically show what suffering fallen man can inflict both on himself and on others, even a nation. The historical books demonstrate that much suffering stems from the mistreatment of other people and disobedience to the covenant Lord.

Larry J. Waters (MDiv, Asian Theological Seminary; ThM, Asia Graduate School of Theology; PhD, Dallas Theological Seminary) is associate professor of Bible exposition at Dallas Seminary. For sixteen years he and his wife, Mary, were missionaries in the Philippines, where they started several churches and a small Bible college, founded the *What the Bible Says* radio broadcast, and trained numerous pastors and Christian workers.

Dr. Waters is the author of Bible curriculum for the Internet Biblical Seminary, associated with BEE World, a missionary organization focusing on Asia. He is the author of several articles on the book of Job for *Bibliotheca Sacra*, the dissertation "Elihu's View of Suffering in Job 32–37," and the book *The Contribution of the Speeches of Elihu to the Argument about Suffering in the Book of Job*. He has also contributed to *Connecting for Christ: Overcoming Challenges across Cultures*.

8

SUFFERING IN THE BOOK OF JOB

Larry J. Waters

The Mission of God in Suffering

Besides displaying one man's faith in God in times of suffering, the book of Job also has a "missionary" purpose. That is, a believer's suffering should be viewed, as seen in Job's experience, as an opportunity to witness not only to God's sovereignty but also to his goodness, justice, grace, and love to the nonbelieving world.

Often the focus of the book of Job is seen simply as the sovereignty of God and man's faith response to God's will. But Job is also part of the progressive revelation of God's purpose and mission, so that in a sense the book is missional and evangelistic. As believers undergo undeserved suffering, they are witnesses to unbelievers of God's goodness, justice, grace, and love. Job is one of the first illustrations of an individual whom God used to demonstrate that mission involves God's redemptive purposes.

Introduction: Who Was Job?

The reader of the book of Job is immediately introduced to the integrity and virtue of the main character. Job "was blameless and upright, one who feared God and turned away from evil" (Job 1:1–2). He was the "greatest of all the people of the east"(v. 4), and there was "none like him on the earth" (v. 8). Job was therefore the most well-known individual, or at least the key individual representative of God, at that time in history.

Job's character is expressed in two other chapters found later in the book. Chapter 29 gives several references to Job's goodness and prosperity. He enjoyed an intimate friendship with God (vv. 4–5); he enjoyed his children and saw them as a blessing from God (v. 5); he was prosperous, his cows gave milk, and his olive groves gave olive oil (v. 6); he was a political leader (v. 7); he was powerful and respected (vv. 8–9); he enjoyed a good reputation (v. 11); he helped the powerless, strangers, orphans, the discouraged, and widows (vv. 12–13, 17); he was honest and performed good deeds (v. 14); he helped the handicapped (v. 16); he prosecuted the godless and oppressors (v. 17a); he freed the oppressed (v. 17b); he was honored and loved by family and friends (vv. 18–20); his advice was valued (vv. 21–23); he encouraged others (v. 24); he was like a king or chief over an army (v. 25a); and he was also a comfort to mourners (v. 25b).

Chapter 31 expresses Job's righteous character in the oath he took before the Lord. Job said that he had not lusted after women (vv. 1–4), lied or deceived (vv. 5–8), committed adultery (vv. 9–12), failed to help his servants (vv. 13–15), or failed to help the poor and needy (vv. 16–23). He had not trusted in his wealth (vv. 24–25), turned to idolatry (vv. 26–28), treated his enemies unfairly (vv. 29–30), been stingy (vv. 31–32), hidden his sins (vv. 33–34), or been unfair to his workers (vv. 38–40). Truly Job was a righteous man.

Since Job was the most well-known individual at that time in history, his experiences were no doubt widely known. What are the implications of his suffering for believers today? First, the emphasis is on hopefully *leading unbelievers to faith*. Suffering believers have untold opportunities to utilize undeserved suffering as an instrument for drawing people to Christ. Second, he was *an example of a believer's faith in the world*. Suffering believers also have opportunity to demonstrate faith in God in spite of suffering and pain.

Satanic Accusation and Attacks

How did Job's undeserved suffering advance God's mission, and how does God work today through the suffering of his people? While Satan is the prime mover behind sin, evil, and suffering, God allowed Satan to inflict Job. Satan was the cause of Job's suffering, and God's people feel the effects of such attacks. God, however, is also at work in suffering. This does not imply that God is detached and uninvolved in what happens to his people. God's ways are far above our ways. God is greater in intellect, power, and knowledge. So his ways are usually past finding out (28:23; Isa. 55:9). God inflicts suffering directly and indirectly for many different reasons: judgment, discipline, refining, and more. But since the fall of mankind, Satan is under God's constraints, in that God is behind all human misery.

Job 1–2 takes the reader into the throne room of God. "Now there was a day when the sons of God came to present themselves before the LORD, and Satan also came among them" (1:6). God then mentioned Job to Satan. Through Job, God was introducing the two concepts of grace and suffering.

The questions of Satan highlight these two concepts. "Does Job fear God for no reason? Have you not put a hedge around him and his house and all that he has, on every side?" (vv. 9–10). That is, does Job fear God, or worship God, on the basis of what he materially gets out of the relationship, and does God buy worshipers through material prosperity? Is man's relationship with God based on grace or works? Is God so impotent that he must purchase human worship through materialism? Or is God worshiped because he is God? Is worship of God based on a *quid pro quo* system of theology? Or does God bless humankind on the basis of grace?

Satan wrongly assumed that since God protected and blessed Job, greed was the foundation of his righteousness rather than Job's personal, intimate relationship based on love, trust, and faith in God (vv. 8–10; 2:3; cf. 1:21–22; 2:10). Satan's accusation was therefore directed toward the foundation of both God's goodness and justice and Job's righteousness.

Undeserved suffering is not traceable to a specific act of personal sin or disobedience as its direct cause. This also includes suffering that is incompatible with preconceived or logical reasons that often seem unfair and unjust. In his undeserved suffering Job lost all he held dear, apparently for no reason traceable to any personal act of sin or disobedience toward God or people. Would God's servant Job serve and worship him regardless of human and material loss? Was God's protection the reason Job served him?

Satan's assumption became more troublesome when the traditional human wisdom of the three friends was applied to Job's situation. Traditional wisdom reasoned that since God is in control of the world and because he is just, the only way wise people can maintain faith in him is to see blessings as evidences of goodness and righteousness, and all suffering as evidence of unrighteousness and sin. Belief in God and service to him would then be reduced to a prosperity or pragmatic religious formula or system of works.

The Suffering of Job

Satan was allowed to attack the hero of the story with viciousness almost beyond comprehension. "While he was yet speaking" (1:16, 17) indicates that within minutes, several catastrophic things happened (vv. 13–21).

First, Job suffered *financial collapse.* A Sabean raiding party rustled all of Job's donkeys and oxen, and murdered all but one of the servants. Fire from the heavens (lightning?) consumed Job's sheep and killed all but one of the servants tending the sheep. A Chaldean raiding party rustled all of Job's camels, killing all but one of the camel's herdsmen.

Second, Job suffered *family loss.* A windstorm caused the collapse of the oldest son's house, killing all ten of Job's children.

Over several days and even months (7:3; 29:2), Job's suffering increased. The seriousness and variety of Job's suffering during that period can be classified in four categories. *Physically,* Job suffered personal pain and disease that included inflamed, ulcerous boils (2:7), itching (2:8), degenerative changes in facial skin (2:7, 12), loss of appetite (3:24), insomnia (7:4), hardened skin, running sores, worms in the boils (7:5), difficulty breathing (9:18), loss of weight (16:8), eye difficulties (16:16), emaciation (17:7; 19:20), bad breath (19:17), trembling of his limbs (21:6), continual pain in his bones (30:17), restlessness (30:27), blackened, peeling skin (30:28, 30), and fever (30:30).[1]

Socially, Job was alienated from family and friends and lost his high status within the community. Job's wife turned against him (2:9) and he was rejected, jeered, and mocked by friends (12:4; 16:10; 17:2, 6), even by children (30:1, 9–11).[2] He was regarded as a fool (5:2–3), sinful (5:7; 18:5–22; 22:5–11), arrogant (8:2; 11:4, 7; 15:11–16; 18:3), evil (11:11; 15:20; 22:5), idle and useless (11:2), stupid (11:11–12), empty (15:2), unteachable (15:8–9), a "byword" or object of scorn (17:6; 30:9), ugly (19:17–20), dishonest (20:19), a persecutor of widows and orphans (22:9), and a worm, scab, or maggot (25:6).

Emotionally, Job was grief-stricken over the loss of his children (1:20–21), lacked a sense of inner tranquility (3:26), generally had no taste for life (9:2), was depressed (3:24–25), experienced troubled thoughts (7:4, 13–14), felt uncertain (9:20), was without joy (9:25; 30:31), and suffered from loneliness (19:13–19).

Spiritually, Job was distressed over his conflict with a theology that implied God was a whimsical deity who delighted in afflicting his followers (6:4; 7:17–19; 19:25). Job was also distressed by God's silence (23:8–9, 15).[3]

---

[1] Roy B. Zuck, "A Theology of the Wisdom Books and Song of Songs," in *A Biblical Theology of the Old Testament,* ed. Roy B. Zuck (Chicago: Moody Press, 1991), 227.
[2] Ibid.
[3] Larry J. Waters, *God, Why?* (Garland, TX: American Tract Society, 2010); www.atstracts.org. See this tract for suggestions on the proper response to these categories of suffering.

If suffering is allowed by God, and if it is part of the conflict with evil and the Evil One, then it would seem likely that God can use suffering in dealing with Satan's lies and the assumptions connected with his lies. The proper response to suffering would then lead to triumphing over the enemy's accusations and reaching the world with God's message of grace. Clearly Job's initial response exemplifies this thinking. "Then Job arose and tore his robe and shaved his head and fell on the ground and worshiped. And he said, 'Naked I came from my mother's womb, and naked shall I return. The LORD gave, and the LORD has taken away; blessed be the name of the LORD.' In all this Job did not sin or charge God with wrong" (1:20–22).

This was followed by his extraordinary answer to his wife's urging that he give up and die. His response to her revealed an understanding of God's grace and the importance of handling suffering in light of that grace: "'Shall we receive good from God, and shall we not receive evil?' In all this Job did not sin with his lips" (2:10). This verse seems to imply that God's blessing and the suffering of life are both instruments of his grace. God's grace, based on Job's statement in 2:10, includes not only the *undeserved blessing* of God for the believer, but also the *undeserved suffering* and *pain* that God allows in the lives of believers. God uses the believer's suffering to communicate his purpose and person to others through conversation, pain management, and attitude.

The Theology of the Three Friends
Since Job was suffering undeservedly, and since the false premise of Satan was the major impetus of his attack against Job and ultimately against God, it would seem logical to assume that Satan's theology would influence the counselors to perpetuate the same false doctrine, namely, that the righteous *never* suffer and the unrighteous *always* do. Each friend suggested the same solution, which was essentially, "Repent of your sins so God can restore your prosperity." Or more directly, "Job, if you want your health, family, and prosperity back, accept our evaluation; admit to sin and wrongdoing."

Interestingly the avowed objective of the three friends was "to go and sympathize with him and comfort him" (2:11). But after a week of silence, this objective was never achieved. A short summary of the speeches of these men reveals this fact.

Following the lamentation of Job over his birth (chap. 3), Eliphaz began the three cycles of debate (chaps. 4–31). His speeches are found in chapters 4–5, 15, and 22. It may be noted that Eliphaz's original appeal was to a mystical experience with a dream spirit (4:13–21). Eliphaz asked questions that immediately revealed his theology.

> Remember: who that was innocent ever perished?
> Or where were the upright cut off? (4:7)

Eliphaz tried to convict Job, on the basis of a wrong premise, of his foolish response to misfortune and to urge him to lay his sin before God (5:8; 15:20–35; 22:5–12). His basic message was that Job must have been sinning, because he was suffering (4:12–5:16; 15:2–5, 20–35; 22:5–15). Eliphaz wanted Job to identify his suffering with many presumed sins (15:11–16, 20; 22:5–11). Once Job admitted his sin, then God's healing hand would come to Job, and his prosperity would return (22:21).

After Job's reply to Eliphaz in chapters 6–7 (see esp. 6:14), Job challenged the friends, saying, in effect, "If I have sinned, show me" (6:24; 7:20–21). Bildad took the challenge (chaps. 8, 18, 25), and in his first speech he appealed to traditional wisdom (8:8, "For inquire, please, of bygone ages, and consider what the fathers have searched out"). The premise, and a correct one, is that God is not unjust or unfair (vv. 2–3). But Bildad's point that Job was totally at fault and must repent of unsubstantiated sin before he could be restored (vv. 4–7) was fallacious. The implication was that God would be unfair to allow undeserved suffering to come to a righteous man and that Job's insistence on innocence was an accusation against the justice and rightness of God (vv. 3, 20). Bildad frankly told Job that he was evil and that he must repent so that God could bring back his laughter, joy, and peace (vv. 21–22, a cruel reminder of Job's losses). Job was accused of not knowing God and of having been rejected by God (vv. 2, 4; 18:4–22).

Zophar's speeches (chaps. 11 and 20) attacked Job's righteousness and integrity (11:2–4), his fear of God (vv. 5–6), and his morality (vv. 6, 14). This is a prime example of Satan's original charge (1:8–9). Zophar appealed to a superior understanding of God and his wisdom. He thought Job was too superficial to understand the deeper things of God, and he stated not only that Job was sinning but also that God had even forgotten some of his sins (11:6). The implication was that Job had sinned a great deal and in fact was not getting all the punishment he deserved (11:5). In his assumed superiority, Zophar accused Job of pride (20:6), of being like dung (v. 7), of being a poor father (v. 10), of loss of vigor because of sin (v. 11), of loss of appetite because of sin (v. 13), and of oppressing the poor (v. 19); and once again Zophar confronted Job with the prosperity issue (vv. 21–22). He hoped this would establish the premise of traditional wisdom and eventually lead Job to repentance. However, chapters 29 and 31 show that these accusations were false.

The effect of the false counsel of the three friends is reflected in Job's responses. In essence, he answered:

- "When will it end?" (chap. 6);
- "What have I done to deserve this?" (6:24);
- "Just forgive me and get it over with" (7:21);
- "No matter what I do, nothing changes" (chap. 9; 10:1–7);
- "Why won't you answer me, God?" (10:1–7);
- "I can't take any more of this!" (14:18–22);
- "Nobody cares about me!" (19:13–22);
- "Nobody understands!" (19:21–22);
- "Where can I get some answers?" (28:12);
- "Everything used to be so perfect" (chap. 29);
- "What good is it to serve God?" (chap. 30).[4]

Job was overwhelmed by false counsel, so he was now ready for a true counselor.

The Intervention of Elihu

Elihu began his discourses with a lengthy introduction and expression of anger toward both Job and the three friends (32:1–10). He felt that both parties had been guilty of perverting divine justice and of misrepresenting God generally (vv. 1–3, 11–22). Elihu was attempting to correct their faulty image of God and how he relates to mankind.

In chapter 33 Elihu established that God was not silent during Job's suffering. In chapter 34 he confirmed that God is not unjust. Furthermore, God is neither uncaring (chap. 35) nor powerless to act on behalf of his people (chaps. 36–37). In chapter 37 Elihu introduced God's response and returned the discussion to the issue of God's sovereignty and plan for Job. Elihu then brought to Job a totally different perspective: his suffering was not because of past sin, but was (1) to keep Job from continuing to accept a sinful premise for suffering, (2) to draw him closer to God, (3) to teach him a true wisdom that reveals God as sovereignly in control of the affairs of life, and (4) to show that God does reward the righteous, but only on the basis of his love and grace.

Elihu identified himself with Job. He was a fellow sufferer, not just an observer (33:6). He helped Job realize that a relationship with God is not founded

---

[4]Mark R. Littleton, *When God Seems Far Away: Biblical Insight for Common Depression* (Wheaton, IL: Shaw, 1987), 53–61. Littleton discusses each of these points.

or maintained by his insistence on loyalty, purity, or righteousness, but is wholly of grace. Elihu did not see the primary basis of Job's suffering as sin, nor did he minimize Job's move toward sin in the dialogue. God rewards the righteous in grace, not because of some human action seeking a deserved response.

The core of Elihu's polemic may be summarized in 37:23:

> The Almighty—we cannot find him;
>> he is great in power;
>> justice and abundant righteousness he will not violate.

Elihu challenged a false belief system in a fixed mechanical formula of compensation that was original with Satan, exemplified in ancient Near Eastern religions, and unwittingly perpetrated by the three counselors. Elihu asserted that Job's suffering was not connected to an external standard of righteousness or to an assumed divine action of compensation that obligates God. Elihu contended that God *is* the standard, he rightly administers justice, and his righteousness is maintained even in Job's initial and continued suffering.

Job 31 records Job's final and passionate oath of innocence and defense of his righteousness.

> Oh, that I had one to hear me!
>> (Here is my signature! Let the Almighty answer me!)
>> Oh, that I had the indictment written by my adversary!
> Surely I would carry it on my shoulder;
>> I would bind it on me as a crown;
> I would give him an account of all my steps;
>> like a prince I would approach him. (vv. 35–37)

God did not answer Job. He remained silent. Job's shrewd attempt to manipulate God into answering his challenge failed. His undeserved suffering had caused him to become obsessed with his own righteousness and God's seeming injustice, so much so that Job's "burgeoning pride" stood "between him and God"[5] and became the major reason for Elihu's entrance into the debate. When Yahweh challenged Job in 40:8, it was because of Job's exaggerated self-image (10:3, 7; 13:18; 16:11; 19:6; 27:2, 6; 31:35–37). Elihu offered several categories of suffering that have nothing to do with acts of past personal sin.[6]

---

[5]Clyde T. Francisco, "A Teaching Outline of the Book of Job," *Review and Expositor* 68 (1971): 518.
[6]These categories are discussed in detail in Larry J. Waters, "Elihu's Categories of Suffering from Job 32–37," *Bibliotheca Sacra* 166 (October–December 2009): 405–20.

Preventive Suffering

Elihu did not minimize Job's move toward sinful comments in the dialogue, nor did he claim that the basis of Job's suffering was punishment for some past sin. Rather, for Elihu suffering became, among other things, a preventive measure that helped keep Job from perpetuating a sinful, false theology. Job's flawed concept of God's justice and providence were challenged and put into correct perspective. Elihu affirmed that God is greater than man (33:12). Yet Elihu also comforted Job, insisting that God sent suffering not to reject Job but to accept him, and to train him to rely on God instead of his own human righteousness and goodness.

Suffering, Elihu said, is preventive in five ways. First, suffering warns and instructs (33:16b; cf. 4:13; 6:4; Ps. 88:15–16). Second, suffering can turn the sufferer from wrongdoing and sin (Job 33:17a; cf. 5:17; 20:6). Third, suffering can keep a person from pride and the destructive conduct connected with arrogance (33:17b; cf. 20:6; 2 Cor. 12:7–10). Fourth, suffering preserves and saves a person from the pit (Job 33:18a, 22, 24, 28, 30). Fifth, suffering can save from divine discipline (v. 18b; cf. 15:22).

Preventive suffering is *instructive, directive,* and *salvific* in that it can deliver from God's disciplinary action. Preventive suffering is used by God to warn (Ps. 88:15–16), to urge obedience (119:67), to keep down pride (Job 33:17; 36:9; 37:24; 42:5–6; 2 Cor. 12:7), and to keep the believer on the right path (Job 33:18, 30). In Job's case it also protected him from violence (15:22) and death (33:22, 24, 28, 30).

Correctional or Disciplinary Suffering

Correctional suffering is the alternative to heeding the warnings of preventive suffering. Correctional suffering is, however, similar to preventive suffering in that it also serves to warn and direct the sufferer who refuses to forsake a sinful or rebellious trend. But it goes beyond warning and actually chastises. Elihu indicated that this category of suffering may have been used in the life of Job to correct the false theology that had surfaced during the debates (32:3, 14). Job misunderstood God's goodness and interaction with humanity (33:19–30), God's justice (34:12, 21–37), and God's righteousness and its rewards (35:2–14). The alternative to heeding the warnings of preventive suffering is therefore disciplinary or corrective suffering (37:13; cf. Prov. 3:11; Heb. 12:5–6).

Educational Suffering

Elihu offered a third category for Job's suffering as pedagogical or educational. The fact that suffering can teach humility is clearly indicated in chapters

36 and 37 (36:24–37:24; cf. 2 Cor. 12:7–10). Suffering produces knowledge and teaches God's will (Job 34:32a; 36:22; Ps. 119:66–67, 71). Suffering teaches the sufferer to look to future glory (2 Cor. 4:17; 1 Pet. 5:10) and to learn obedience and self-control (Job 33:17b; 35:12–13; 36:9; 37:19–20; Ps. 119:67; Rom. 5:1–5; Heb. 5:8). Suffering teaches patience and perseverance (Job 35:14b; Rom. 5:3–4), as well as sympathy for others who suffer (2 Cor. 1:3–7), and encourages a life of faith (Job 13:14–15; Rom. 8:28–29; James 1:2–8). Suffering helps the sufferer to understand God's gracious purpose (Job 36:15; Jer. 29:11), to share in Christ's suffering and represent him to others (cf. 2 Cor. 4:8–10), and to pray and give thanks in time of trouble (cf. 1 Thess. 5:18; 2 Cor. 1:11). Suffering can glorify God (Job 1:21; 2:10; John 9:1–4; 11:4), deepen one spiritually (cf. Rom. 5:3–4), and teach humility (Job 36:24–37:24; 1 Pet. 5:6–7) and contentment (cf. 2 Cor. 12:10; Phil. 4:11). The ultimate objective of Elihu's presentation of educational suffering is to lead the sufferer to a deeper understanding of a true relationship with Yahweh, the definitive teacher (Job 36:22; 37:19–24).

Glorification Suffering

Suffering can also be a glorification process in which the sufferer brings glory to God by remaining faithful during the suffering. The testimony of the repentant person glorifies God for personal restoration after suffering (33:26–27). God is also glorified when he promotes the righteous person after a period of suffering (36:7; 36:15; cf. 42:10–16). In human suffering God is often glorified when his work is displayed and he is praised (36:22–26; cf. John 9:3; 11:4). Job was a witness to all sufferers throughout history that even when one does not know the reason for his suffering and when there is no reason given, there is indeed a reason, namely, God's glory (Job 36:15–16; 37:22–23; 42:5; Pss. 59:16; 92:5–6; 138:5–6; Rev. 15:3).

Revelational or Communicational Suffering

According to Elihu revelational suffering helps the sufferer gain a deeper understanding of God's relational attributes of love, grace, and mercy. God is gracious and forgives (Job 33:24, 26). He redeems his people and turns them back to himself (33:27–30; 34:32). He is loving and persuades those he loves to proper action (36:15–16, 22–23, 26, 31). He is the great and sovereign God who gives grace and mercy even in punishment (37:7, 13b). In the revelational sense suffering is also communicational, for God uses suffering as a means of communicating his will to people (33:19–33).

Organizational Suffering

Suffering can be organizational in that it prioritizes what is important in one's life and relationship to God (37:7, 14, 23–24). Weather can confine and restrict human activity on earth (v. 7), thereby forcing people to consider their dependence on the power of the Creator and to acknowledge that he is the source of such storms. The desired result is that people will acknowledge God's creative work (v. 7b), considering what is important in life. Organizational suffering can help the sufferer see what is important and can lead him to rely on God (cf. 2 Cor. 1:9–10), to spend more time in prayer (cf. Pss. 50:15; 77:2; James 5:13), and to keep on the right path (Job 33:18, 30). Suffering forces the believer to depend on God (cf. Phil. 4:12–15), and it teaches him to number his days and to use time wisely (Job 37:14; Ps. 90:7–12). Organizational suffering can focus the sufferer's mind and hope on the grace that will be revealed when Jesus Christ returns (cf. 1 Pet. 1:6, 13).

Relational Suffering

Suffering can also be a stimulus to develop a believer's relationship with God. It can lead him to cry out for deliverance (positively, Job 33:26; 34:28; negatively, 35:9–12). The sufferer sees God's face, prays to God, and is restored (33:26; exactly what Job did in 42:5–6). God hears the cries of the poor and needy (34:28). God woos or pursues the sufferer during his suffering (36:16), and "he delivers the afflicted by their affliction and opens their ear by adversity" (v. 15). God is personally related to and involved in the suffering of his people. God wants the sufferer to focus on divine blessings (cf. Ps. 77:1–2, 10–12). Job, like all believers, experienced God's comfort *in* the suffering (cf. Matt. 5:3), and this deepened his faith, trust, and certainty in his relationship with the Lord (cf. Rom. 8:28–31). Suffering can lead the believer to offer thanks in all circumstances (cf. 1 Thess. 5:18) and to know that God's purpose and plans are not hindered by suffering, but are often moved forward (cf. Jer. 29:11).

Proclamational or Declarational Suffering

Suffering can be proclamational or declarational in that it magnifies God in several areas. First, suffering reveals the nonarbitrary nature of God's actions (Job 34:10–15). Elihu declared that God acts in accord with his perfect nature. Second, Elihu declared the preeminence of God's justice (vv. 16–17). In light of Job's insistence on his innocence (v. 6b, "I am without transgression"), this is significant because Job, not the three, was accusing God of being unjust and biased. Third, Elihu emphasized the purity of God's character and the greatness of his person (v. 10; 36:26; 37:23). God will do nothing that is not good; nor is he even capable of doing anything that is unjust. Fourth, Elihu pointed out the nonmanipulative nature of God (35:4–8). Elihu maintained (a) that God's ways are higher than human ways (vv. 5–8); (b) that God's silence is justified and does not imply that he is uninvolved with humanity's suffering (vv. 9–11); and (c) that God's silence does not mean that he does not hear his own (vv. 12–14). Fifth, Elihu praised the greatness of God's person and his omniscience (36:26–33). He said that God is unquestionably "great" and "we know him not" (v. 26). The way in which God uses his power to bless or afflict, to save or destroy, is beyond human understanding (vv. 26, 29; 37:5; cf. Ps. 139:6; Eccles. 8:17; Isa. 55:9; 1 Cor. 13:12). Job's problem was that he was seeking to comprehend the workings of the incomprehensible God (Ps. 102:28). The lesson for Job was that God is worthy of praise and is not subject to scrutiny or a legal claim against him.[7]

Conclusion

Elihu genuinely cared for Job, who had become embittered because of his continued suffering, poor advice, and acceptance of a faulty theology that was not compatible with his experience (Job 33:6–7, 23–24, 32; 36:6–7, 15–16; 37:19–24). Therefore, Elihu was attempting to show Job that God's justice is in perfect harmony with his essence, and that God's justice is beyond human understanding. However, Elihu did not attempt to offer an answer for Job's initial undeserved suffering. Elihu did not presume on God's prerogative. That answer resides with God, for he alone knows all the facts. For Elihu, suffering is not an enemy but a neutral force, a vehicle used by God to clarify and enhance the divine-human relationship. Therefore, since God goes to such lengths to develop this relationship, suffering becomes the supreme opportunity for humans to represent this relationship with God to the world. The sufferer may not always know all the facts. Nor is that at all necessary for living a life of faith, for suffering can be endured with faith and trust in an all-knowing, loving, and gracious God even when there is no logical or rational answer immediately available.

God Speaks to Job

Speaking in a whirlwind, God charged Job with darkening his counsel by "words without knowledge" (38:2; as Elihu said twice, 34:35; 35:16). God did not address Job's suffering directly during this discourse, nor did he answer Job's attacks on his justice. God spoke to Job about divine sovereignty and omnipotence as

---

[7]John Hartley, *The Book of Job*, New International Commentary on the Old Testament (Grand Rapids: Eerdmans, 1988), 479.

demonstrated in the creation of the earth, the sea, the sun, the underworld, light and darkness, the weather, and the heavenly bodies (38:4–38). Animate creation testifies of God's sovereignty and power without complaint: the lion (vv. 39–40), the raven (v. 41), the mountain goat and the deer (39:1–4), the donkey (vv. 5–8), the ox (vv. 9–12), the ostrich (vv. 13–18), the horse (vv. 19–25), the hawk (v. 26), and the eagle (vv. 27–30). Then God asked Job:

> Shall a faultfinder contend with the Almighty?
>> He who argues with God, let him answer it. (40:1–2)

Of course Job remained silent (vv. 3–5).

Job 40:8–14 presents the power of God versus the power of man. God addressed his own justice, but he did not defend or explain it. God did say that he is just and fair in the lives of his creatures. God alone administers and regulates justice—not Job, not the three friends, and certainly not Satan. The "Ode to the Behemoth" follows, in which God stressed the power that is in his hands in opposition to that of man or Satan (vv. 14–24). The second poem (41:1–34) is the "Ode to the Leviathan," which represents the same essential principles. What the behemoth and the leviathan represent is contested in scholarly circles, but the message is that man has no power over these creatures, nor can man explain the purpose for their creation or existence. God is sovereign, omnipotent, just, loving, and perfectly righteous toward all his creation.

God did not ask Job to repent so that his pain would be explained, so that he, Job, would be vindicated, or so that his losses would be restored. What God did was bring Job to a face-to-face meeting with himself. Then Job repented of his misconception of God and God's freedom, not of the alleged sin that was the focus of the three friends (42:7–9). Still, God commended Job, because even in the face of doubt and pressure from false theology, Job maintained a personal relationship with God and brought his doubts directly to the Lord. Therefore Satan's hypothesis, that Job would curse God once his protection and prosperity were removed (1:9–11; 2:3–4), was proven false. Job finally rejected the approaches of tradition, logic, and all wisdom that was foreign to what he learned about God and himself. All attempts to explain God and his actions either logically, historically, or traditionally failed. Job was left with God and God alone. Interestingly, God did not address the prosperity issue. Job's prosperity was returned only after everyone involved understood that all blessing comes by God's grace alone, not by the activity and piety of Job or through a false theology.

Conclusion

The answer to the question, why do the righteous suffer? cannot be satisfied by one explanation. The many reasons given in Scripture for personal suffering must all be examined in light of God's grace. Suffering taught Job that he was righteous because he had a grace relationship with the Righteous One, not because he had earned it. Job knew God and responded with humility, love, and godly fear for God's sovereignty (42:1–2), realized God's inscrutability (v. 3), reflected on God's superiority (v. 4), refocused on God's intimacy (v. 5), and repented of serving God from wrong motivation (v. 6).

However, the book of Job is not restricted to an expression of God's sovereignty. Job's struggle and ultimate triumph give those who suffer many important lessons:

1. God is not held to a preconceived, limiting concept of compensation theology.
2. Sin is not always the basis for suffering.
3. Accepting false tenets about suffering can cause one to blame and challenge God.
4. Life under a compensation theology is a legalistic system that not only distorts the application of the true precepts of God's law but also confines God and his grace to human standards of interpretation.
5. Satan is behind this false system and delights in using it to afflict the righteous.
6. The Devil's world is unfair and unjust, and a relationship with God is the *only* place where a person will know justice.
7. Life is more than a series of absurdities and unexplainable pains that one must simply endure; it is linked with God's unseen purposes.
8. Mankind does not always know all the facts, nor is that at all necessary for living a life of faith.
9. God's wisdom is above human wisdom.
10. God's protection and blessing are based solely on grace, not on a traditional, legalistic formula.
11. Suffering can be faced with faith and trust in a loving, gracious God even when there is no apparent logical reason to do so.
12. God does allow suffering, pain, and even death if it best serves his purposes.
13. Prosperity theology has no place in God's grace plan.
14. Suffering can be preventive rather than simply merited.

15. The greatest of saints struggle with undeserved suffering and will continue to do so.

16. Because God's people are intimately related to him, suffering is often specifically designed to glorify God in the unseen war with Satan and to bring others to salvation and a deepened relationship with God.

Undeserved suffering becomes a living demonstration of God's grace and man's faith. As Job finally stated,

> I had heard of you by the hearing of the ear,
>> but now my eye sees you. (42:5)

Ronald B. Allen (ThM, ThD, Dallas Theological Seminary; DD, Rocky Mountain Bible College and Seminary) is senior professor of Bible exposition at Dallas Seminary. He has written more than a dozen books, principally on the Psalms and worship, as well as commentaries on the books of Numbers and Micah. He is one of the senior editors for the *New King James Version*, Old Testament, and is the Old Testament editor for *Nelson's New Illustrated Bible Commentary*.

Dr. Allen leads study tours to Israel and other countries of the Middle East and Western Europe, and has preached and taught in numerous countries in Asia, the South Pacific, Europe, and Africa.

9

Suffering in the Psalms and Wisdom Books

Ronald B. Allen

Have mercy on me, O Lord, for I am in trouble;
My eye wastes away with grief,
Yes, my soul and my body! —Psalm 31:9[1]

Patterns, Genres, and Forms

The Hebrew Scriptures (or the Old Testament) abound with varied genres and forms of literature. Patterns of writing range widely from robust epic narratives, such as the Exodus, to rather dreary tales of lust and lax morals, such as those in the book of Judges, to what for the modern reader are mind-numbing details of ritual and obligation, as in the book of Leviticus, to war songs and taunts scattered among battle narratives, and to lively love poetry with surprising sexual frankness, as in the Song of Songs. Along the way of course are splendid paeans of praise to the might, majesty, wonder, and especially the loyal love of Yahweh, the living God.

Bible scholars have developed names and descriptions for these varied literary categories. Some of these are broad; others are more narrow and more tightly defined. Thus one may speak of prophetic literature as a genre (*genre*

---

[1]All Scripture quotations in this chapter are from the New King James Version.

works best as a broad term), and then speak, for example, of the *rîb*[2] oracle as a distinctive form within the larger genre of prophetic speech (*form* works best as the more narrow word).

Wisdom Literature—in Two Groupings

Wisdom literature is used broadly by some writers but with more precision by others. Some say all the so-called poetic books are wisdom literature. Others regard as "wisdom texts" only those writings that fit more specific categories.

In this chapter the term *wisdom literature* is used both broadly and narrowly. Broadly the wisdom books include Job, Proverbs, and Qohelet (Ecclesiastes), as well as the Song of Songs and the book of Psalms. In the more narrow use of the term, *wisdom literature* refers to the book of Psalms, which displays the broad genre of hymnic literature and includes several recognized forms (the more narrow term) within that genre, such as psalms of individual lament, royal psalms, and wisdom psalms.

Broadly speaking the wisdom books (or the poetic books) of the Old Testament may be divided into two categories with respect to their orientation toward life, God, and the human condition.

One group of these books presents a solidly positive view toward life, a warm embrace of faith in God, and an optimistic approach to the human condition. Among these writings are the book of Proverbs and some of the categories of the psalms: wisdom psalms, royal psalms, praise psalms—both descriptive and declarative (thanksgiving hymns)—and psalms of trust.

A second group of these wisdom books looks at life, God, and the human condition from the stance of disappointment, discouragement, and dissatisfaction, and yet these books also affirm the goodness, power, and wonder of God. Even people of faith experience disappointment, discouragement, and dissatisfaction, which makes these passages so difficult, and so very real. If a person has no hope of experiencing God's goodness, then there is no great disappointment when life seems to go wrong. Randomness, luck, karma—all such ideas regard disappointment as less dramatic when an experience of goodness seems not to have been realized.

The challenge of pain in the life of the faithful person has led to the writing of this second cluster of books, which includes Job, Ecclesiastes (Qohelet), and within the book of Psalms the psalms of lament (both of the individual and of the community).

---

[2] A *rîb* oracle is a literary device in which the prophet spoke metaphorically of the nation of Judah, for example, being called into the heavenly court of Yahweh to face judgment. Examples are in Isaiah 1 and Micah 6. The Hebrew term *rîb* means "judicial complaint."

Christians believe in the essential goodness of God, not just as an article of faith—an affirmation—but also as their *personal* faith, something they hold to very dearly. "If God is good," one surmises, "then he will be good to me!" However, when the vagaries of life, particularly those of deep misfortune, impose themselves on a person who has expectations of ordinary mercies, the believer may be confounded by a deeper sadness than the person with no real belief in God, with belief in a passive God, or with belief in God that is so vague as not to lead to a firm expectation of heavenly mercy.

> *For my life is spent with grief,*
> *And my years with sighing;*
> *My strength fails because of my iniquity,*
> *And my bones waste away.* —PSALM 31:10

For those whose outlook is a view of randomness, bad things are as likely to show up in one's life as good things. "After all," they surmise, "is not life just a gamble?" As someone recently said to me, "You can't expect to get the good parking spots all the time." Others, and their numbers are increasing in the West, think in karmic terms. Bad things in one's life now are the result of bad actions earlier in this life or in a former life. Meritorious actions in this life may ease one's experience in the next life. I have spent several months in Thailand in recent years and I have learned firsthand a bit about karmic logic in Buddhist thought. This is sometimes simplified in the maxim, "What goes around, comes around." One friend expressed things this way: "The universe just wants to even things out, so don't take good or bad things too personally—these things are really not about you."

Two Options

In recent years within the broad context of the Judeo-Christian tradition two attractive (to some) but erroneous ideas about misfortune and misadventure in one's life have made their mark. One comes from a kindly looking rabbi; the other from a serious biblical scholar. Both of these writers are highly regarded, making their viewpoints all the more troubling.

Harold Kushner

The publication in 1981 of Rabbi Harold S. Kushner's best seller, *When Bad Things Happen to Good People*,[3] not only was met by critical acclaim among

---

[3]New York: Schocken, 1981; repr., New York: Anchor, 2004.

book reviewers, but also (and this is troubling) was received with enthusiasm by a number of people in Christian circles.[4] The gentle rabbi "wrote in such personal terms," one Christian counselor said some years ago, "and with such candor and openness, that I just loved the book. I promote it all the time."

One can certainly have a strong sense of empathy with the Kushner family as this book was prompted by the illness and death of a child—something that my wife and I deeply understand, as will be noted shortly. The Kushner son Aaron was born with progeria, a horrible condition that causes rapid, premature aging. Aaron Kushner died two days before his fourteenth birthday. The father told the son's story in a very moving manner. Nonetheless, the underlying tenet of the book is alarming. God, Kushner avers, is good. But he is not powerful enough to do all the good he would like to do. Kushner cannot bring himself to doubt God's goodness, but he allows the notion of limitation in the effectiveness of that goodness. But the leukemia-stricken child who lives, lives because of the mercy of God and his goodness. The leukemia-stricken child who dies, dies not because God does not care, but because he cannot prevent the child's death. Chapter 7 of the book is titled "God Can't Do Everything, but He Can Do Some Important Things."

> *I am a reproach among my enemies,*
> *But especially among my neighbors,*
> *And am repulsive to my acquaintances;*
> *Those who see me outside flee from me.* —PSALM 31:11

Walter Brueggemann

A second work that has received much critical acclaim is the serious and immensely learned Old Testament theology by Walter Brueggemann.[5] In this tome the scholarly and articulate author presents two contrary ideas about God that he believes are taught in varied scriptural passages. One is that God is good. This is the dominant viewpoint and the one that believers rightly celebrate. Part 1 of his book is titled "Israel's Core Testimony,"[6] in which he presents a focus on normative elements in Israel's belief structures about Yahweh.

---

[4]A not-untypical positive response to the book is found on the Amazon.com page on this book: "Rabbi Harold S. Kushner offers a refreshing point of view that differs from those who think everything occurs on earth because God wants it that way, and at the same time provides a surprising comfort in the fact that events actually can, and do, take place for no reason at all" (J. Lizzi, July 7, 2000, accessed December 3, 2009).

[5]Walter Brueggemann, *Theology of the Old Testament: Testimony, Dispute, Advocacy* (Minneapolis: Fortress), 1997.

[6]Ibid., 115–313. "Israel's core testimony is able to affirm, in the splendor of its faith, that Yahweh's 'steadfast love endures forever'" (ibid., 313).

But there is another portrait of God in the Hebrew Scriptures, Brueggemann suggests, that is not good at all. This is a presentation of God as decidedly adversarial to his people and their lives. Brueggemann develops this idea in part 2, "Israel's Countertestimony."[7] He writes, "The countertestimony, rooted in Israel's lived experience of absence and silence, ends in an articulation of Yahweh's hiddenness, ambiguity, and negativity."[8]

Any reading of Scripture affirms the twin experiences of mercy and sadness, of expectations and disappointments, of triumph and disaster. But the troubling experiences are not attributable to the limitations of a loving God or to dual natures attributed to God in a dialogical encounter. The simple facts are that God is good and that life may be tough.

> *I am forgotten like a dead man, out of mind;*
> *I am like a broken vessel.* — PSALM 31:12

My "Credentials"

I am acquainted with grief. I do not wish to be guilty of overstatement here. But one who writes on a theology of pain and suffering should, it seems, have a few scars. Somewhat in the manner of Paul in 2 Corinthians 11:22–33, here are my credentials, as it were.

My Father

My father, Barclay Allen, was a dance-band pianist in the 1940s. For a brief period he was nationally known and had recordings that were big sellers in the postwar years. I have written his dramatic life story in one of my books.[9] The element of that story that fits in this present chapter is the aftermath of his serious automobile accident in August 1949, when he was thirty years old and I was a lad of seven. My father's car accident nearly took his life. But he

---

[7] Ibid., 315–403. It is in the countertestimony that Brueggemann places the writings that speak of the troubles believers face in life (psalms of lament, the book of Job, the book of Ecclesiastes). He writes, "At the very edge of the Old Testament, culturally and epistemologically, the Book of Ecclesiastes gives us the residue and outcome of that shrill and incessant voicing of negativity" (ibid., 393). See also his newer work, *An Unsettling God: The Heart of the Hebrew Bible* (Minneapolis: Fortress, 2009). Amid many splendid ideas he presents about Yahweh are these troubling words: "The partner [Israel] who suffers is often perpetrator, but also sometimes victim. Sometimes the partner is victim of YHWH's negligence, whereby the hosts of the Nihil run rampant in the earth; sometimes the partner is victim of YHWH's mean-spirited irascibility" (*Theology of the Old Testament*, 172). Waltke has criticized Brueggemann's approach of dialogical theology, calling it "flawed," "heretical," and "failed" (Bruce K. Waltke with Charles Yu, *An Old Testament Theology: An Exegetical, Canonical and Thematic Approach* [Grand Rapids: Zondervan, 2007], 69–72).
[8] Brueggemann, *Theology of the Old Testament*, 400.
[9] Ronald B. Allen, *Lord of Song: The Messiah Revealed in the Psalms* (Portland, OR: Multnomah, 1985), 157–74.

lived on for seventeen years as a paralytic. His brilliant career was over. Now he was paralyzed from the high chest down.

The hero of the story is my mother, Vantoria Allen. She had been the long-suffering wife of a famous musician whose personal life had become askew. At the time of his accident my mother was actually about to begin divorce proceedings against my father. But the news of his accident led her to fly to Reno, Nevada, where he was first hospitalized and to be by his side for weeks of initial recuperation. Then, when he was flown back to Hollywood by a hospital plane, she began many years of constant care for her invalid husband. In my book I tell about his dramatic conversion story. I just hint in that chapter about the rigors of family life when the breadwinner was now crippled and his wife had to learn a skill that could gain her employment—all the while caring for her crippled husband and her two small children.

My father lived with constant pain and needed constant care. When you see a person in a wheelchair, you may have no idea of the nature of his or her disability. That person might be ambulatory, but weak. Or he or she may suffer from debilitating ravages of diabetes or from post-polio syndrome. Such people may need the use of the wheelchair just to get around, but not because of the loss of the use of their legs. Those who suffer paralysis from spinal injuries have varying levels of disability. Joni Eareckson Tada has a very high level, as her injury was in the cervical spine. Thus she is a quadriplegic—all four limbs are involved. My father's level was in the high thoracic area of the spine. Having suffered a broken neck and an impaired spinal column, he was permanently paralyzed from the high chest downward.

After twenty-one months of being in and out of the hospital, my father spent the rest of his life in a hospital bed in our home, and for short periods of time, in a wheelchair. My parents had our house remodeled, nearly doubling the footage. All of this was to provide a very large bedroom for my dad, a large wheelchair-accessible bath, and a greatly enlarged kitchen where he could also roll around in his chair. The front of the house was a bit of squeeze, but we made it work, for that is where the piano was.

My mother realized she now had to go to work. She had few skills, but she did the best she could. She got a graveyard-shift job processing checks ("punching"), went to night school to learn secretarial skills, cared for my sister and me—and all this in addition to helping my father. Eventually she got a job at an aviation company and moved up the secretarial ladder until she became the executive secretary of a highly placed group of engineers. We are very proud of her!

To my mother fell Dad's daily care. This was far more than preparation of meals and standard issues of housekeeping. A person who is paralyzed at the level of my father's case no longer has independently functioning bowels. My mother had to give him enemas several times a week. Nor could my father take a bath unaided. He worked very hard on his upper body strength—already having very strong arms and hands from his piano virtuosity. With Mom's help he could lower himself into the tub, using the special bars that had been installed in the bathroom. But there were times when he would fall or slip—times my mother would scream in panic and then in frustration. We would then call the church office for help. Duties for our youth pastor began to include helping out at the Allen home at odd intervals.

And my life was impacted—as was the life of my sister, Peggy, who is two years younger than I. When my mother became more and more affected by painful arthritis, Peggy learned to help her. It fell to me to be Dad's part-time aide before and after school. In one of many articles written about my father, a local paper included a picture of me bringing him a tray with a pitcher of lemonade. Not published was a picture that Dad also asked the news photographer to take, one of me taking my dad's urinal to the bathroom to empty and to rinse—something I did several times a day.

I also learned to stretch his legs. Muscles atrophy when they are no longer used. If the disuse is prolonged, the atrophy leads the muscles to become merely connective tissue—an irreversible situation. We all knew that my father's leg muscles would never work again, but neither was it desirable that they disappear. Muscles do not care if they are moved actively or passively so long as they are moved. So when I was still a very young boy I was taught how to stretch my father's legs. I would move each leg so that his knee was high on his chest, hold it, then extend it out again. I would do this ten times for each leg, then repeat the process three times.

I learned how to iron his sheets. In those days cotton sheets were prone to wrinkle more than modern fabrics do. A few wrinkles on a bed would disturb a drill sergeant, though perhaps not a homemaker. But for my father, wrinkles in his sheets could lead to decubitus ulcers, horrible bedsore wounds that might take months to heal. Our church raised funds for a mangle iron, an ironing contraption designed for sheets. I was the "chief mangler" for many years; I still iron all my clothes to this very day.

So I grew up with a paralyzed father. I loved him dearly—and miss him greatly. But our family life was always a struggle because of his permanent injury. Struggles were emotional and financial—issues of constant pain and stress. The marvel, of course, is that my father came to Christ. And the second marvel is that Mom, who had planned on divorcing him before the accident, faithfully—but not always happily—cared for him for many, many years.

For I hear the slander of many;
Fear is on every side;
While they take counsel together against me,
They scheme to take away my life. —Psalm 31:13

Our Daughter

Our daughter Rachel provides another instance of my "credentials" in writing on the theology of pain and suffering. Perhaps nothing hits parents so deeply as the serious illness (or death!) of one of their children. When our youngest child, Rachel, was just twenty-one months old, she was diagnosed with acute lymphoblastic leukemia. I have also written her story.[10]

When she was admitted to the children's oncology unit of the University Medical Center in Portland, Oregon, in March 1979, our life as a family took on turns that were enormously stressful. All of our focus was on her. Along the way, our three older children (Laureen, Craig, and Bruce), while never outwardly resentful, were well aware that this was now "Rachel time." For the first seven weeks my wife, Beverly, stayed with Rachel in the hospital night and day. I would come and spend hours at a time after teaching my classes at Western Seminary. My mother (still the hero) came from California and stayed with our children while we were both at the hospital.

Many things have improved in the procedures and protocol of caring for leukemia patients since our experience three decades ago, but the levels of hurt, sadness, pain, and angst remain the same for parents and other family members. As Beverly and I watched Rachel suffer, we both knew that, if given a chance, either of us would gladly change places with her.

I have so many memories of those days—and Beverly's memories of these things are sharper than mine. I recall the first time Rachel's hair began to drop (and *drop* seems the best term) off her head in "gobs" (as Bruce, her brother put it). She was not even two years old, but the loss of her hair was tragic in her young life and small world. She actually grieved for the loss of her hair. Beverly would lovingly tape little ribbons on Rachel's head when the hair could no longer sustain them, or when it was finally all gone. Rachel took some small solace in the ribbons.

I remember the breakdown of her outer sphincter and the pain this produced in bowel movements—pain that was so intense she seemed instinctively to reduce her eating so that there would be fewer occasions for sphincter

---

[10]See "Rachel—God's Lamb," in Ronald B. Allen, *Praise! A Matter of Life and Breath* (Nashville: Nelson, 1980), 225–38; also in Allen, *And I Will Praise Him: A Guide to Worship in the Psalms* (Grand Rapids: Kregel, 1999), 225–38.

pain. I recall the sores in her mouth that made even drinking liquids painful. I think of countless "sticks" with needles into veins all over her body—as her treatment period took place before Dr. Robert Hickman in Seattle developed a catheter implant that significantly reduced this trauma. I remember also the times when I would hold her in a fetal position, with her spine exposed as fully as possible, and a doctor would use a needle to punch into that arc to draw out spinal fluid to be used to determine the progress—or lack of such—in the chemotherapy. I remember once when Rachel was placed on a metal table for radiation therapy and the radiologist had failed to place a lead apron over her lower body. I shouted out that she needed protection. The work-haggard technician said resignedly, "Okay. But you know she will not live anyway, so protection is not really needed."

Despite all, the radiation technician was wrong. Rachel not only survived those early weeks, but at the time of this writing she has survived for thirty years! Our joy in God's goodness in sparing the life of our daughter is boundless. But even when she was in remission, family life was still troubled—for years! During the three years of her continuing chemotherapy, Rachel was at risk for invasive infections that would be new threats to her life. Twice she was in a near-critical situation with pneumocystis pneumonia, an infection that took the lives of many HIV/AIDS patients in those years. And on two occasions we had to send Bruce (aged five) "into exile" for several days because it was thought that he had been exposed to chicken pox, which would likely have been fatal to Rachel if she were also exposed. Bruce's "first exile" was to stay with a loving family in our church. His "second exile" was to my study, at the time a separate building from our home. I would go out and stay with him in the evening. We both nearly destroyed our thumbs playing Intellivision, the video game of choice back in that day.

God blessed our family in enormous ways. But the experience of a sustained, critical illness of a young child makes a mark on each member of the family. That mark is indelible.

> But as for me, I trust in You, O LORD;
> I say, "You are my God." PSALM 31:14

My Head

Then there is the matter of my so-called head. I woke up today with head pain. I woke up yesterday with head pain. I have been waking up with head pain now, at the time of this writing, for eight years. I don't say "headache," as that sounds too trivial to me. A headache is something that might be treated with

Advil or Excedrin. My head pain is intractable, constant, and has what I now know to have very clear triggers that raise the levels of pain through the day. The triggers are what I do: teaching, preaching, studying hard, reading with deep concentration, speaking intently, and—perhaps saddest of all, taking part in the music of Christian worship. Each of these triggers intensifies the pain that is already there. In postsurgical pain clinics (twice for six months each) I have learned to use a "number" to describe the pain. When I get to what I call a "four" I am moaning. When I get to a "five" I am tearing. At "six" I am weeping. Again the pain is not something that comes and goes; it is always there.

My head pain is the result of brain surgery in October 2001. I sustained a bicycling accident in July 2001.[11] Two months to the day after my accident, and two days after 9/11, I began having seizures. A number of tests were done to find the cause of my pain. It turned out that when I fell in the bicycling accident and hit pavement with the left side of my body, my head hit particularly hard. My helmet shattered.[12] Unknown to me at the time, my brain bounced in a *coups–contra-coups* action, leaving a brain injury on the right side. This injury gradually led to a massive subdural hematoma that covered the entire right hemisphere and was, at the deepest point, an inch and a half deep.

When I met with an esteemed brain surgeon, he told my wife and me that only craniotomy surgery would save my life; without it I would likely not live more than three or four more weeks. A portion of my skull was sawed out and the massive blood clotting was removed; then the skull piece was put back in place with titanium plates and small screws. (If I misspeak from time to time, it may be that a screw is loose.) I am enormously grateful for the surgery! But it left me with this always-present and sometimes-debilitating head pain. This has been the case now for eight years.

After many medications and a number of therapies failed to help, I found that the only thing that actually relieves my head pain to any extent is massage. When I get a full-body massage, my whole body is relaxed and the head pain goes down. The story is long and detailed, but I decided that since massage is such a help to me, I might learn to do it. Now here is the remarkable point—*doing* massage reduces my head pain significantly as well. I went to night school in Dallas and learned the skills of massage, took the state examinations, and am

---

[11]My friend Gary Mahone and I spent our early life together when our fathers were traveling in the "band years." Gary suffered a motorcycle accident around the time of my bicycle accident. He sustained a serious brain injury, was in a coma for a period of time, and has lasting pain issues as well. He likes to speak of the two of us as "Brains R Us."

[12]I am often asked whether I was wearing a helmet. Of course! And I am so grateful; the helmet likely saved my life.

now a licensed massage therapist (LMT). I have even taken comprehensive and advanced training in Thai massage in Chiang Mai, Thailand, and am certified in that field as well.

My days now swing like a pendulum between periods of significant head pain and wonderful periods of relief. Now massage (both as receiver and as giver) is the help that God has given me in his mercy.

In none of this do I wish to appear maudlin, nor do I look for sympathy. It is just that when one writes on a topic in which there is no personal investment, the writing may remain somewhat unconvincing. It is the personal experience of Rabbi Kushner, after all, that commends respect and hearing.

> *My times are in Your hand;*
> *Deliver me from the hand of my enemies,*
> *And from those who persecute me.* —PSALM 31:15

The Psalms and the People

Believing people over the centuries have turned to the book of Psalms for comfort, for encouragement, and for patterns in the expression of joy. Some Christian communions still use the Psalms as their only repository of worship songs, some set to the tunes established in Geneva at the time of John Calvin.

I began my first book on the Psalms with these words: "Only a Philistine could fail to love the Psalms."[13] I still take pride in that remark; it is correct on so many levels.

But the sad truth is that there are *Christians* who do not like the Psalms—and they are not Philistines! These are people who find themselves very uncomfortable with the psalms of lament—and even more so with the imprecations that are sometimes a part of these poems.

One of the happiest days in the life of a writer is a publisher-sponsored book signing. In some ways this is even better than opening the envelope with the first royalty check. Multnomah Press honored me many years ago with such a privilege. Beverly and I were seated at a table in a lovely ballroom at the Christian Bookseller's Convention, held that year in Dallas, Texas. We had just arrived from Israel, where we had spent several weeks. I remember that I had brought with me a very large *shofar*, a horn from the kudu antelope. Several hundred people came to my table and waited while I signed copies of my new book. They were there for me!

---

[13]Allen, *And I Will Praise Him*, 17.

It did not matter at all that the table behind me was manned by Dr. Charles Swindoll, and that he was also signing his new book! To get to Swindoll, they had to get through Allen! Ha. Whenever there was a lull, Beverly would go to the refreshment table and bring me coffee and a snack. I would use the opportunity to blare on my *shofar*. Dr. Swindoll would laugh and respond, "There he goes again, blowing his own horn." What a night!

And then . . . it was ruined. Don Wyrtzen, a musician, composer, and writer,[14] came up to me during a break and said he had something to tell me. Don said that a very well-known Christian writer wanted him to tell me that he wishes that "Allen would quit writing books on the Psalms." I thought Wyrtzen was kidding at first. Then I saw his pained expression. Don was sent by this Christian writer, who did not wish to speak to me in person, to tell me that the book of Psalms has wonderful passages, but they also include scandalous sections in which people lash out against God. "These passages are sub-Christian," the writer wished me to be told. "Please, I beg you, cease making a big deal out of the Psalms. They do not fit into the pattern of the Spirit-filled life!"

That was a message to quell my joy! I recall not picking up my *shofar* the rest of the night, even when Swindoll said, "Well, are you going to toot on that thing again?" I said, "No, I'm no longer in the mood." He must have wondered what in the world was the trouble.

Make Your face shine upon Your servant;
Save me for Your mercies' sake. —PSALM 31:16

Discoveries of Patterns
Only a hundred years ago a biblical scholar discerned the pattern of the psalms of lament and other forms in the book of Psalms. Hermann Gunkel made his pioneering discoveries in the 1910s–1930s concerning forms in biblical texts.[15] In midcentury Claus Westermann published his significant work on the Psalms.[16] David Hubbard, then president of Fuller Theological Seminary, told me that my own book on the Psalms (the 1980 edition) may have been the first to present these ideas for the nonscholarly reader. Now of course these

[14]Don Wyrtzen, *A Musician Looks at the Psalms: 365 Daily Meditations* (Nashville: Broadman, 2004).
[15]Hermann Gunkel and Joachim Begrich, *Introduction to Psalms: The Genres of the Religious Lyric of Israel*, trans. James D. Nogalski (Macon, GA: Mercer University Press, 1998). Gunkel's first work on the Psalms was published in German in 1904.
[16]Claus Westermann, *Praise and Lament in the Psalms* (Atlanta: John Knox, 1981). Westermann has written numerous works on biblical themes.

ideas are commonplace among Bible teachers, but I suspect they are still not appreciated by the larger number of lay Bible readers.

> *Do not let me be ashamed, O LORD, for I have called upon You;*
> *Let the wicked be ashamed;*
> *Let them be silent in the grave.* —PSALM 31:17

The Pattern of the Psalms of Individual Lament

Psalms of individual lament generally follow the following pattern:

- an introductory cry
- the lament, with three pronouns (*I, you, they*)
- the confession of trust
- the petitions, with three verbs (*hear, save, punish*)
- the motifs—giving suggestions to God as to the reasonableness of the prayer
- the vow of praise

However, many psalms of lament have only some of these elements. Apparently poets of the Bible had considerable latitude in their use of the forms, even as they showed daring and ever-creative patterns in the mechanics of parallelism. Since many psalms have only parts of this "master scheme," the nature of the overall pattern was not easily discovered and described. This was the great achievement of Gunkel. A stunning restatement of the pattern was developed by Westermann, whose approach I follow.

An Introductory Cry

The introductory cry is based on a personal relationship with the living God. Today the words "Oh, my God" have become so trivialized in common usage (e.g., texting and tweets of "OMG") that they hardly have any of the force such words had in the writings of the poets of ancient Israel. "Oh, my God" in many uses in contemporary society is just an expression of surprise or fear, but with no real content or meaning beyond a gasp. Barely a hiccup for many, "OMG" has nothing to do with God. It is similar to "Valley Girl" talk: "I mean, oh, my God—I mean, like, totally."

But in the poems of Israel and in the lives of God's people today, meaning is imperative! It is precisely because he is God that the devaluing of this phrase is so consequential.

139

The opening words of many psalms are the shocked words, "Oh, my God," or the equivalent. The poet is astounded; something distressing has happened in the life of a person of deep faith in Yahweh! How could this be? "Oh, my God!"

The Lament—with Three Pronouns

The dramatic elements in the lament include the use of three pronouns to express the comprehensive nature of the pain, the perplexity, and the problems facing the poet. The writer speaks of self ("I" and "my"), to God ("You"), and concerning others ("they").

The Pronouns I and My

Psalm 31:9, quoted earlier in this chapter, includes the "I" and "my" in a powerful way.

> Have mercy on me, O LORD, for *I* am in trouble;
> *My* eye wastes away with grief,
> Yes, *my* soul and *my* body!

The totality of the person is indicated by the use of pronouns and the enumerating of body parts. The poet is in shock, disarray, and ruin. These laments, however, are not voiced in ordinary times. They come when one feels one's world has collapsed—and the distress is magnified with the question, How could such happen when one is related to the living God?

The Pronoun You

The most shocking element of the psalms of lament is their accusations of disinterest thrust at God. Again, only because one has great expectations from God does the issue even matter. Only a person who has deep, resilient faith in God can truly bring charges against him when his or her world caves in. Secularists might use the same type of language, but it is hollow. Since they do not believe in God, since they have no deep expectations from God, their calls to God are more a sort of "I told you so" than real lament.

But when the person of faith charges God with not being active, with not being attentive, with not being of help—these are the substance of genuine pain.

> How long, O LORD? Will *You* forget me forever?
> How long will *You* hide *Your* face from me? (Ps. 13:1)

Here is the wonderful thing about these terrible words—*they may be spoken!* These are the very kinds of words that led Kushner to describe God's limitations. These are the very kinds of words that led Brueggemann to suggest a countertestimony.

These words are presented as the anguished expressions of real people with real feelings in real times facing real life! This *is what one feels!* When all expectations fail, and the totally unexpected comes crashing in, the response of the believer may very well be to call out to God in strong, even harsh words—to scream aloud and to shout, "Where are you, oh, my God?" Again, it is the "oh, my God" element that makes these words so powerful!

These words do not contradict what we know about God; they express the experiences of people who find themselves completely overwhelmed when life is tough!

The Pronoun They

The third pronoun refers to one's enemies. For David these would often be military leaders, but ambiguity in many of these charges is valuable. In Psalm 3 the enemies specific for David would be the forces allied with his rebellious son, Absalom.[17] But in the psalm itself the language is vague and general. The enemy is not specified; thus people in any era can think of things from their own perspectives, as they face their own demons.

> Lord, how *they* have increased who trouble me!
> Many are *they* who rise up against me.
> Many are *they* who say of me,
> There is no help for him in God. (Ps. 3:1–2)

With three pronouns (*I, you, they*) the poet is able to express a comprehensive picture of stress with a remarkable economy of words. The poet says: "I am hurting. You don't care. They are winning."

The Confession of Trust

Most remarkable in these poems is the conjunction of lament and trust.

> *But You*, O Lord, are a shield for me,
> My glory and the One who lifts up my head. (Ps. 3:3)

---

[17]This is suggested in the superscription, ". . . when he fled from Absalom his son." Unfortunately most contemporary biblical scholars give scant notice to these superscriptions.

The same poet who said that God is of no help now speaks of him as altogether adequate for his needs. This very fact disproves the notion of Brueggemann concerning countertestimony. The same poem has both despair and affirmation—God is both silent and trustworthy. Sometimes these statements of lament and of trust interplay one with the other, as is the case in Psalm 22:

> Verses 1–2 are lament.
>> Verses 3–5 are confession of trust.
> Verses 6–8 are lament.
>> Verses 9–10 are confession of trust.
> Verses 11–18 are lament.

Here is the point: Psalms of lament express what one *feels* at the time of distress. One's feelings are in a blender. Everything is awhirl. One says all kinds of things, and among them are words of confidence and expressions of distress.

Martin Luther had this idea when he said, "There are times when our hope despairs; these are the times our despair must learn to hope." This is not countertestimony, but contradictory feelings colliding in and all around when one is experiencing deep grief—and when one has profound belief in the living God and deep hope in his loyal love.

The Petition—with Three Verbs

In the heart of these psalms are the psalmists' requests to God. These requests are based on faith—as are all the elements in the psalm. The psalms of lament are not just random screams in the night; they are the real expressions of pain of real people who exercise real faith in the living God.

> *Arise*, O Lord,
> *Save* me, O my God!
> *Strike* all my enemies on the cheekbone;
> *Break* the teeth of the ungodly. (Ps. 3:7, my translation)[18]

Basically these psalms ask for three things, using three verbs: "hear," "save," and "punish."

---

[18]The NKJV reads the last two cola, "For You have struck all my enemies on the cheekbone; / You have broken the teeth of the ungodly." But in fact these things had not yet happened, or the issues of the lament would be moot. A knowledge of the pattern helps to reveal the force of the verbs in these psalms.

The verb "hear!" In the lament section the psalmist has screamed out to God that he appears not to be paying attention to the psalmist's needs. This is the "you" element in the lament. Here the psalmist shouts to God to "rise" or to "listen." The verb "hear" calls for attention.

The verb "save!" Salvation here is deliverance from the pressure of the lament. This is what the poet wants God to do to deliver him from overwhelming distress.

The verb "punish!" The call for God's judgment on enemies is great, but it is disliked by many; today some view this as "sub-Christian." However, the development of the concept of imprecation ("cursing"—calls for God's judgment) on one's enemies fits both the Old and New Testaments! "Vengeance is Mine, I will repay" (Rom. 12:19; cf. Deut. 32:35). Calling on God to bring judgment on one's enemies leaves the decisions in the proper hands! Further, as J. Carl Laney has shown, calling for judgment on one's enemies was in full agreement with the words of promise that Yahweh had given to Abraham at the beginning.[19] Yahweh promised to bless those who brought blessing on Abraham and his descendants; he also promised cursing on those who did not treat them with worth and respect (Gen. 12:1–2). In this regard the poet was simply calling on God to do as he has promised!

The Motifs of Motivation

The idea here is that the poet may add elements to the poem to express the fitness of his request to the living God for help. The poet may put it in terms such as this: "If you answer my prayer, dear Lord, not only will I be delivered, but also your name will be exalted." Negatively, "If you do not answer my prayer, my enemies will give credit to their gods, and your name may be denigrated by them."

The Vow of Praise

The psalms of individual lament conclude, almost always, with a vow of praise.[20] This vow brings resolution to the poem as a document of faith. The more difficult the situation, the more faith is demanded by the poet. He demonstrates great faith in saying, in essence, "When God has brought me through this mess, I

---

[19]See J. Carl Laney, "A Fresh Look at the Imprecatory Psalms," *Bibliotheca Sacra* 138 (January–March 1981): 35–45.

[20]The exception is Psalm 88, a lament psalm admirably suited for the experience of the Savior on the night of his arrest and when he was held in the house prison of the high priest. In this psalm the poet feels desperate and bemoans the absence of friends. The location of the house of the high priest Caiaphas is not known. One suggestion is that it lay a bit south of the Ottoman walls surrounding today's city of old Jerusalem. The Church of Saint Peter in Gallicantu ("Where the Cock Crowed") is built over the foundations of a first-century house. Beneath the church and the ancient home are two disused cisterns. One was a pit for flogging. The other is a possible short-term holding pit for prisoners. In this second pit Psalm 88 is printed in a score of languages and is bound as a book for pilgrims to read. To read this psalm in this pit is an unforgettable experience.

will go before the people of God (and others) and I will magnify his name by telling them what he has done."

Perhaps the most glorious of the vows of praise at the conclusion of psalms of individual lament is that which ends Psalm 22. Many know that Psalm 22 prophetically describes the suffering of the Messiah in almost clinical detail (in vv. 12–18). But it is less known that this poem also has a vow of praise that becomes predictive of both his resurrection and the spread of the gospel throughout time. The vow begins,

> I will declare Your name to My brethren;
> In the midst of the assembly I will praise You. (v. 22)

The vow then moves to the praise that should extend to both Jewish people (v. 23) and Gentiles (v. 27), from the poor (v. 26) to the wealthy (v. 29), and to all peoples throughout all time.

> A posterity shall serve Him.
> It will be recounted of the Lord to the next generation,
> They will come and declare His righteousness to a people who will be born,
> That He has done this. (vv. 30–31)

What a comprehensive vow of praise! And what an ending to this glorious psalm!

What Does It All Mean?
During the couple of weeks when I was preparing for the classroom presentation of these materials, I had interactions with four persons who had experienced deep shock, sorrow, and grief. Each one is related to the seminary in some way; all four are women.

The first is a woman who had endured a grueling year and a half of treatment for breast cancer. Hers was a very difficult case, and her treatment had been unusually taxing, both physically and emotionally. But then she received some tragically bad news that was unrelated to her cancer. I will never forget her despair when she told me that report was worse than facing cancer treatment all over again.

The second was an e-mail from one of my students. She wrote some very nice things about my class session, but then she told me she had to drop the course. Her mother had died unexpectedly in the summer, and she was finding that her grief was uncontrollable; she needed a break from classes to have time and energy to face her loss.

The third was an alumna who was being stalked by a fellow she had dated briefly. In the midst of filling out reports with the sheriff's department, she went to the counselor of women at her church to ask for advice concerning a temporary restraining order. The counselor turned around and contacted the fellow who then "dished a lot of dirt" about the young woman. Then the counselor took it on herself to send e-mails to ministries and friends of this young woman, accusing her of dishonesty and immorality. Most shocking to her (and to me) was that the pastor of the church took no step either to help her or to redress the treachery of the counselor! The outrageous breach of confidentiality and unprincipled behavior are nearly unbelievable. The hurt of the young woman is beyond measure. If there is any place where a single woman, a believer in Christ, should feel safe, it is in the church. Not so for her!

The fourth was a woman who learned that her sister's husband, while riding his bicycle home from the school where he was a teacher, was killed by a hit-and-run driver. My friend was understandably devastated by this seemingly random violent death. The man who died was dearly loved at the school where he taught, as was evidenced in the outpouring of grief from the student body. But the grief of my friend was compounded by the insensitive remarks she received from others. "He was not even your family; he was your sister's husband. Why are you so upset?" Gasp!

Each of these situations is unique. But what was shared by all four of these women was the kind of pain and loss, shock and grief, sorrow and anger that mark the psalms of lament in the Bible.

Two things are remarkable here. One is that the biblical psalms of lament mirror our own pain. The second is that in each case the story is not over. There will be an end to the pain. Psalm 31, from which many verses have been cited in this chapter, ends in these words:

> Oh, love the LORD, all you His saints!
> For the LORD preserves the faithful,
> And fully repays the proud person.
> Be of good courage,
> And He shall strengthen your heart,
> All you who hope in the LORD. (Ps. 31:23–24)

IO

SUFFERING IN THE WRITING
PROPHETS (ISAIAH TO MALACHI)

Stephen J. Bramer

The writing prophets include the five "major" prophetic books (Isaiah, Jeremiah, Lamentations, Ezekiel, and Daniel) and twelve "minor" prophets (Hosea, Joel, Amos, Obadiah, Jonah, Micah, Nahum, Habakkuk, Zephaniah, Haggai, Zechariah, and Malachi). Of course, the terms *major* and *minor* refer to the contrasting length of the books, not to their importance or inspiration. The book of Lamentations is traditionally included in the listing of the major prophets, though it is not lengthy, nor is it representative of the more traditional prophetic genre. In this chapter these books will be discussed in the order in which they were written.

The writing prophets make two points clear: God warned of the consequences of exile, and he wanted his people to repent in order to avoid those consequences. In fact he promised to bring them back "if they confess their iniquity . . . if then their uncircumcised heart is humbled and they make amends for their iniquity" (Lev. 26:40–41). And he promised in Deuteronomy 30:1–3, "So it shall be when all of these things have come upon you . . . and you return to the LORD your God . . . then the LORD your God will restore you from captivity" (NASB).

The preexilic prophets emphasized the avoidance of sin so that suffering because of disobedience would not come on them. The exilic and postexilic prophets emphasized both the need to repent and the need for obedience so that they could experience God's blessings.

Writing Prophets of the Northern Kingdom (Eighth Century BC)—Amos and Hosea

Two writing prophets, Amos and Hosea, prophesied to the northern kingdom of Israel. The nonwriting prophets Elijah and Elisha also ministered to the northern kingdom. Their ministry and messages are recorded in 1 Kings 17–19 and 2 Kings 1–9, 13. Interestingly, the accusations of Elijah and Elisha against the nation were similar to what Amos and Hosea declared later in the eighth century.

Amos

The prophet Amos (ca. 760 BC) began by declaring that fire would come as a punishment to each of the surrounding nations (1:4, 7, 10, 12, 14; 2:2, 5). As a covenant-enforcement mediator, a spokesman for God, he essentially said, "On the basis of this covenant, I am here to enforce God's standards." The covenant most often enforced by the prophets when they spoke to nations other than Judah and Israel was the Noahic covenant (Gen. 9:1–7). This covenant focused on the value of human life because humans are created in the image of God. As a result, and as seen in Amos 1–2, the prophets usually declared that judgment (i.e., suffering) would come on a nation because it had not treated people properly.

Amos also reminded the people of God's promises, promises that would be realized by God's gracious acts, not because of obedience. Amos 9:11–12 presents a wonderful message of hope, namely, that God would restore David's fallen booth (tent). That is, he would restore the Davidic kingship over the entire nation.

Ultimately Israel would be restored. After speaking of the surrounding nations, Amos concentrated on the fact that Israel was suffering because of how they too had treated people. Amos detailed several social sins of Israel: they mistreated the poor, they molested the righteous, and father and son abused the same girl (Amos 2:6–8, 11–12).

Hosea

Prophesying soon after Amos (ca. 750 BC), Hosea declared, in essence, "God's love brought you to him as his people, yet you have spurned his love, and like my wife, Gomer, you have wandered away from him." But Hosea continued, "God will keep pursuing you because he has an everlasting love for you."

Gomer, Hosea's unfaithful wife, finally came home. She had suffered greatly because of her infidelity. Perhaps surprisingly, God basically told Israel, "You need to be in isolation for a little while" (Hos. 3:3–5). Israel would go into exile as part of God's disciplinary suffering so that when they returned from exile, God's people would have learned not to worship idols. Suffering in Israel served as a consequence of sinful actions, but it also taught the people lessons for future obedience. Chapters 4–14 reveal God's restorative love in spite of Israel's unfaithfulness.

Israel chose not to have a Davidic king as their sovereign, not to worship at the temple in Jerusalem, and not to have Levitical priests, all of which were demanded in the Mosaic Law. They were warned by the prophets, but then they were disciplined by suffering. Some of the suffering came upon them quickly, but some suffering, such as the exile, did not occur until two hundred years later. God's people suffered when they disobeyed God's Law under the Mosaic covenant and when they did not treat people properly according to the Noahic covenant. Unbelieving nations are not held accountable to the Mosaic covenant, which was for Israel, but they are held to the standards of the Noahic covenant, which was made with Noah, the head of the entire human race.

Writing Prophets of the Southern Kingdom (Eighth Century BC)—Isaiah and Micah

The southern kingdom lasted longer in the land than did the kingdom in the north (approximately 354 years compared with 210 years). The messages to the southern kingdom included the same emphasis on judgment as the message to the northern kingdom, but they also included a clear messianic hope. Isaiah and Micah were prophesying in the south when Amos and Hosea were prophesying to the north.

Micah

Micah warned of coming judgment, but he also held out hope for a deliverer and for peaceful security in a coming kingdom. Like Isaiah, he declared that someday

> they shall beat their swords into plowshares,
>   and their spears into pruning hooks;
> nation shall not lift up sword against nation,
>   neither shall they learn war anymore. (Mic. 4:3; cf. Isa. 2:4)

149

The United Nations has this statement engraved in the side of its building, but without reference to the person—the deliverer, Jesus the Messiah—who will make this possible. However, both Micah and Isaiah make it clear that nations can live in peace only when they recognize God's word and his authority.

> Many nations shall come, and say:
> "Come, let us go up to the mountain of the LORD,
>   to the house of the God of Jacob,
> that he may teach us his ways
>   and that we may walk in his paths."
> For out of Zion shall go forth the law,
>   and the word of the LORD from Jerusalem.
> He shall judge between many peoples,
>   and shall decide for strong nations far away. (Mic. 4:2–3a)

People will never be able to create a world of peace until the Messiah, the one who will break open the way, comes (2:13). He will be born in Bethlehem (5:2). Until the Messiah comes and reigns, man has no hope of being spared from the many conflicts that cause suffering in this world.

Isaiah

In chapters 1–12, Isaiah wrote of the judgment that was coming on Judah. His indictments, like those of other prophets, explained how Judah had not kept God's Law given through Moses and therefore why God would need to bring suffering on the nation. The judgments coming on surrounding nations are detailed in chapters 13–23. Like Amos 1–2, Isaiah indicated the reasons nations suffered, either because they did not treat people properly or because they did not bless God's chosen people, the Jews. This second reason was especially true of Edom, Moab, and Ammon. The nation Edom descended from Esau, and Moab and Ammon from Lot's two daughters. These nations were accountable not only for the Noahic covenant and their general treatment of people but also because of their familial relationships to the Jews, for the Abrahamic covenant says, "I [God] will bless those who bless you [Abraham], and him who dishonors you I will curse" (Gen. 12:3).

Isaiah 24–39 gives additional information about judgment on Israel, as well as the nation's future restoration. Isaiah then wrote in chapters 40–66 about the time when Judah would be restored to her land and would worship, but also when much of the suffering caused by the cursed earth (cf. Genesis 3) would be removed. In fact in Isaiah 65 he spoke of a new heavens and a new earth. Apparently this would occur not when the curse has totally disappeared (as in

Revelation 21–22). Instead this refers to the millennial kingdom, Christ's reign on the earth for one thousand years (Revelation 20).

Though Isaiah did not refer to it as the thousand-year-millennial kingdom, he did emphasize the restoration of creation. Because the curse will no longer be in effect,

> The wolf and the lamb shall graze together;
>> and the lion shall eat straw like the ox. (Isa. 65:25)

In verses 20–21, he described the life of blessing in the millennium.

> No more shall there be in it
>> an infant who lives but a few days,
>> or an old man who does not fill out his days,
> for the young man shall die a hundred years old,
>> and the sinner a hundred years old shall be accursed.
> They shall build houses and inhabit them;
>> they shall plant vineyards and eat their fruit.

This shows that suffering in this fallen world does not last forever in God's plan.

In Isaiah 53 the prophet discussed the One who would become known as the Suffering Servant (Isaiah 42, 49, 50, 53). His suffering and death would be vicarious, and he would take care of the sin that has brought much temporal and eternal suffering (53:4–7).

Writing Prophets to Assyria (Eighth and Seventh Centuries BC)—Jonah and Nahum

Jonah and Nahum discuss the nation Assyria. Jonah wrote that this cruel, pagan nation responded in repentance when presented with God's threat of judgment (Jonah 3:5). Jonah made it clear that God is "a gracious God and merciful, slow to anger and abounding in steadfast love, and relenting from disaster [suffering]" (4:2). He desires that people, even the cruelest of all, repent and acknowledge him.

Writing approximately a hundred years later, Nahum detailed the final judgment that came on Nineveh, the capital of Assyria. This time there was no repentance, and the Assyrians suffered at the hands of the Babylonians. This was because of the extent of their wickedness, which included violence and witchcraft (Nah. 3:1–4) and "unceasing evil" (v. 19). Once again, as in Jonah, Nahum was careful to depict the character of God in such a manner that he could not be seen as evil or unloving.

The LORD is a jealous and avenging God;
  the LORD is avenging and wrathful;
the LORD takes vengeance on his adversaries
  and keeps wrath for his enemies.
The LORD is slow to anger and great in power,
  and the LORD will by no means clear the guilty. (1:2–3)

He is also the one of whom it is said,

The LORD is good,
  a stronghold in the day of trouble;
he knows those who take refuge in him. (v. 7)

God's punishment stems from his holy and good character.

Writing Prophets of the Southern Kingdom (Seventh and Sixth Centuries BC)—Zephaniah, Habakkuk, Jeremiah, and Lamentations

After the northern kingdom had gone into exile in 722 BC and Isaiah and Micah passed off the scene, the still-existing southern kingdom also failed to learn obedience. Therefore God sent more prophets. Today people tend to think that prophets merely predicted the future. But perhaps less than five percent of the recorded words of the writing prophets pertains to the distant future. They were usually talking about current conditions in their society. Prophets primarily showed up when priests and kings were not completely doing their jobs. A priest's job included explaining the Old Testament Law, and a king's job involved making sure the Old Testament Law was enforced. But when a priest did not teach properly and became disobedient, or when a king was not a faithful ruler, then God called in a prophet, who declared that whether the king was obedient or not, God would appear and would judge his people.

Zephaniah

Before the three exiles in 605, 597, and 586, Zephaniah appeared (ca. 635 BC). His message was something like this: "The day of the LORD will come with certain judgment on evil. Only a humble remnant will survive." In no other Old Testament book is the day of the Lord such a major part of the message. Zephaniah almost reversed the creation as he wrote of God's consuming man, beast, birds, and fish (Zeph. 1:2–3). The day of the Lord will ultimately affect all of creation.

Most often the day of the Lord is associated with the nations of the world. The final day of the Lord is when all the nations of the earth will be gathered together and God will declare judgment. It is a day of future accountability. Amos said, in essence, "You're not longing for the day of the LORD, are you?" (Amos 5:18). Even God's own people should not be longing for a day when they are accountable unless they faithfully rest on God's grace. Only then could one be confident that it will be a time of great blessing.

> "I will utterly sweep away everything
> from the face of the earth," declares the LORD.
> "I will sweep away man and beast;
> I will sweep away the birds of the heavens
> and the fish of the sea,
> and the rubble with the wicked.
> I will cut off mankind
> from the face of the earth," declares the LORD. (Zeph. 1:2–3)

What will prevent a person from undergoing this terrible judgment? Humble repentance, for only the humble person realizes that he cannot make it on his own. A humble person realizes he is a sinner.

Zephaniah 3 develops this message of hope.

> But I will leave in your midst
> a people humble and lowly.
> They shall seek refuge in the name of the LORD,
> those who are left in Israel;
> they shall do no injustice
> and speak no lies,
> nor shall there be found in their mouth
> a deceitful tongue. (vv. 12–13)

> The King of Israel, the LORD, is in your midst;
> you shall never again fear evil. (v. 15)

> The LORD your God is in your midst,
> a mighty one who will save;
> he will rejoice over you with gladness;
> he will quiet you by his love;
> he will exult over you with loud singing. (v. 17)

> "At that time I will bring you in,
> at the time when I gather you together;

> for I will make you renowned and praised
>> among all the peoples of the earth,
> when I restore your fortunes
>> before your eyes," says the LORD. (v. 20)

Having declared that judgment is coming, Zephaniah stated that there is hope for those who respond properly. Suffering does not have to be the continued experience of God's people even when the judgment they suffer here on earth is deserved.

Habakkuk

The prophet Habakkuk had a wonderful message to those who suffered. He was an unusual prophet because, rather than speak to the people as a typical covenant-enforcement mediator on behalf of God, he spoke first of his own concerns and then on behalf of the people to God with their concerns. He first asked, in effect, "God, are you not going do something? Look at your people. They are sinning. Will you not do something?" (Hab. 1:2–3). And God answered, "Yes, I'm doing something. I'm bringing the Babylonians" (see v. 6). Habakkuk then responded, "Oh no, not the Babylonians. They are not good people!" (see vv. 12–17).

God can use some very sinful people to cause believers to suffer. This allows learning to take place in two ways: first, learning to stop doing one's own sinful actions; second, realizing that what the evil agent of suffering is doing is not right either. It was as though God said to Habakkuk in 2:4, "Rather than talk about the Babylonians, take a look at yourself and learn to trust me." Habakkuk realized that the just must live by faith. With such a terrible time coming on both sinful Judah and Babylon, those who trusted God would need to keep on trusting.

> Yet I will quietly wait for the day of trouble
>> to come upon people who invade us. (3:16)

How should a believer respond when facing suffering and judgment, judgment that may not be personally deserved? Habakkuk 3:17–19 reads,

> Though the fig tree should not blossom,
>> nor fruit be on the vines,
> the produce of the olive fail
>> and the fields yield no food,
> the flock be cut off from the fold
>> and there be no herd in the stalls,

yet I will rejoice in the LORD;
    I will take joy in the God of my salvation.
GOD, the Lord, is my strength;
    he makes my feet like the deer's;
    he makes me tread on my high places.

Thus God's Word suggests that believers can suffer and yet be victorious. Though they suffer, they need not grumble and complain. They can suffer and trust in the Lord without depending on circumstances. This is a great lesson taught by a prophet in the midst of terrible evil and suffering. He said, in essence, "I am going to rejoice and rest in the Lord, and I will be renewed by the Lord."

In a world in which sometimes there is unjust, undeserved suffering, the prophet understood that God's plan is bigger than merely his own life. And therefore he was willing to commit his life to the Lord and to keep on trusting.

Jeremiah

Jeremiah began prophesying in 626 BC and continued until after 586, when the third exile to Babylon occurred. His is the longest of all the prophetic books. This book reveals much about the struggle of the prophet himself.

The book of Jeremiah enables the reader to identify with the prophet as he delivered a message of covenant violation and judgment. At times Jeremiah wept; it was not easy for him to keep going in life. Jeremiah gives an inside look at what sometimes occurs in a person's emotional struggles.

Some people in Jeremiah's day were upset with him for stating that they would experience suffering in exile. When they did go into exile, they were upset that he had prophesied such a thing. They implied that if he had not prophesied, it would not have happened (e.g., Jer. 11:21–23).

Jeremiah's message was that if the people would repent, the Lord would protect a remnant among them from certain, just national judgment. The nation would go into exile, but beyond that, restoration and renewal would come for the descendants of those who experienced the exile. Jeremiah 31–33 teaches that Israel and Judah would be restored. Nations that crushed her would be crushed. This would come about under a new covenant. And this new covenant would be wonderful for people who suffer, because it would deal with sin. There would be forgiveness and a new Spirit.

When the Spirit would come on Israel and Judah, people would realize that sin was not the ultimate victor, that someday God would have people living as he intended them to live, and that sin, Satan, and the curse would not be the ultimate victors.

Lamentations

Traditionally thought to be written by Jeremiah, Lamentations places the blame for the destruction of Jerusalem squarely on the shoulders of the disobedient nation Judah. Though developed in a creative acrostic, the message of the book is clear: terrible destruction has occurred. Lamentations was a national cry of recognition and of repentance—recognition that what had happened to the temple, to Jerusalem, and to Judah were legitimate consequences of sin. Furthermore, in the middle of this book God is said to be faithful.

> The steadfast love of the LORD never ceases;
>> his mercies never come to an end. (3:22)

How could the writer be stating what he does in the book and not be upset with God? How can God be good in view of human suffering? The answer is that in the middle of all that suffering, God is faithful, merciful, and the one to whom people can turn and know that he is a good and merciful God.

Obadiah

The date of the writing of the book of Obadiah is difficult to determine with precision. The prophet Obadiah discussed the nation of Edom and its rejoicing that God's people suffered. The Edomites were descendants of Esau, who must have known the promises of God to his grandfather, Abraham. Obadiah pointed out that these proud people who rejoiced when God's chosen people were being judged would themselves end up being cursed (Obadiah 15). A future day would come, a day of the Lord, which would be a blessing for God's people but judgment for those who have not turned to the Lord.

Many prophets point out that God's people are not exempt from the consequences of rejecting the covenant they made with God. Others, like Obadiah, also pointed out that other nations would suffer because they did not treat Abraham's descendants properly (Gen. 12:3). This was especially true of such nations as the Edomites, Moabites, and Ammonites, who descended from Abraham and should have been cognizant of the Abrahamic covenant.

Joel

As with the book of Obadiah, the dating of the book of Joel is uncertain. Yet the exact historical context is not needed in order to appreciate the message of the book. Joel wrote about a locust plague that illustrates God's treatment of his people. A people insensitive to God's judgment must repent and find protection through blessing. When they are experiencing suffering and judgment because of sin, the solution is repentance. Joel's depiction of the locusts causes the reader to realize that the repeated nature of the plague was to make sure God's people did not ignore his judgments. Under the Mosaic covenant certain curses (and suffering) would come about because of the people's sins.

Writing Prophets of the Exile (Sixth Century BC)—Ezekiel and Daniel

During the exile, when the Jews were away from the Promised Land and all the warning judgments detailed in Deuteronomy 28 and Leviticus 26 had fallen, two prophets, Ezekiel and Daniel, were ministering.

Ezekiel

Ezekiel's duty was to help God's people accept the exile as a just judgment from God. But Ezekiel was also responsible for encouraging the exiles to have hope. They were to trust that God would someday fulfill his promises about his kingdom in the land of Israel. Ezekiel's message is therefore twofold: first, covenant judgment had come on Judah; second, God in his mercy would restore the nation and give them his Spirit. The exiles would know that national hope rests in the Lord.

Regarding suffering, Ezekiel wrote about individual responsibility. He argued against the use of a common proverb, "The fathers have eaten sour grapes, and the children's teeth are set on edge" (Ezek. 18:2). Apparently the exiles felt that the overriding principle God was using was that the sins of the fathers resulted in the suffering of the next generation. But Ezekiel wanted his people to understand that while God sometimes brought about corporate punishment because of the national covenant, God's discipline called for each person to take responsibility for his own actions. "The soul who sins shall die. The son shall not suffer for the iniquity of the father, nor the father suffer for the iniquity of the son. The righteousness of the righteous shall be upon himself, and the wickedness of the wicked shall be upon himself" (v. 20). Sometimes a person suffers because he himself chooses not to do what is right and proper.

Ezekiel 37 discusses how God will cause the dried bones, that is, the nation of Israel, to come to life again. In the millennium the temple will be rebuilt, some sacrifices will be offered, and worship will be in the land (Ezekiel 40–48). Despite the present suffering of the nation, God has a plan for restoration. Faith, then, must be maintained in the midst of suffering.

Daniel

The second exilic prophet, Daniel, prophesied that ultimately only the Son of Man would deliver Israel from judgment under Gentile world sovereignty.

The people in exile would continue to suffer because of God's judgment for their disobedience to the Law (2 Chron. 36:21). Daniel 9 states that the seventy years of exile were just about up. But Daniel realized that the purpose of the exile was to urge the nation to repent of their sins (9:13). In keeping with God's word in Leviticus 26:18–19, the Lord revealed through Daniel that there would be seven times the punishment until God's mercy is extended toward them in restoring their kingdom. There would be 490 years of suffering under Gentile rule—suffering the Jews could have avoided if they had responded in repentance. This "time of the Gentiles" would continue until the Messiah returned. God expects his people to learn from the suffering that he brings or allows to come upon them. When they do not repent, God often brings additional suffering so that learning takes place. Suffering can involve punishment, but it usually is about learning the lessons God has for his people.

Daniel 3 details the suffering of Shadrach, Meshach, and Abednego. They were threatened with the loss of their lives because they were to be thrown into a fiery furnace. They simply refused to bow down to an idol, and they believed that God's hand is powerful, that he would deliver them from the fire. They believed not only in God's omnipotence but also in God's wise sovereignty ("Even if He does not," Dan. 3:18, NASB), and that is a great lesson to learn in the midst of suffering. Daniel's message is that God would ultimately deliver Israel from Gentile domination and allow his kingdom to prevail.

Though absolutely blameless, Daniel was thrown into the den of lions. He suffered because of the jealousy of others. But he was true to the Lord, and the Lord delivered him. Some people reading Daniel 3 and 6 may think that God always comes through supernaturally to deliver his people. But they forget that Daniel 9 talks about the seventy years of exile, and Daniel 11 talks about the wise who suffer as part of God's design. Some have died being faithful to the Lord. Daniel 12:2 speaks of a resurrection of some "to everlasting life, and some to shame and everlasting contempt." The suffering of this world is not always "fair," as Daniel could testify. But a time of justice and fairness is coming in which everyone will receive his just reward.

Writing Prophets of the Postexilic Era (Sixth and Fifth Centuries BC)— Haggai, Zechariah, and Malachi

Historically the suffering of the exile was over, but God's people were still not who they were meant to be in his plan. They did not have a Davidic king ruling over them. They did not have peace and security in the land. They were still waiting for God's promises to be fulfilled. While they waited, these postexilic prophets came with a message of hope, a message that said, "Until God finally does what he plans to do, your responsibility is to obey, to worship, and to trust."

Haggai

Haggai confronted the remnant in Israel about their lack of commitment to build the temple. How could God's people worship biblically if they did not have a temple that was required by their covenant with God? Haggai's message was that obedience to God's commands (which for Israel included building a new temple) would lead to his blessings. God's people were to express their faith in him by seeking to do what he requires. If not, they would not experience life as they could.

Zechariah

Building on Haggai's message, Zechariah desired that the worshiping remnant understand that God was concerned not only about an outward building, but also about an inner spiritual rebuilding that must take place. The Israelites would not be getting a king for many years. Zechariah said, in essence, "Obey God, and let him take care of the future. Meanwhile, obey his commands and allow his presence and associated blessings to be in your midst."

God's people have never received all the blessings that will come to them someday. Suffering in its various forms reminds believers that they are not yet "home."

Malachi

In Malachi, the Lord ended the Old Testament by challenging his people to understand that there was coming a day of the Lord, a day of decision, which would be heralded by a forerunner. In the New Testament this forerunner is John the Baptist (Matt. 17:11). He would prepare the people for the coming King. But when Jesus came, the people were not ready for him, as the Gospels reported. Their suffering could have come to an end had they recognized their King and responded to his offer. But they rejected him, and human suffering continued, as seen in the New Testament.

Conclusion

These seventeen books of Old Testament prophecy vary in length from sixty-six chapters (Isaiah) to one chapter (Obadiah), but a common thread runs through them: sin leads to suffering, but repentance results in blessing—both nationally and personally. To disobey God is to experience his punishment, but to obey him results in abundant blessing both now and in the future.

Mark L. Bailey (MDiv, ThM, Western Conservative Baptist Seminary; PhD, Dallas Theological Seminary; DD, Dallas Baptist University) is professor of Bible exposition and president of Dallas Seminary. Previously he was vice president for academic affairs, academic dean, and provost. He has pastored in several churches, is in demand for Bible conferences, and has led numerous tours to Israel and the Middle East.

Dr. Bailey is the author of *To Follow Him: The Seven Marks of a Disciple* and coauthor of *Nelson's New Testament Survey*.

II

A Biblical Theology of Suffering in the Gospels

Mark L. Bailey

One cannot watch much of what is called Christian television before getting the impression that a believer should not have to suffer. In fact, like the friends of Job in their rounds of dialogue, many view suffering as an indication that something is wrong in the life of the sufferer, whether sin or a lack of faith. Suffering seems unfair since it seems to serve no good purpose. Some would even say that there can be no real joy in the midst of suffering. What is often forgotten is that where there is physical suffering, there is also emotional suffering, often unnoticed by the casual observer. All these distortions lead some to see no redeeming value in suffering. However, a study of the life of Jesus in the four Gospels overturns every one of these inadequate views of suffering.

John Stott has well stated the enigma of suffering in a world created and sustained by the all-powerful yet loving God: "The fact of suffering undoubtedly constitutes the single greatest challenge to the Christian faith, and has been in every generation. Its distribution and degree appear to be entirely random and therefore unfair. Sensitive spirits ask if it can possibly be reconciled with God's justice and love."[1]

---

[1] John R. W. Stott, *The Cross of Christ* (Downers Grove, IL: InterVarsity, 1986), 311.

The justice and love of God come together in an amazing way in Jesus's work, as recorded in the Gospels. As Dan McCartney has written, "A thesis of the New Testament, perhaps *the* thesis, is that the answer to the problem of suffering and death lies in the suffering and death of Jesus Christ."[2] The life and ministry of Jesus can transform the way we think about suffering.

Jesus is the ultimate example of how to endure suffering. In Peter's first epistle, he wrote:

> For to this you have been called, because Christ also suffered for you, leaving you an example, so that you might follow in his steps. He committed no sin, neither was deceit found in his mouth. When he was reviled, he did not revile in return; when he suffered, he did not threaten, but continued entrusting himself to him who judges justly. He himself bore our sins in his body on the tree, that we might die to sin and live to righteousness. By his wounds you have been healed. For you were straying like sheep, but have now returned to the Shepherd and Overseer of your souls. (1 Pet. 2:21–26)

Suffering in a Fallen World

Human suffering originates from a combination of the natural consequence of living in a fallen world, the effects of demonic attacks, the work of a sovereign God accomplishing the purposes of his wisdom and desires, and the invitation of Jesus for his followers to identify with him in suffering for his cause.

The natural results of sin are seen in the diseases, disabilities, disasters, and death that come with living in a fallen world. Suffering may be emotional, such as a troubled spirit, fear, worry, or even the impending threat of death. Physical suffering identified and addressed by Jesus throughout his life included temporary issues, such as hunger, fever, general sickness, and imprisonment. Also he and his disciples confronted people with long-term diseases or disabilities such as impaired hearing, speaking, walking; or illnesses such as leprosy, paralysis, and epileptic seizures; or various combinations of physical difficulties and demonic control.

Satan's tactics for unbelievers and believers include deception and destruction, which have as their goal the disruption of God's plan for an intimate relationship of trust and obedience with his creatures. Satan even used his menacing methods against Jesus in the temptation accounts (Matt. 4:1–11; Luke 4:1–13), in Jesus's agony in the garden of Gethsemane (Matt. 26:36–46; Mark 14:32–42;

---

[2]Dan G. McCartney, "Suffering and the Goodness of God in the Gospels," in *Suffering and the Goodness of God*, ed. Christopher W. Morgan and Robert A. Peterson (Wheaton, IL: Crossway, 2008), 79 (italics his).

Luke 22:39–42), through Judas at the time of his betrayal (Luke 22:3), and in Peter's denial of the Lord in the courtyard of the high priests (Luke 22:31–34).

The purposes of a sovereign God in suffering are seen in three specific accounts in John's Gospel. With the healing of the infirm man at the pool of Bethesda (John 5), Jesus taught that sin may be the cause of suffering and sickness. In healing the man born blind, Jesus stated that the reason for the man's blindness was neither his sin nor his parents' sin, but that the work of God might be shown (9:3). And Jesus intentionally delayed his arrival at Bethany so that he and his Father would be glorified when he raised Lazarus from the dead (11:4).

A final reason for suffering is so that Jesus's followers can voluntarily identify with their Lord in a life of committed discipleship. The fact that suffering is an expected and characteristic feature of being a follower of Jesus Christ is a consistent theme in the Gospels, as well as in the entire New Testament. This is especially clear from the center section of Mark's Gospel, framed around the cyclical announcements of the inevitable and impending death of Jesus and his corollary calls to discipleship. Woven into the cycles is also the recurring theme of the frequent misunderstandings of the disciples.

The Suffering of Jesus as a Divine Necessity

In any contemplation of the cross it is imperative that one move beyond the human causes in order to see the divine purpose. Several Gospel passages show that suffering was a central "must" (Greek, *dei*) in the will of God for his Son in his earthly ministry.

The Expressions of the Divine Necessity

From that time Jesus began to show his disciples that he must [*dei*] go to Jerusalem and suffer many things from the elders and chief priests and scribes, and be killed, and on the third day be raised. (Matt. 16:21)

And he began to teach them that the Son of Man must [*dei*] suffer many things and be rejected by the elders and the chief priests and the scribes and be killed, and after three days rise again. (Mark 8:31)

The Son of Man must [*dei*] suffer many things and be rejected by the elders and chief priests and scribes, and be killed, and on the third day be raised. (Luke 9:22)

Nevertheless I must [*dei*] go on my way today and tomorrow and the day following, for it cannot be that a prophet should perish away from Jerusalem. (Luke 13:33)

For as the lightning flashes and lights up the sky from one side to the other, so will the Son of Man be in his day. But first he must [*dei*] suffer many things and be rejected by this generation. (Luke 17:24–25)

Other references include Luke 22:37; 24:7, 44; John 3:14; 12:34; and 20:9.

With this preponderance of references, R. T. France comments, "It is on such grounds that many believe that Isaiah's Servant figure was a major factor in Jesus' understanding of his own mission and the crucial basis on which his followers found it possible to make sense of his death as the fulfillment of Scripture."[3] For an expanded discussion of the debate as to whether Isaiah 53 is the background for Jesus's own understanding of his suffering, see *Jesus and the Suffering Servant: Isaiah 53 and Christian Origins*.[4]

Many of the verses cited earlier are from the Gospel of Luke. Regarding this concentration in Luke's accounts, Joel B. Green notes, "In Luke Jesus evinces a purposefulness about the cross that is without parallel in the Synoptic Gospels."[5]

The divine purpose for Jesus's suffering and death was completely misunderstood by the disciples. This occurred in six separate historical contexts: on the journey of ministry with Jesus, in the garden of Gethsemane, at the moment of Jesus's arrest, at the time of Jesus's trials, during the events of the crucifixion, and in the aftermath of Jesus's resurrection.

The Explanation of the Divine Necessity
The need for Jesus to suffer and thus fulfill the Father's will during his ministry and passion can be seen in the following fifteen purposes. (This list is limited to the four Gospels. Many more could be added from the rest of the New Testament.) Jesus suffered:

1. To obey the will of the Father (John 17:4)
2. To satisfy the just demands of a holy God against sin (Matt. 27:46; John 3:14)
3. To pay the ransom to set sinners free from sin and death (Matt. 20:28; Mark 10:45)
4. To free people from the slavery of sin (John 8:32–34)
5. To establish an eternal covenant through his shed blood by which forgiveness and redemption were accomplished (Matt. 26:28)

[3]R. T. France, "Servant of Yahweh," in *Dictionary of Jesus and the Gospels*, ed. Joel B. Green and Scot McKnight (Downers Grove, IL: InterVarsity, 1992), 746.
[4]William H. Bellinger and William R. Farmer, eds., *Jesus and the Suffering Servant: Isaiah 53 and Christian Origins* (Harrisburg, VA: Trinity, 1998).
[5]Joel B. Green, "The Death of Jesus," in *Dictionary of Jesus and the Gospels*, 160.

6. To show the supreme depth of God's love for sinners (Matt. 20:28; John 3:16; 15:13)
7. To make provision for the forgiveness of sins (Matt. 26:28)
8. To provide the means for ultimate healing (Matt. 8:16–17; Luke 6:19)
9. To give eternal life to all who believe (John 3:16; 3:36; 17:13)
10. To deliver from the Evil One (John 12:31; 17:15)
11. To grant access to the Father (Matt. 27:51)
12. To enlist a band of faithful followers who would identify daily with Jesus whether by life or by death (Matt. 10:38; Luke 9:23)
13. To proclaim the message of salvation to all nations (Matt. 28:19–20; Luke 24:46–47; John 1:29)
14. To gather together believers from among Jews and Gentiles to be in a unified flock under one Shepherd (John 10:16; 11:51–52)
15. To deliver from the coming wrath of God (Matt. 3:7)

John Piper has chronicled fifty different purposes for the suffering of Jesus. He concludes:

> But the most astonishing thing is that evil and suffering was Christ's appointed way of victory over evil and suffering. Every act of treachery and brutality against Jesus was sinful and evil, but God was in it. The Bible says, "Jesus [was] delivered up [to death] according to the definite plan and foreknowledge of God" (Acts 2:23).[6]

Central Themes of Suffering in the Gospels

A study of the life of Christ reveals (1) suffering and disability on the part of the people to whom Jesus ministered, (2) what his disciples experienced as they identified with Jesus, (3) the suffering Jesus experienced during his earthly life, and (4) his agony on the cross as he gave his life as the sacrifice for sin. Not always taken into account in a discussion of suffering is the judgment of God that will be meted out by Jesus in the end times. The theology of suffering found in the Gospels can be considered by an examination of ten major themes.

Suffering of Others besides Jesus in the Gospels

Emotional

The most common emotional suffering recorded in the Gospels is *fear*. That fear may be alarm in the presence of angelic messengers or a response to intimidation

---

[6]John Piper, *The Passion of Jesus Christ* (Wheaton, IL: Crossway, 2004), 119.

from those who did not share the disciples' faith. The cosmic events of Jesus's crucifixion and resurrection were also accompanied by fear. *Anxiety* is another emotional stress. Such worry may be about material provisions or materialistic distractions. Even Mary and Joseph were anxious when looking for Jesus when he stayed behind to interact with the leaders at the temple.

Mourning was expressed over the loss of a child or at the thought of Jesus's departure. The absence of leaders brought a sense of distress and depression to the people. *Grief* was a noted emotion at the prospect of the death of Jesus and guilt following his own disciples' betrayal and denial of him. *Doubt* that Jesus would be able to save the disciples in a storm or that he had been resurrected following his death was understandable, though mistaken on both occasions.

Physical

Physical sufferings recorded in the Gospels were related to *storms* of nature, *ailments* Jesus healed, or warnings of the *mistreatment* that may be experienced by the disciples for their public testimony. In addition to general statements about Jesus's healing all kinds of sickness, specifics included fever, epilepsy, paralysis, leprosy, lunacy, and impairments of speech, hearing, and walking. He even restored a severed ear, and he raised the dead. Jesus realistically predicted that his disciples would suffer the same kinds of verbal abuse and physical persecution that the prophets had endured, including martyrdom. Neither Jesus's forerunner, John the Baptist, nor his close friend Lazarus was spared physical death.

Spiritual

The suffering and disability Jesus healed went beyond the physical. Both Jesus and his disciples faced temptations by the Devil. On numerous occasions Jesus cast out demons and cured illnesses and diseases caused or aggravated by demons. The effects of satanic attacks are also seen in spiritual interference with people's receiving and understanding the Word of God. An often-repeated theme is the opposition faced by messengers of the Word of God. Several times Jesus predicted that his followers would be arrested and tried by religious and political leaders. Legalism, opposition, manipulation of defenseless widows, selfish and dishonest gain, and killing of God's messengers were all a part of the hypocrisy Jesus condemned.

Social

Jesus's followers also faced social disenfranchisement. Sometimes it was by their own families as the choice to follow Jesus offended family members who rejected him. Guilt by association was also a tactic of the religious leaders against Jesus and his disciples. Intimidating questioning and testing by religious leaders was an expected part of following Jesus. Those not normally invited to banquets included the poor, the crippled, the blind, and the lame. The disciple Judas even criticized his fellow followers for wasting resources on Jesus that could have been given to the poor.

The Suffering Jesus Experienced in the Course of His Prepassion Ministry

In addition to Jesus's suffering as he was tried and crucified, a surprising amount of suffering faced him throughout his earthly ministry before the final week. The following fifty experiences are especially noteworthy, given that only portions of fifty-two days of the entire life of Jesus are represented in the four Gospels:

1. Jesus's life was threatened by Herod at his birth (Matt. 2:13–21).
2. Jesus was tempted by Satan when he was hungry in the wilderness (Matt. 4:1–11; Mark 1:12, 23; Luke 4:1–13).
3. An attempt was made on the life of Jesus in Nazareth after his synagogue message (Luke 4:16–30).
4. Jesus had no permanent place of residence (Matt. 8:19–22; Luke 9:27–62).
5. Jesus was chased out of the region of the Gadarenes (Matt. 8:34; Luke 8:37).
6. Jesus was charged with blasphemy when he claimed to forgive the sins of a paralytic (Matt. 9:3; Mark 2:7; Luke 5:21).
7. Jesus was questioned by the religious leaders for eating with tax collectors and sinners (Matt. 9:11; Mark 2:16; Luke 5:30).
8. Jesus was questioned as to why his disciples were not fasting (Matt. 9:14; Mark 2:18; Luke 5:33).
9. Jesus was ridiculed with laughter when he raised Jairus's daughter (Matt. 9:23; Mark 5:40; Luke 8:53).
10. Jesus was charged with performing miracles by the power of Satan (Matt. 9:34; 12:24; Mark 3:22, 30).
11. Jesus was maligned as a glutton, a drunkard, and a friend of sinners (Matt. 11:19; Luke 7:34).
12. Jesus was challenged about his disciples' violating the Sabbath (Matt. 12:2; Mark 2:24; Luke 6:2).

13. The Pharisees were planning to accuse Jesus of violating the Sabbath if he healed the man with a withered hand in the synagogue (Matt. 12:10; Mark 3:2; Luke 6:7).
14. The furious Pharisees and the Herodians plotted to kill Jesus following his healing activity in the synagogue (Matt.12:14; Mark 3:6; Luke 6:11).
15. Jesus's family sought to take control of him because they thought he was out of his mind (Mark 3:20–21).
16. The Pharisees and the scribes demanded a sign from Jesus (Matt. 12:38; cf. 16:1; Mark 8:11–12).
17. Jesus was doubted at home in Nazareth (Matt. 13:57–58; Mark 6:1–6).
18. Some attempted to make Jesus a king after he fed the five thousand (John 6:15).
19. Jesus experienced racial discrimination and rejection by the Samaritans, since he had determined to go to Jerusalem (Luke 9:51–53).
20. Jesus was aware of his rejection and that of his followers (Luke 10:16).
21. Jesus was tested about the doctrine of eternal life by a young lawyer (Luke 10:25).
22. After he healed the speech-impaired man, Jesus was charged with getting power from Beelzebul (Luke 11:14–15).
23. Others asked Jesus to show them a heavenly sign even after he had performed many miracles (Luke 11:16).
24. The scribes and Pharisees sought to question Jesus on many subjects with great hostility in order to trap him (Luke 11:53–54).
25. Jesus experienced the indignant response of the synagogue officials after healing the demonized woman with spinal difficulties (Luke 13:14).
26. Jesus endured the grumbling of the Pharisees and scribes because of his associations with sinners (Luke 15:1–2).
27. The Jews grumbled against Jesus when he said he was the Bread of Life (John 6:41).
28. Jesus was challenged as to whether he paid the temple tax (Matt. 17:24–27).
29. In their unbelief, Jesus's brothers challenged him to manifest himself in the feast at Jerusalem (John 7:1–3).
30. Jesus was charged with having a demon at the Feast of Tabernacles (John 7:20).
31. The Jews were seeking to seize Jesus at the feast (Luke 7:44).
32. The Pharisees sought to trap Jesus when he was talking with the woman caught in adultery (John 8:6).

33. Jesus exposed their desire to kill him throughout his address at the feast (John 8:37, 40).

34. Jesus was called a Samaritan and was accused of being demon-possessed (John 8:48, 52; 10:20).

35. The Jews attempted to stone Jesus (John 8:59).

36. At the Feast of Dedication, after his claim to be the Good Shepherd, Jesus was charged with having a demon and being insane (John 10:20).

37. Believing that Jesus had committed blasphemy, Jews took up stones to kill Jesus (John 10:31).

38. Jesus experienced deep emotional stress at the death of Lazarus (John 11:33, 38).

39. The Pharisees sought to entrap Jesus with questions about marriage and divorce (Matt. 19:1–9; Mark 10:1–12).

40. People thought of Jesus as no more than a prophet (Matt. 21:11).

41. The Pharisees demanded that Jesus rebuke his disciples for the adulation he was given in his triumphal entry into Jerusalem (Luke 19:39).

42. The religious leaders plotted how they might destroy Jesus (Luke 19:47–48).

43. The religious leaders continued to seek a way to seize Jesus and kill him (John 11:53).

44. Jesus reminded his disciples of the persecution and hatred he had experienced, which they too would have to experience (John 15:20, 23–25).

45. The indignation of the religious leaders was manifest against the children who were praising Jesus in the temple (Matt. 21:15).

46. The chief priests and elders challenged Jesus's authority (Matt. 21:23; Mark 11:27–28; Luke 20:1–2).

47. The chief priests and the Pharisees looked for ways to arrest Jesus (Matt. 21:45–46; Mark 11:12; Luke 20:19).

48. Jesus was challenged by the Pharisees and Herodians about paying taxes to Caesar (Matt. 22:15–22; Mark 12:13–17; Luke 20:20–26).

49. The Sadducees, who said there was no resurrection, questioned Jesus about the resurrection (Matt. 22:23–33; Mark 12:18–27; Luke 20:27–40).

50. The Pharisees sought to entrap Jesus with a question about the most important commandment in the Law (Matt. 22:34–40; Mark 12:28–34).

The Passion Events Predicted by Jesus

While there may have been some early veiled references to the fact that Jesus would be rejected, it was not until Peter confessed that Jesus is the Messiah, the Son of God, that Jesus began to predict openly to his disciples his rejection, death, and resurrection. The passion predictions are found in the following passages in the Synoptic Gospels: Matthew 16:21; 17:22–23; 20:18, 29; Mark 8:31; 9:12, 31; 10:33–34; 14:21; Luke 9:22, 44; 18:31–33. In a few of these references the terms *cup* and *baptism* are used as a reference to the coming death of Jesus. For example *baptism* is used of his death in Mark 10:38–39 and Luke 12:50.

The Challenge of Suffering in Discipleship

Mark's Gospel includes a cyclical pattern of announcements, misunderstandings, and discipleship implications as Jesus traveled with his disciples on the road to Jerusalem (see table 3).

Table 3. A cyclical pattern in Mark's Gospel

Mark 8:31–9:2	Mark 9:30–41	Mark 10:33–52
Passion prediction	Passion prediction	Passion prediction
Misunderstanding	Misunderstanding	Misunderstanding
Discipleship	Discipleship	Discipleship
Leadership lesson	Leadership lesson	Leadership lesson
Elders, chief priests, scribes	Into the hands of men	Chief priests, scribes, Gentiles
Peter—human Interest	The disciples—human greatness	James /John—human positioning
Deny self, take up cross, follow Christ	First-last: servant of all	Greatness = servanthood
Listen to Christ	Identify with Christ	Follow Christ

Each of these contexts includes Jesus's prediction of his passion and an accompanying call to discipleship. In each cycle the disciples were revealed as lacking the discernment necessary for faithful followers of Jesus Christ. A correcting instruction by Jesus was intended to bring the disciples along in their faith and commitment to follow him in spite of the coming persecution and threat of death. According to Mark 10:45 (cf. Matt. 20:28), the ultimate purpose of Jesus's suffering was not only to provide the means of redemption from sin, but also to be a model of humble service for his disciples.

The point in all of this is that rejection, suffering, and death were all necessary (Greek, *dei*) before Jesus would be resurrected, exalted, and enthroned to reign ultimately as the messianic King. True discipleship means following the pattern of Jesus by imitating his model of servanthood under the shadow of the cross. This theology of the cross is the seedbed for the theology of sanctification that is central to the Christian life, as explained later in the New Testament Epistles. Paul referred to "carrying in the body the death of Jesus, so that the life of Jesus may also be manifested in our bodies" (2 Cor. 4:10). And Paul wrote, "Consider yourselves dead to sin and alive to God in Christ Jesus" (Rom. 6:11). Therefore suffering is neither meaningless nor arbitrary; it is purposeful and powerful in the lives of those who choose to identify with Jesus, the Suffering Servant of the Lord.

Suffering in the Passion Narratives

The word *passion* comes from the Latin word meaning "suffering." The passion of Christ was absolutely unique, and in his resurrection three days later, God vindicated what the death of Christ would achieve for humanity. Jesus finished the work God gave him to do, and the resurrection was proof that God was satisfied with the sacrifice of his Son (John 17:4).

While the song of the Servant in Isaiah 53 is debated by such authors as Rudolph Bultmann and Morna Hooker, most evangelical scholars see it as the background for both the self-understanding of Jesus and the explanation of the apostles' preaching.[7]

The impending plots and threats of death against Jesus were especially noted by John (7:1, 19, 25; 8:37; 11:16). And Jesus escaped a series of threats of arrests and stonings (7:30, 32, 44; 8:20, 59; 10:31, 39) until it was his hour to go to the cross.

In John the suffering of Christ for sins is described ironically as his being "lifted up," which refers not only to the work of Christ on the cross as a sacrifice for sin, but also to the ultimate exaltation of Jesus when he returned to glory and the Father in heaven (12:32). This "lifting" is expressed as well in terms of divine necessity (*dei*), as seen in John 3:14 and 12:34.

The suffering Jesus endured extended throughout the passion narrative from the murderous plots of the leaders to the final moments of crucifixion on the cross. The following pages reveal the extent to which the Savior suffered for his own.

The Plot of the Leaders

The continual plotting and planning of the religious leaders to rid themselves of Jesus was complicated by his popularity among the people and the timing of the Passover Feast (Matt. 26:1–5; Mark 14:1–2; Luke 22:1–2). Their desire was to seize him by stealth and to kill him, but they did not want that to happen during the Feast of Passover and Unleavened Bread.

---

[7]See the debate in Bellinger and Farmer, *Jesus and the Suffering Servant.*

The Betrayal of Judas

The work of Satan behind Judas's betrayal of Jesus is notable (Luke 22:3–6; John 13:2, 27). The chief priests paid Judas thirty pieces of silver to betray Jesus (Matt. 26:14–16). Judas was constantly looking for an opportunity to betray him when a crowd was present (Mark 14:11; Luke 22:6).

The Last (Lord's) Supper

During the Passover meal, Jesus predicted both his betrayal (Matt. 26:21; Mark 14:18; Luke 22:21; John 13:21) and the failure of all the disciples, in fulfillment of Zechariah 13:7, "Strike the shepherd, and the sheep will be scattered" (Matt. 26:31; Mark 14:27). He also predicted that before the cock crowed, Peter would deny him three times (Matt. 26:34; Mark 14:30; Luke 22:34; John 13:38).

Jesus initiated the symbols of the bread and cup to clarify the purposes of his death. The bread represented the sacrifice of his body, and the cup signified the blood of the new covenant poured out for the forgiveness of sins (Matt. 26:26–30; Mark 14:22–26; Luke 22:17–20). The blood is the physical evidence of life (Gen. 9:4; Lev. 17:11, 14; Deut. 32:23). The Lord's Supper thus became a symbolic demonstration of the ransoming and redeeming work of Jesus Christ that would be accomplished on the cross. According to Matthew 26:28 Jesus knew that the giving of his life through the shedding of his blood would provide for the forgiveness of sins.

When Jesus identified his own blood with the wine of the Passover meal, he was identifying himself as the Passover Lamb who would suffer as the substitute for those who would become his people. The Servant Songs in Isaiah 40–55 predicted that the Messiah must die as the vicarious sacrifice for the sins of humanity.

In the Last Supper Jesus announced the suffering he would endure in his passion. The supper also called on the disciples to identify with those sufferings as his followers who would take his message to the world in an atmosphere of hostility (Mark 10:39). The context of his statement in Mark 10:45 that he would suffer and give his life a ransom illustrates the kind of servant-hearted leadership demanded of his followers. The roots of this idea of ransom are to be found in the substitutionary suffering of the Servant of the Lord, as explained in Isaiah 53.

The Agony in Gethsemane

The agonizing prayer of Jesus about his impending "cup of death" was made all the more vivid by the sleeping of his disciples. Jesus's severe emotional distress is described in detail as sorrow, grief, anxiety, distress, and a troubled spirit (Matt. 26:37). As Mark recorded, Jesus said, "My soul is very sorrowful, even to death" (Mark 14:34).

Much of Jesus's sorrow was no doubt caused by the fact that both his Father and his followers would desert him. As Green has stated, "Gethsemane, then, does not so much demonstrate Jesus' anguish in the face of death as his fear of being abandoned before God. The humanity of Jesus could hardly be emphasized more acutely."[8]

The example of Jesus facing the greatest of tests revealed his followers' need for prayer and spiritual preparation in order to be submissive to the will of God. Just as Jesus's instructions frame the account, so the central thrust stands as an example of Jesus's agonizing, prayerful submission to God.

In the garden of Gethsemane the disciples continued to show their lack of understanding, as evidenced in their inability to stay awake and pray with Jesus. They even abandoned him when the betrayer and opponents came to arrest Jesus.

Jesus submitted his will to the Father in the imagery of the "cup" of suffering (Matt. 26:39, 42; 44; implied in Mark 14:36, 39 and Luke 22:42). After struggling in prayer, Jesus announced that the hour of his passion had arrived as he was betrayed into the hands of sinners, represented by the religious and civil leaders who arrived to arrest him (Matt. 26:45; Mark 14:41).

The Arrest in Gethsemane

Judas betrayed Jesus with a kiss (Matt. 26:49; Mark 14:44–45; Luke 22:48).

Jesus was arrested like a common criminal by a crowd of people, including the chief priests, elders, scribes, soldiers, and other officials of the Pharisees who were armed with swords, clubs, torches, and lanterns (Matt. 26:47–50; Mark 14:43–46; Luke 22:47–48; John 18:2–9). When Jesus was arrested, all the disciples fled (Matt. 26:56; Mark 14:50), including the one disciple who left his robe in the clutches of the captors (Mark 14:51).

The Religious Trial of Jesus

After a religious trial before Annas, Caiaphas, and the Sanhedrin, when Jesus was charged with blasphemy, the Jewish leaders brought before Pilate the additional charge of sedition against Jesus. Pilate conducted a political trial. False testimony was solicited against Jesus in order to condemn him to death

---

[8]Joel B. Green, "Gethsemane," in *Dictionary of Jesus and the Gospels*, 266.

(Matt. 26:59–60; Mark 14:55–59). Jesus was charged with blasphemy, which carried a death sentence (Matt. 26:65–66; Mark 14:64).

The mistreatment of Jesus included his being struck in the face before Annas (John 18:22), spit on the face, blindfolded, struck with fists, slapped, and mocked to prophesy in answer to the taunting question, "Who is it that struck you?" The guards also joined in and beat Jesus (Matt. 26:67–68; Mark 14:65; Luke 22:63–64). Luke added the personal touch that along with the previous mistreatments many other insults were leveled against Jesus (Luke 22:65).

Peter denied Jesus three times during the religious trials (Matt. 26:69–75; Mark 14:66–72; Luke 22:54–62; John 18:15–18, 25–27). The chief priests and elders came to the decision to put Jesus to death (Matt. 27:1; Mark 15:1; Luke 22:66–71).

Roman Trial

The trial of Jesus before Pilate involved a separate set of charges that envisioned a death sentence. Whereas the Sanhedrin charged Jesus with the religious sin of blasphemy, these rulers urged the Romans to find Jesus guilty of treason against the state. The charges included subverting the nation, opposing payment of taxes to Caesar, claiming to be the Messiah, and stirring up the people to rebel (Luke 23:2, 5, 14).

Jesus was bound and led away to the Praetorium to appear before Pilate, the Roman procurator (Matt. 27:2; Mark 15:1; Luke 23:1–2; John 18:28). Jesus was questioned by Pilate about being the king of the Jews, and he was harshly accused by the chief priests and the elders (Matt. 27:11–14; Mark 15:1–5; Luke 23:1–5; John 18:28–38). One of the interchanges John recorded concerns the issue of truth and its definition.

As an accompanying episode, Matthew recorded Judas's confession that he had betrayed innocent blood and his subsequently hanging himself (Matt. 27:3–10). Jesus was sent to Herod where the chief priests continued to accuse him vehemently (Luke 23:6–12). Herod and his soldiers mocked Jesus, robed him in purple, and sent him back to Pilate. The people demanded the release of Barabbas and cried repeatedly that Jesus be crucified (Matt. 27:15–26; Mark 15:6–15; Luke 23:13–25).

Jesus was flogged and handed over to be crucified (Matt. 27:26; John 19:1). Jesus was humiliated before the Roman cohort with extreme and cruel mistreatment. Those actions included being stripped and robed with a scarlet (purple) robe; being "crowned" with a crown of thorns; having a reed staff put in his right hand; being mocked by people kneeling before him and saying,

"Hail, King of the Jews"; and being spat on, struck on the head with a staff, and slapped in the face.

The tragic irony, as recorded by John, is that the one charged with being the "imposter king" went to the cross. He who really was the King of the Jews died for the very ones who had called for his crucifixion. John recorded that the leaders acted out of fear and envy (John 11:45–53).

Crucifixion

Jesus was crucified between two thieves at Golgotha, the place of the skull (Matt. 27:58; Mark 15:28; Luke 23:32–33; John 19:18). Jesus's garments were divided, and lots were cast to see who would win them (Matt. 27:35; Mark 15:24; Luke 23:34; John 19:23). A sign with the "identifying charge" was posted on the cross in three languages (Matt. 27:37; Mark 15:26; Luke 23:38; John 19:19–20).

Jesus was verbally abused by onlookers, the religious leaders, and even the two robbers crucified on either side of him, all challenging him to save himself since they said Jesus had claimed he could save others (Matt. 27:39–44; Mark 15:29–37; Luke 23:35–43).

Darkness fell from the sixth hour to the ninth (Matt. 27:45; Mark 15:33; Luke 23:44). At the ninth hour Jesus cried out, "Eli, Eli, lema sabachthani?" ("My God, my God, why have you forsaken me?" Matt. 27:46; Mark 15:34). Jesus experienced thirst as he was dying on the cross (John 19:28). He cried with a loud voice, "Father, into your hands I commit my spirit!" (Luke 23:46), said "It is finished" (John 19:30), breathed his last (Mark 15:37), and "yielded up his spirit" (Matt. 27:50).

Jesus was confirmed to be dead, and he was buried in the tomb of Joseph of Arimathea (Matt. 27:57–60; Mark 15:42–47; Luke 23:50–56; John 19:31–42).

According to Luke 24:25–26, the suffering of Jesus was no mere accident or simply the consequence of jealous Jewish leaders. The passion of Jesus, which climaxed with his death and resurrection, was the very purpose of God.

Postresurrection Appearances

After his resurrection Jesus explained to his disciples that his suffering and death were a necessary part of the plan of redemption predicted by God in the Old Testament. To the two on the road to Emmaus, he said, "O foolish ones, and slow of heart to believe all that the prophets have spoken! Was it not necessary that the Christ should suffer these things and enter into his glory?"(Luke 24:25–26). Later, to the Eleven he said, "Thus it is written, that the Christ should suffer and on the third day rise from the dead" (Luke 24:46).

Therefore the suffering of Christ was no unfortunate coincidence or accident of history. It was a central message anticipated in the Old Testament and fulfilled in Jesus.

Afflictions and Persecutions in the Present Age

Jesus warned the disciples that they would experience rejection for their identification and representation of Christ in this world. Such treatment would mean they would be delivered up to religious and civil authorities to face accusation, imprisonment, and even martyrdom (Matt. 10:16–18). Even intrafamily betrayals and hatred might be their plight (Matt. 10:21). With the death of Jesus they would experience temporary sorrow and grief (John 16:20) before experiencing joy over his resurrection (John 16:20). Followers of Christ can expect hatred and persecution by the world (John 15:18–20). While Jesus announced that he had overcome the world, until such a time when this world is renovated by him, there will be tribulation (John 16:33).

Temporal Disciplinary Judgments of God

Suffering as the consequences of sin can be chronicled on both national and individual levels. Jesus predicted the destruction of the temple and the city of Jerusalem and the fall of the nation of Israel at the hands of their enemies (Matt. 21:43; 23:37–39; Luke 13:6–9). The transfer of custody for the message and responsibility of kingdom leadership in the present age may be seen as a temporary judgment against Israel (Matt. 21:43–45; Mark 5:25).

Disease or disability may in exceptional cases (as noted earlier) be the result of persistent sin (John 5:14). Jesus also announced that judgment comes to individuals for misjudging others (Matt. 7:1–2). The loss of opportunity or even life may result from failure to produce the fruit God expects (John 15:1–6).

Suffering in the Great Tribulation

While some elements in the Olivet Discourse may prefigure the destruction of Jerusalem in AD 70, the final suffering of God's people will be experienced during the tribulation leading up to the second coming of Christ. The judgments of the fall of Jerusalem in the generation of Jesus and those of the future tribulation are called the "days of vengeance, to fulfill all that is written" (Luke 21:22).

The unparalleled distress of that time will include wars, earthquakes, famines, and death (Matt. 24:4–8; Mark 13:5–8; Luke 21:8–11). During that same tribulation those who will identify with Christ will suffer the persecution of severe trials, mistreatment, hatred, family rebellion and betrayal, arrests, and even martyrdom for the sake of Christ and the gospel (Matt. 24:9–14; Mark 13:9–12; Luke 21:12–24).

The midpoint of the seven-year tribulation will be marked by the abomination of desolation, a desecration of the temple and the maniacal, ego-motivated self-promotion of a pagan world leader, as predicted by Daniel (Dan. 9:24–27; Matt 24:15). In the latter half of the period false christs and prophets will mislead with fraudulent signs, and many will be deceived (Matt. 24:15–28; Mark 13:14–23). All tribulational suffering before the messianic kingdom was regarded by the Jews as the "birth pangs" before messianic deliverance (Isa. 26:17–19).

Final Judgment

To Jesus all judgment has been delegated by the Father (John 5:22–27). Jesus taught that all need to repent in order to avoid perishing in future judgment (Luke 13:1–8). Suffering will be eliminated as the righteous and the wicked experience the reversal of fortunes in the eschatological future (Matt. 16:13–31; Luke 6:20–26). Jesus spoke of the realities of final judgment probably more than any other person in the New Testament.

Judgment would come on Israel for rejecting the messengers of God because the nation had been privileged to receive more direct revelation, as well as the messianic miracles (Matt. 11:16–19). As a result, Jesus pronounced the collective and accumulative guilt of the nation (Matt 23:36–39). Then would occur the destruction of the temple and the city of Jerusalem and the continuation of the times of the Gentiles until the end of the present age (Matt. 24:1–2; Luke 21:24). Jesus lamented on numerous occasions the failure of Jerusalem and Israel's failure to respond to the call of God to repentance (Matt. 23:36–39; Luke 13:34–35; 19:41–46). Judgment would take the form of the abandonment of Israel to her enemies, a judgment reminiscent of that announced by Jeremiah (Jer. 7:25–34) and Hosea (Hos. 9:15–17; 10:13–15).

Jesus taught that a final judgment will come on all when he returns to establish his kingdom on earth (Matt. 7:22; Luke 17:30–35). The judgment is described as a separation of the wise from the foolish (Matt. 7:24–27), a separation of the wicked "sons of the evil one" from the righteous "sons of the kingdom" (Matt. 13:38), and a separation of the "sheep" from the "goats"—all of which describe those going into judgment in contrast to those entering into eternal life (Matt. 25:31–46).

Judgment will be meted out according to works that demonstrate the presence or lack of faith (Matt. 7:21–23; 12:36–37; 25:31–46; John 5:28–29). Examples of criteria include causing little ones to sin (Mark 9:42), mistreatment of the poor (Luke 16:19–31), and wrongly judging others (Matt. 5:22; 7:1–2). The most critical criterion is the response to the person and message of Jesus (Mark 8:38; Luke 10:8–16; 11:29–32; 12:8–9). The result is the entrance into or expulsion from the presence of the Father and the Son.

Judgment to life is described metaphorically as a place at the banquet table of the Father in the kingdom of heaven (Matt. 8:11; Luke 13:28–29). Judgment to condemnation is described as being unending, intolerable, irreversible, and incendiary. The descriptions include unquenchable fire (Matt. 5:22; Mark 9:43, 45, 48; Luke 12:5) where there is weeping and gnashing of teeth (Matt. 13:42, 50; Luke 13:28). Matthew 25:26 and 41 state that the judgment is a curse of fiery judgment that lasts for eternity, and Mark 9:48 states that in hell "the worm does not die and the fire is not quenched" (NIV).

Responses to Suffering in the Gospels

The Responses of Jesus

Jesus's responses to suffering are best seen both in passages that mention his compassion and mercy and in the miracles he performed to alleviate suffering. In his compassion and mercy he helped the hopeless and helpless while addressing a wide variety of needs. His compassion extended to the people because of their lack of spiritual leadership (Matt. 9:36; Mark 6:34), their sicknesses (Matt. 14:14), and their human needs (Matt. 15:32; Mark 8:2); he restored sight (Mark 8:25), cured leprosy (Mark 1:41), and gave life to a widow's dead son (Luke 7:13). Jesus's mercy extended to the blind who received back their sight (Matt. 9:27), a self-destructive demoniac who was cured and sent back with the message of God's mercy (Mark 5:19), a foreign mother whose demonized daughter was healed in response to her faith (Matt. 15:28), a father whose lunatic boy was likewise delivered from demons (Matt. 17:15), two blind men healed between the Old Testament ruins and the New Testament site of Jericho (Matt. 20:30–31; Mark 10:47; Luke 18:38–39), and a leper who cried out for healing (Luke 17:13).

The Place of Miracles in the Life of Christ

Most of Jesus's miracles were performed during his Galilean ministry with a decreasing number after the sign ministry of Jesus reached a climax in Galilee. As he came closer to his crucifixion, the number of his miracles decreased. Jesus worked four kinds of miracles: nine miracles in nature, seventeen healings, six exorcisms, and three raisings from the dead. All his miracles were beneficent except that of cursing the fig tree.

The diseases Jesus healed included fever, leprosy, palsy or paralysis, blindness, speech and hearing impairments, dropsy, and uncontrolled bleeding. Many of these conditions were accompanied by or caused by demon oppression.

The place of faith in the miracles of Jesus is so varied that no predictable pattern is seen. Only five of the thirty-five miracles showed that faith was exercised by the one healed. Twelve times faith was present in those interceding for the person who needed healing, whereas in eighteen cases faith was not mentioned at all.

The Gospels also reveal a variety of means Jesus used. Ten miracles note the importance of his powerful word. Seven miracles record his touch in healing someone. Seven additional miracles combined the touch and the word of Jesus. Another seven record no method at all. On one occasion a woman was healed who touched Jesus, and in three cases Jesus performed the miracle at a distance.

Several purposes for Jesus's miracles may be suggested. The compassion he felt for the suffering person is noted in the healing of the leper (Matt. 8:2–4; Mark 1:44–45; Luke 5:12–15). Another purpose was to show Jesus's authority as the Messiah. One example is the statement Jesus made when he healed the paralytic: "But that you may know that the Son of Man has authority on earth to forgive sins . . . Rise, pick up your bed and go home" (Matt. 9:6; Mark 2:10; Luke 5:24). A third reason for the miraculous ministry of Jesus was his discipling of his followers. Typical of this is the lesson in faith Jesus desired to teach his disciples during the stilling of a storm (Matt. 8:23–26; Mark 4:35–41; Luke 8:22–25) and his testing the disciples as to his power and provision in the feeding of the five thousand (Matt. 14:13–21; Mark 6:32–44; Luke 9:10–17; John 6:1–4). A fourth and most important purpose was Jesus's desire to glorify his Father. The healing of the man born blind (John 9:3) displayed the work of the Father, and the raising of Lazarus brought glory to both the Father and the Son (John 11:4). The miracles of Jesus served to authenticate his person and work as the Messiah. As he presented himself to Israel, his miracles proved to be the signs of the kingdom authenticating him as the Messiah (Isa. 35:5–6; Matt. 11:1–6; 12:28).

The miracles signified that the Messiah was present, and as the Messiah, Jesus had the power and prerogative to establish the kingdom of God by the will of God and the power of the Spirit of God. The expectation from the Old Testament was that the kingdom of God would bring about justice, restore a peaceful environment, and deliver people from all pain and sorrow. Sorrow and suffering in this life give ample reason for the need of the kingdom of God and the reign of his Messiah. Miraculous deliverances of people from the powerful throes of Satan are signs of the coming kingdom of God that will mean the ultimate defeat of the Devil (Matt. 12:28).

The ultimate miracle was the resurrection of Jesus. The New Testament links the suffering and hope of the believer with the suffering and resurrection of Jesus Christ. The interplay between the two shows that for neither of them is suffering meaningless. Meaning in suffering is best understood in light of the suffering of Jesus.

Appropriate Responses to Suffering

Followers of Jesus should display various responses to both those who cause suffering and those who suffer.

Responses to Those Who Cause Suffering
- Bless them (Luke 6:28; cf. Rom. 12:14; 1 Pet. 3:9).
- Do good to them (Luke 6:27, 35).
- Do not be afraid of them (Matt. 10:26, 28).
- Do not repay evil for evil (Matt. 5:39; cf. Rom. 12:17).
- Do not resist them (Matt. 5:39).
- Love your enemies (Matt. 5:44).
- Pray for those who persecute you (Matt. 5:44).
- Forgive them (Luke 23:34; cf. Acts 7:60).
- Love them (Matt. 5:44; Luke 6:27–28).
- Turn the other cheek (Luke 6:29).

Responses to Those Who Suffer
- Reflect the love of Christ to others (John 13:34–35; 15:12, 17).
- Meet the legitimate needs of others (Luke 10:30–37).
- Be merciful as God is merciful (Matt. 18:27; Luke 10:37).
- Feed the hungry (Matt. 15:32; Mark 8:2).
- Give water to the thirsty (Matt. 10:42).

Conclusion

The response of believers to suffering should be similar to Jesus's emotional response as he suffered on the cross. The worst suffering is spiritual, not just physical. For those who have faith in Christ, spiritual life is the result, including the final remedy for all physical disease and disability, because resurrection is the promise. For those who have not yet believed in Christ as their Savior, final judgment is the worst suffering about which they should worry.

Jesus talked more than any other person in the New Testament about eternal judgment. The implications for this life in light of final judgment are enormous. One dare not miss them. No one suffered as Jesus did, and no one needs to benefit from his suffering more than those yet to hear. So the best response to suffering of those who have a relationship with Christ through faith is to lead people to the only One who can take care of their suffering. For the person without faith in Christ, suffering the throes of judgment will last for eternity. In Luke 13:3, 5, Jesus reminds everyone that life is tenuous and repentance is necessary before death makes faith impossible.

Stanley D. Toussaint (ThM, ThD, Dallas Theological Seminary) is senior professor emeritus and an adjunct professor of Bible exposition at Dallas Seminary. A pastor-teacher, he has taught at Dallas since 1960 and pastored for more than twenty years. He has also taught in Christian schools in the Middle East, Australia, and the Far East and has ministered in churches around the world.

Dr. Toussaint is author of *Behold the King*, a commentary on Matthew, and is coeditor of *Essays in Honor of J. Dwight Pentecost*.

12

Suffering in Acts and the Pauline Epistles

Stanley D. Toussaint

Why is there so much suffering in the world? And why do good people suffer? Many answers may be given.

First, people suffer because sin has consequences, as is seen in many aspects of life. If a person participates in an immoral sexual lifestyle, bad things happen—sexually transmitted diseases, hurt relationships, broken marriages, and so on. People suffer because of sinful practices.

Second, evil people cause much suffering. One can scarcely find better illustrations of this than Hitler, Stalin, and Mao Tse-tung. These three villains were responsible for the deaths of tens of millions of people. More recently the terrorists who destroyed the Twin Towers in New York City killed nearly three thousand people. And many people have been killed or permanently injured by drunk drivers. Wicked people have caused much suffering.

Third, the fallen world accounts for much suffering. When I was a lad of eleven years of age, I was afflicted with a serious case of polio. I do not believe I was stricken with polio because I was more wicked than other children my age who lived in the tiny town of Hinckley, Minnesota. It is just that sickness, disease, and death are part of living in a fallen world.

Fourth, many Christians suffer because they are aliens in this world system. Their priorities, philosophy of life, and goals differ from people who are driven by this world system. Sometimes because of this believers are misunderstood, maligned, or even persecuted.

Other reasons can be given for suffering. But often one must say, "I do not know why" or "I don't understand." More than once as a pastor I have stood before a little white casket of a tiny baby with the parents standing at my side. The infant may have died a few minutes after birth, or because of infant death syndrome at the age of two months. At times like these anything I would say to the parents would be meaningless. All I could do was hug them, weep with them, and love them. There are times when we must say, "I do not know why."

However, in 2 Corinthians 1:3–11 Paul states three reasons why Christians suffer: (a) so they can comfort others (vv. 3–7), (b) so they might learn their own inadequacy and God's sufficiency (vv. 8–10), and (c) to encourage them to praise God if he gives deliverance (v. 11).

To Comfort Others (2 Cor. 1:3–7)

Interestingly, Paul begins this paragraph by praising God. His first word is "blessed" (*eulogētos*). A verbal adjective, this word is used only of God in the New Testament. The English word *eulogy* derives from it. In the Greek language words that begin with *eu* speak of something good. For instance, a eulogy is a good word spoken on behalf of someone who is deceased. Here in 2 Corinthians 1:3 *eulogētos* refers to something spoken well of God. The translation "blessed" is a good one. God is to be praised. The translation "Blessed be" could better be rendered, "Blessed is."

Paul then refers to God as "the God and Father of our Lord Jesus Christ." On the cross Jesus cried, "My God, my God, why have you forsaken me?" This was Jesus speaking as a suffering human being. But Paul also called God Christ's "Father." When Jesus prayed in the garden before his arrest, he did not say, "Our Father"; he said, "My Father." This refers to Jesus as divine. Because Christ is both human and divine, God is called "the God and Father of our Lord Jesus Christ."

Paul then takes the same two names of God and relates them to Christians. The first is "the Father of mercies." The term "mercy" is directed toward misery. When one sees the noun "mercy," he is always to look for someone in miserable circumstances. Mercy and misery may be thought of as the "M & M sisters" of the New Testament. God as "our Father" saw people in their misery and reached out to them in mercy. Thus he is called "the Father of mercies."

The term "Father" logically goes with mercy because as an ideal Father he is merciful to believers.

He is also the "God of all comfort." The word "comfort" (*paraklēseōs*) often means much more than just encouragement. The word in both English and Greek emphasizes strength and help. "Fort" of course suggests strength. The Authorized Version translates the noun *paraklētos*, referring to the Holy Spirit, as "Comforter," though many translations render it "Helper." The Greek word basically means "one who is called alongside to help." So the Holy Spirit strengthens believers, as is stated in John 14:16. In 2 Corinthians 1:3 God is called "the God of all comfort" because he is able to help believers in times of difficulty.

God is given two names here—"the Father of mercies" and "the God of all comfort." Of these two names, the only one Paul develops further is "the God of all comfort." Nothing more is said of "the Father of mercies." God "comforts us in all our affliction, so that we may be able to comfort" others (v. 4). This is commonly taken to mean that believers go through certain sufferings so they can help people who are facing the same kinds of affliction. For example, someone who is blind can come alongside another blind person to encourage and strengthen him. But the verse says much more than this. God comforts believers in all their afflictions so that they can comfort "those who are in any affliction." What believers learn in one kind of suffering can transfer to people who are experiencing different kinds of suffering. In other words, we learn transferable concepts in suffering. When we suffer, we are comforted and strengthened so that we may be able to comfort and strengthen others. My experience with polio gave me a sympathetic heart for handicapped people in wheelchairs, people who are on crutches, people who limp and are physically limited. But what I learned from having polio can also apply to people who are experiencing financial hardships or other types of difficulties. In all these situations the same principles apply—God's sovereignty, trust, joy, faith, and so forth.

To be effective, believers must know several things. Verse 5 says that they learn of the *sufficiency* of Christ's comfort. "For as we share abundantly in Christ's sufferings, so through Christ we share abundantly in comfort too." No one can "out comfort" Christ's comfort. If one suffers for one day, God's comfort is for twenty-five hours. No matter how one may measure his suffering and comfort, Christ's suffering and comfort are more than sufficient.

Verse 5 refers to "Christ's sufferings" as being Paul's experience. Normally when people think of the sufferings of Christ, they think of his sufferings on the cross. But the phrase "Christ's sufferings" is broader. It can also refer to the believer's suffering. Much as Christ was misunderstood, so believers may be misunderstood. Believers may suffer as Christ did because they stand up for principles that conflict with the world's philosophy. Or they suffer simply because they are Christians. Similarly, in Philippians 3:10 Paul refers to "the fellowship of [Christ's] sufferings" (NASB). So in 2 Corinthians 1:5, Paul is referring to his sufferings as a result of serving the Lord Jesus (cf. 5:10–12).

Another principle is given in 1:6. Verse 5 says that believers cannot "out-suffer" God's comfort; verse 6 says that if one's comfort is to help others, he must live for other people: "If we are afflicted, it is for your comfort and salvation; and if we are comforted, it is for your comfort, which you experience when you patiently endure the same sufferings that we suffer." One's suffering and God's comfort do not automatically result in comfort for others. The sufferer must be committed to others. Whether Paul was being afflicted or comforted, it was for the sake of the believers in Corinth. Verse 7 confirms their participation in God's comfort: "We know that as you share in our sufferings, you will also share in our comfort."

To Learn Our Own Inadequacies (2 Cor. 1:8–10)

In verse 8 Paul refers to some heavy affliction that came on him and his associates in Asia (the province in far west Asia Minor). Since he does not state what the affliction was, this has given birth to much speculation as to what happened to him. Most probably it looks back to the riot that occurred while he was in Ephesus. It was indeed a dangerous time. In fact Paul says, "We despaired of life itself." And in verse 9 he adds, "We felt that we had received the sentence of death." The word "sentence" conveys the idea, "We asked ourselves, is there any way out of this? and we answered no." It was certainly a dire situation. The purpose of it "was to make us rely not on ourselves but on God who raises the dead."

Many times suffering will do this for us. People learn about their own insufficiency and are left with only one alternative, namely, to trust in God. A brief poem by Samuel Johnson says it well.

> I bless thee, Lord, for sorrows sent
> To break my dream of human power;
> For now my shallow cisterns spent,
> I find thy founts and thirst no more.

How true this is of believers. They soon learn their inability and the need for trusting in Christ (cf. 2 Cor. 12:9–10). In Paul's case God did deliver him, and his trust was that in the future God would deliver him again.

To Give Thanks to God (2 Cor. 1:11)

Verse 11 is difficult to translate; the Greek text is just as complicated as the English translation seems to be: "You also joining in helping us through your prayers, so that thanks may be given by many persons on our behalf for the favor bestowed on us through the prayers of many" (NASB). Paul is stating that if God gives deliverance, all the people who are praying for deliverance will turn their faces upward and give thanks to God. God may or may not rescue them, but when he does, they will praise him for that.

In August 1998 my wife had a very serious fall. She is hypoglycemic and must have a consistent diet of protein. Because of a very busy schedule that day, we had not eaten properly. That night around 12:30 she got up to get some protein and fainted, hitting her head. I dialed 911 for an ambulance, and they took her to the hospital. The emergency ward was extremely busy, and she was shuttled aside. They had taken X-rays and felt she only had a concussion. About two hours later she was given a CAT scan. Immediately, the medical team leaped into action because she had developed an epidural hematoma, which was causing severe trauma to the brain. A brain surgeon was immediately called, cut off the flow of blood to the hematoma, which by that time was the size of a fist. Her life was hanging in the balance.

Normally a person recovers from this kind of surgery in three to five days. After five days my wife was still in a semicoma condition and could not breathe on her own. Nor could she breathe on her own after ten days. Fourteen days later her condition was still unchanged. At that time one of the doctors informed me that I better find a nursing home to take care of my wife because I would not be able to care for her.

It was prayer-meeting night, and I had wanted to attend, but I was so distressed that I drove right past the church and went on home. I just lay in my bed and groaned. For the first time in my life I began to understand Romans 8:26–27, which talks about prayer that can be expressed only in groans. During those two weeks, I had been sending e-mails literally around the world, requesting people to pray for my wife. The next day I went to visit her, and she had suddenly taken a turn for the better. She was able to breathe on her own. From then on her recovery was almost miraculous. For the next two weeks she had therapy and then was released to come home. She was determined to prepare a meal for me when she got home, which she did.

The doctor called her recovery a miracle. Of course, everybody praised God, especially those who had been praying. She has recovered with no residual effects. To this day people who knew about the situation still thank God and praise him for what he did.

Why did Paul begin 2 Corinthians 1:3–11 by saying, "Blessed be God"? Because a proper view of suffering must begin with a proper view of God. If a person begins with himself, he will be bitter and self-centered. But when he begins with God, he will focus more on God's attributes, God's character, and the benefits of suffering. A proper view of suffering ultimately will lead to worship. Paul had learned this lesson, and he wanted to relate it to his readers.

Suffering as Discipline (1 Cor. 11:24–34; Acts 5:1–11)

The preceding section considered only one passage, 2 Corinthians 1:3–11. In this section various aspects of suffering will be considered. When a pastor preaches on doctrine, it is often best to find a key passage and teach the doctrine from that passage. At other times it is advantageous to look at a doctrine from a number of passages, as we will here.

Abuses at the Lord's Table reflected an old problem at Corinth—divisions in the church. Some were eating before others, and some who were hungry were being deprived of food. In fact some were even becoming drunk. Obviously the Corinthians did not recognize the significance of the Lord's Table and the elements in it. They were participating in an unworthy manner.

Because of this Paul wrote in 1 Corinthians 11:29–30, "For anyone who eats and drinks without discerning the body eats and drinks judgment on himself. That is why many of you are weak and ill, and some have died." In other words, God was disciplining the church physically even to the point of death because of this sacrilege. Verse 32 states, "When we are judged by the Lord, we are disciplined so that we may not be condemned along with the world." This verse indicates that chastisement evidences a believer's salvation. In a sense this parallels Hebrews 12:8. God's chastisement evidences his love and care for his children.

Another passage on discipline is 1 Corinthians 5:1–5. Paul describes the sin of the offender in verse 1. Evidently the man at fault was a professing believer and the woman was not; this can be inferred because no discipline was applied to the woman. The situation was ongoing. Apparently the woman was the man's stepmother, which seems to be the significance of the words "his father's wife." As great as the man's sin was, the sin of the church was greater. The church did nothing about the situation (v. 2).

Verses 3–5a indicate that Paul needed to step in and take apostolic action. It seems he had already delivered the man "to Satan for the destruction of the flesh." Who has this kind of authority? Apparently delivering a person to Satan was an apostolic prerogative. This action is mentioned twice in the New Testament; the other passage is 1 Timothy 1:20. In both cases Paul was the one who delivered the person to Satan. The church does not have this kind of authority.

Paul authorized the church to come together to declare this sentence on the man. As in 1 Corinthians 11:32, the purpose of this discipline was to guarantee the salvation of the man. What happens to a person who is delivered to Satan? "The destruction of the flesh" refers to some physical difficulty that would bring about his repentance. The church was to do two things—pronounce the Pauline sentence on the man and cut off any fellowship with the offender (1 Cor. 5:11).

Very likely 2 Corinthians 2:5–9 is discussing the same person. If so, this indicates that the discipline worked and the man repented.

A graphic illustration of suffering to the point of death as a means of discipline is seen in Acts 5:1–11. Ananias and Sapphira lied to God and put the Spirit of the Lord to the test. For this they received the ultimate discipline, namely, death. Apparently they were believers.

A number of principles can be drawn from this subject of discipline. The first is the need to serve God with an obedient and reverent heart. Another is that God disciplines believers because of his love for them. If he did not care for them, he would not be concerned for them (Prov. 3:12; Heb. 12:6). A third principle is that God in his wisdom knows exactly how to discipline each believer according to his personality, background, and needs.

Suffering in the Hope of Future Glory (Rom. 5:1–8; 2 Cor. 4:16–18)

Several passages contrast present suffering with the believers' future glory. One commonly misunderstood passage is Romans 5:1–8. Many refer to this passage as "the results of justification." But that is not Paul's point in these verses. Instead the passage is emphasizing the endurance of believers in suffering. Romans 4 defends justification by faith as God's method of salvation in all dispensations. Yet someone may well object that faith is nebulous and is like a fine gossamer thread that could break under stress. Paul is stating the opposite. Faith is a strong cable that will not break under the severest of stresses.

A key word is "hope," mentioned in verse 2. "We have also obtained access by faith into this grace in which we stand, and we rejoice in hope of the glory of God." A critical factor in all suffering is hope, a virtue that is either misunderstood or not understood at all. Hope is desire with expectation. It is not desire by itself or expectation by itself. The two must go together. It used to be common for a single woman to have a hope chest—a cedar box with items to be used after marriage, including pillow cases, sheets, towels, and so forth. That hope chest was a tangible expression of desire with expectation. In Romans 5:2 the believers' hope is for the glory of God. That is the background of verses 3–5: "We rejoice in our sufferings, knowing that suffering produces endurance." However, suffering by itself does not produce perseverance and endurance.

189

It may cause bitterness, disappointment, and frustration. Suffering produces endurance only when there is hope. Hope causes endurance. That is why Paul adds, "and endurance produces character, and character produces hope" (v. 4). In other words, it is a spiral, beginning with hope and ending with hope. And that is why verse 5 adds, "and hope does not put us to shame." Hope does not disappoint because of God's love, which Paul then discusses in verses 5–8.

The hope of God's glory gives strength to endure suffering and to mature in one's faith. For those who are facing any kind of affliction, hope is an essential ingredient. The hope may not result in present deliverance, but it certainly will result ultimately in the glory of God.

Another passage that contrasts present circumstances with future glory is 2 Corinthians 4:16–18. Verse 16 says, "So we do not lose heart. Though our outer self is wasting away, our inner self is being renewed day by day" The "outer self" of course refers to the physical body, and the "inner" is the reborn individual. As one ages, the body deteriorates. But while the body is decaying, believers are being spiritually renewed each day.

Few passages stress the need for daily revival more than this one. The reason believers need to be renewed daily is that "light momentary affliction is preparing for [them] an eternal weight of glory beyond all comparison." "Light momentary affliction" stands in contrast to "eternal weight of glory." In Hebrew the word for "glory" refers to something that is heavy. That is why Paul uses the words "weight of glory." Interestingly, this is like an investment. Suffering produces a great return, namely, glory. But this investment is not tit for tat. The glory far exceeds the suffering. Given the extent of Paul's sufferings in 2 Corinthians 11:23–29, it is amazing that he would call them "light momentary affliction." If they are light and momentary, how great must be the glory!

Second Corinthians 4:18 describes a believer's outlook on life. "We look not to the things that are seen but to the things that are unseen." The first words are present participles that literally say, "while not *looking* at the things which *are seen*, at the things which *are* not *seen*." This describes the proper attitude while one is suffering. Things that are seen are only temporary, but eternal things are not seen. During their suffering, believers are to be focused on eternity.

Many other passages teach this truth, such as Romans 8:18–30, 35–36; 1 Corinthians 4:10–13; 15:30–32; 2 Corinthians 13:4; and 2 Timothy 4:7.

Suffering as a Means to Display God's Glory (2 Cor. 4:8–12; 11:30)
One's weakness magnifies God's power. This truth is often seen in Scripture. It is illustrated by Moses's rod before Pharaoh, Gideon's army of three hundred, David and Goliath, the boy who gave five barley loaves and two small fish for the

Lord to use to feed five thousand, and many other incidents. The first passage to be considered here is 2 Corinthians 4:7–12, which speaks about God placing the treasure of the gospel in humans, like clay pots, so that God's power might be seen. It may well be that Paul here was thinking of Gideon in Judges 7. Just as those clay pots were broken and the Lord was glorified, so God magnifies himself by using frail human creatures.

Paul makes the application of this basic principle in 2 Corinthians 4:8–12. We are "afflicted in every way" (that's the clay pot), "but not crushed" (that's the power of God). "Perplexed" (that's the clay pot), "but not driven to despair" (that's the power of God). This contrast is made all the way through verse 12, where Paul says, "So death is at work in us" (the clay pot), "but life in you" (the power of God). In spite of the believer's weaknesses, God works through them for his glory.

A more graphic illustration is found in Paul's thorn in the flesh. In 11:30, Paul states, "If I must boast, I will boast of the things that show my weakness." His weakness is his thorn in the flesh (12:7), given to him because of his surpassing visions, one of which is described in 12:2–4, where Paul says he was caught up into paradise.

Speculation abounds as to what the thorn in the flesh was. Paul never identifies it. From Galatians 4:12–14 one may conclude that it was repulsive. This would constantly remind Paul to walk humbly before the Lord.

Physical infirmity does not limit God's ability to use people. The most loathsome may ultimately become the most effective means of displaying God's power and glory. What an encouragement this is for suffering saints! Many times the greater the infirmity, the greater the opportunity to display God's glory.

Suffering as Servants of Christ (2 Cor. 6:4–10; 11:23–29; 2 Tim. 1:11–12)

Sometimes Christians are called on to suffer simply because they are serving the Lord Jesus. Paul states this more than once. One illustration is 2 Corinthians 6:4–10, in which he offers a long, descriptive list of his various sufferings. They can be cataloged in the following manner: (1) In verses 4–5 he discusses endurance in sufferings, including such things as beatings, imprisonments, sleeplessness, and hunger. (2) In verse 6a he looks at four moral qualities that are involved—purity, knowledge, patience, and kindness. (3) In verses 6b–7 he discusses powers that are operative in his life: the Holy Spirit, love, the word of truth, and the power of God. (4) In verses 7b–8a he refers to three conditions in which he ministers: by the weapons of righteousness for the right hand and the left, by glory and dishonor, and by evil reports and good reports. (5) And in verses 8b–10 he describes seven seeming contradictions in his ministry. These verses indicate that while there is suffering in ministry, many other factors are involved. One must have a well-rounded walk with God to endure sufferings for Christ. In 2 Corinthians 11:23–29, Paul uses his sufferings as proof of his servanthood. These sufferings are in contrast to the false teachers at Corinth who also claimed to be servants of Christ.

Another illustration of Paul's suffering as a servant of Christ is found in 2 Timothy 1:11–12. Here he says he was appointed to be a preacher, an apostle, and a teacher for the gospel. He then adds, "For this reason I also suffer these things" (NASB). "These things" perhaps look back to verse 8, where he refers to being a prisoner suffering for the gospel. As Paul wrote Timothy his last letter, he was in a dungeon in Rome about to suffer martyrdom. In other words, he was about to die as a martyr simply because he was a servant of Christ. He says much the same thing in 2:9, where he talks about the gospel and then adds, "for which I am suffering, bound with chains as a criminal."

Again this principle of suffering simply because one is serving Christ is also often illustrated in Acts (cf. Acts 5:40–41; 7:54–60; 8:1; 9:1–2, 23, 29; 11:19).

The lesson is obvious. Suffering does not necessarily imply that one is under discipline or out of the will of God. Instead it may actually show that the person is in the center of God's will.

Suffering as a Part of Living the Spiritual Life (Phil. 3:10; Col. 1:24)
Suffering is an essential part of spiritual growth. It is often used in believers' lives to bring them to spiritual maturity. One passage that says this is Philippians 3:10: "That I may know him and the power of his resurrection, and may share his sufferings, becoming like him in his death." Knowing Christ in one's daily experience often means suffering for the sake of Christ. This of course leads to spiritual growth. That is why Paul adds in verse 12, "Not that I have already obtained this or am already perfect, but I press on to make it my own, because Christ Jesus has made me his own."

A similar concept is found in Colossians 1:24, which is a difficult statement: "In my flesh I am filling up what is lacking in Christ's afflictions for the sake of his body, that is, the church." The term "afflictions" is never used of Christ's sufferings on the cross. It is as if Christ left behind an empty bowl called "Christ's afflictions," which refers to sufferings believers endure for his sake. This does not mean we seek to suffer, but when it occurs, we use it to grow spiritually.

Suffering as a Result of Spiritual Failures and Lapses
Failures and lapses that cause suffering may be classified into three groups: failures in ourselves, failures in churches, and failures in disloyal friends and associates.

In Romans 7:24, Paul exclaims, "Wretched man that I am!" This of course is the conclusion to his struggles in trying to keep the Law without the strength of the Holy Spirit. Such a struggle is doomed to failure and will lead to despair. When Christians fail morally and spiritually, it leads to a terrible sense of discouragement. Few sufferings are worse than this.

A second cause of suffering is our experiences with churches. When Paul lists his sufferings in 2 Corinthians 11, he concludes, "Apart from other things, there is the daily pressure on me of my anxiety for all the churches" (v. 28). This is found many times in Paul's grief over various church's failures. For instance in Galatians 4:19, he talks about being in labor pains for the Galatian churches until Christ is formed in them. Few pains are as intense as birth pangs. When Paul wrote to the Corinthians, he referred to not having rest until he found out about their spiritual condition (2 Cor. 2:12; 7:5). In Colossians 2:1, Paul talks about the struggle in his heart because of the churches in Colossae and Laodicea. Addressing the Ephesian elders in Miletus he says, "I did not cease night or day to admonish everyone with tears" (Acts 20:31). Churches may be a great source of comfort and encouragement, but they also may be the cause of profound heartache.

A third source of suffering is disloyal friends and associates. No book illustrates this more poignantly than 2 Timothy. In 1:15 Paul mentions that Phygelus and Hermogenes turned away from him in Asia. Two others who hurt Paul were Hymenaeus and Philetus, mentioned in 2:17. Demas proved to be a huge disappointment during Paul's final days, as seen in 4:10. People can be tragic sources of grief and heartache. Thankfully, in spite of these Paul can say that the Word of God is not bound (2:9).

Conclusion

The subject of suffering in Acts and the Pauline Epistles is almost endless. But one cannot help but notice what Paul says about God's love for believers in Romans 8:35–39. Nothing, absolutely nothing, can separate us from the love of God in Christ Jesus our Lord.

James E. Allman (ThM, ThD, Dallas Theological Seminary) is professor of Bible exposition at Dallas Seminary. He was professor at Mid-South Bible College/Crichton College for eighteen years before joining the Dallas faculty. He has also been a visiting lecturer in Australia, Ukraine, India, and Siberia.

Dr. Allman served as a translator for the *Holman Christian Standard Bible*, and he has written articles for *Life and Work Directions* for the Baptist Sunday School Board.

13

SUFFERING IN THE NON-PAULINE EPISTLES

James E. Allman

Of the non-Pauline epistles, Hebrews, James, and 1 Peter center their messages on the suffering of God's people. James focuses on general suffering, the hardships of life that God uses to bring his people to maturity. Second Peter and Jude focus mainly on persecution. The Johannine epistles address specific issues, as will be noted below. James is probably the earliest book of the New Testament, while Hebrews and 1 Peter were written about two decades later, when persecution was a growing reality for the church. This chapter examines what these books teach about suffering in Jesus's life, the lives of Christians, and the lives of unbelievers.

The Suffering of Jesus

Hebrews and 1 Peter offer significant teaching on Jesus's suffering, with 1 Peter making Jesus's sufferings the basis of his argument. These two books describe Jesus's passion and then use it as a pattern for the suffering of his people.

Several passages refer to Jesus providing salvation through his suffering. First Peter 1:18–19 declares, "You were ransomed from the futile ways inherited from your forefathers, not with perishable things such as silver or gold, but with the precious blood of Christ, like that of a lamb without blemish or spot." John alludes to this in 1 John 5:6. Peter continues his discussion in 1 Peter 2:6, describing Jesus as the stone Isaiah 28:16 predicted: an elect, precious "stone"

Yahweh would be "laying in Zion" as the chief cornerstone in whom people should believe. The stone imagery occurs again in Psalm 118:22. There the stone refers to the victorious king whom God snatched from sure defeat, giving victory and deliverance to his people (vv. 10–14). He thus has become the cause of both salvation for believers and judgment to the unbelieving. Having suffered death, Jesus can set free all those who have been held in bondage by the fear of death, freeing them from the Devil's sway (Heb. 2:14–15).

Jesus endured deep suffering to bring salvation. As John wrote, Jesus came as a true man and died as a true man, for he came by the water and the blood (1 John 3:5, 8). Redemption is available because of the valuable blood of Christ (1 Pet. 1:18–19). He suffered, "the righteous for the unrighteous," dying on the cross for mankind's sins (3:18; cf. 1 John 4:8–10), bearing not only the shame and horror of the cross (1 Pet. 2:21) but also the wrath of God (Heb. 12:2). His suffering was profound, affecting him even before the cross (5:7–8). He prayed in Gethsemane with strong crying and tears. No one can know the depth of his sufferings, but something of it can be seen in his agony in the garden.

Jesus's suffering was linked to his role as High Priest. Suffering was the rite that ordained[1] him, as he brought "many sons to glory," to be "the founder of their salvation" (2:10). To be high priest, one must be human (5:1). So, "since therefore the children share in flesh and blood, he himself likewise partook of the same things" (2:14). One of the goals of his incarnation was to free believers from the Devil's power and to deliver them from their bondage to the "fear of death" (vv. 14–15).

The incarnation also opened Jesus to various sufferings other than his atoning passion. As incarnate, he was tempted (4:15; cf. James 1:13), bearing the affront of Satan's onslaught. Yet he remained sinless, for he is the Son of God. Surely temptation could have no impact on him, for "in him there is no sin" (1 John 3:5; cf. 2 Cor. 5:21). Yet since he is truly human, he had to be genuinely subject to temptation and its power, even as Adam was. Thus Jesus bore the full force of Satan's attack and drained it of its potency. He remained "without sin" (Heb. 4:15). Thus he is able to deal with believers in compassion as they face any temptation, and his throne becomes a "throne of grace" where believers can find grace to help in their times of need (v. 16).

A high priest must have certain qualities (5:1–4). First, he must be like the people he represents (v. 1). Second, he must be subject to weakness (v. 2). Otherwise he may be harsh, especially with those who sin ignorantly and who are wayward. Third, he must be divinely appointed.

---

[1] The exact meaning of the key verb in Heb. 2:10, *teleioō*, is not clear. However, it was used in the Septuagint, the Greek Old Testament, to refer to Aaron's "ordination" as high priest. Such a thought is not entirely foreign to Heb. 2:10.

Jesus meets each of these qualifications. Psalm 110:4 states that God had long ago appointed David's heir and Lord (v. 1) as "a priest forever after the order of Melchizedek" (v. 4; Heb. 5:6). Then Hebrews 5:7–9 addresses the weakness Jesus suffered in his humanity.

While it is difficult to associate weakness with Jesus, this was part of his humanity. But because of his experience, he can genuinely understand the weakness of the human heart. Further, only he who had "life in" himself (John 5:26) can genuinely know the horror of death. Only he who had known eternally perfect fellowship with the Father can know the dreadful abandonment by the Father. So "in the days of his flesh, Jesus offered up prayers and supplications, with loud cries and tears, to him who was able to save him from death, and he was heard because of his reverence" (Heb. 5:7). Believers then may "with confidence draw near to the throne of grace" (4:16). Clearly, then, Jesus's suffering demonstrates God's love for believers (1 John 4:8–10).

A major task of the high priest was to offer atonement. Jesus's sacrificial death on the cross provided propitiation for humanity (Heb. 2:17; 1 John 2:2; 4:10). Bible students have long discussed whether *hilasmos* should be translated "propitiation" or "expiation." To propitiate means simply to appease, that is, to avert the anger of God. By contrast "expiate" comes from the Latin *expio*, which means "to purify anything defiled by a crime."[2] Thus the Greek word focuses on removing God's wrath or on canceling or removing sin.

The words translated "propitiation" (*hilasmos*) and "to propitiate" (*hilaskomai*) occur over one hundred times in the Septuagint. These terms are used in the context of averting wrath (Gen. 32:21; Ex. 32:14). However, *hilaskomai* is also used to mean "to expiate," that is, "to cleanse from defilement" (see Ex. 30.10, Lev. 4:20, 26, 31, 35; 5:6, 10, 13).

Therefore, *hilaskomai* includes the ideas of both expiation and propitiation. God's wrath rests on mankind because sin has defiled each individual, making him or her unfit for worship of and service to God. But God in his love sent Jesus, his one and only Son, who gave himself as a propitiation for mankind, thereby removing God's wrath from the believing sinner. In addition, Jesus's sacrifice of himself also cleanses the believing sinner of spiritual defilement (Heb. 9:14).

In a sense unbelievers are spiritually unfit because of their love for the darkness and hatred for the light (John 3:19). In his suffering the Savior was wooing unbelievers from love for the darkness to love for the light. Jesus's suffering impacts hard hearts, drawing them mercifully to the light. How could one not love a Savior who endured such travail to give them life?

---

[2]Charlton T. Lewis and Charles Short, *A Latin Dictionary* (Oxford: Clarendon, 1962), 695.

Another group of texts present Jesus's suffering as an example for his people of how and why to suffer. The most important passage is 1 Peter 2:21–25. Christ himself suffered, Peter wrote, leaving us "an example" (v. 21, *hypogrammon*, a "copy-book model")[3] to follow in suffering. This model is detailed in verses 22–24. Jesus did not sin or attempt to use cunning deceit. He did not threaten or abuse those who abused him. Rather he committed himself to the One "who judges justly" as "he himself bore our sins in his body on the tree" (vv. 23–24). He is the model of enduring suffering, given to those who bear the name Christian (4:16).

Two passages in 1 John address Jesus's suffering. His death on the cross demonstrates what God's love is like. "By this we know love, that he laid down his life for us" (1 John 3:16). Jesus suffered for his enemies to reconcile them to God. Therefore, "if God so loved us, we also ought to love one another" (4:11). Jesus's sufferings demonstrate God's love for believers so that they can respond to each other with love.

Jesus's suffering has taught us love (3:16). This distinguishes us from the children of the Devil, who do not love God's people. Sharing in the sufferings of others demonstrates that believers are children of God since they live as God's Son lived. Believers voluntarily assume the needs of others by providing resources for them.

The Suffering of God's People
Most of the material on suffering in Hebrews, 1 and 2 Peter, and Jude deals with suffering experienced by humanity in general, but especially God's people.

Suffering of People in the Old Testament
Passages that refer to suffering in the Old Testament are Hebrews 11:24–27, 35–38; and 2 Peter 2:8–9. In the verses in Hebrews two kinds of experience are mentioned. First, Moses intentionally chose to join in the sufferings of his people since he considered the "reproach of Christ [Messiah] greater wealth than the treasures of Egypt." Second, Hebrews 11:35–38 rehearses the sufferings of those who, like Moses, endured great suffering "so that they might rise again to a better life" (v. 35). All these are witnesses to the teaching that endurance is worthwhile to receive what was promised (cf. 10:32–39; 12:1–11).

The other passage, 2 Peter 2:8–9, speaks of Lot's suffering because of his living in the corrupt society of Sodom. He "felt his righteous soul tormented day after day by their lawless deeds" (v. 8, NASB).

---

[3]Literally, a "model or pattern to be copied in writing or drawing."

The Suffering of New Testament Believers

The Fact and Certainty of Christian Suffering

It is a sad reality, but godly people do suffer. Hebrews 10:32–36 refers to hardships faced by the earliest recipients of the book. They lost their social status, and some even went to prison. Some lost their property and homes. Others in the community were "partners with those so treated" (v. 33). And 1 Peter 4:12–19 reminds readers, "Do not be surprised at the fiery trial" that comes upon God's people. Their proper response must be to rejoice (v. 13) "because the Spirit of glory and of God rests upon" them (v. 14). Indeed, the suffering of the godly is part of the necessary divine judgment of humanity (vv. 17–18). "Therefore . . . those who suffer" should commit themselves to their "faithful Creator while doing good" (v. 19).

Causes of Suffering

The General Epistles identify five causes of suffering. First, God's people suffer because of Satan's activity. James 4:7 urges believers to resist the Devil. The Son of God came to the earth to destroy the Devil's works (1 John 3:8). Though believers are in conflict with Satan, Jesus, the captain of their salvation, is their champion.

The most important reference on this subject is 1 Peter 5:6–11. Peter calls his readers, in the face of Satan's depredations, to humble themselves under God's mighty hand and to be sober-minded and alert (vv. 6–8). They are also to be confident of God's care (v. 7). This struggle is the common allotment of God's people (v. 9) and yet is temporary, even brief ("a little while," v. 10). The outcome will mean spiritual advancement for those who suffer (v. 10).

Second, some Christians suffer because they fear death (Heb. 2:15). Jesus assumed flesh and blood (v. 14) to render powerless the Devil, who had "the power of death." The result is that now Jesus can deliver from the fear of death those who have been in lifelong slavery (v. 15). Of special importance here is Jesus's own agony in the face of death (5:7). His death delivers believers from the fear of it.

Another cause of suffering is temptation (2:18). Through Jesus's own experience of temptation, believers can find help from him. Still another cause of suffering is persecution for the faith. The messages of both Hebrews and 1 Peter focus significantly on such suffering, along with Jude 3. Hebrews 10:32–39, which mentions contending for the faith, discussed already in this chapter, reminds the recipients of earlier persecution and warns of similar times to come.

First Peter adds two passages, 3:13–17 and 4:12–19. Peter states that his readers would escape much harm as they committed themselves to "what is good" (3:13). Even so, it remained possible ("if you should suffer," v. 14)[4] that persecution would arise. Perhaps the local situation of his readers made persecution a less immediate prospect than either Paul or the author of Hebrews saw for their readers. The other Petrine passage, 1 Peter 4:12–19, however, takes the reader much further along this line of thought. Peter's audience must expect a "fiery trial" and not be surprised. In it they would be "insulted for the name of Christ" (v. 14). The development of his thought here seems to suggest that to face this divine judgment would mean escaping God's condemnation of the world (vv. 17–19). To be shamed by God's enemies is to receive honor from God.

Third John adds another cause of suffering, this time at the hands of people in the Christian community (3 John 9–10). John sent messengers to one of his churches, but the local leader Diotrephes refused to receive them. This no doubt led to some hardship for the messengers and John, but also for those who, like Gaius (v. 1), were faithful to God and his apostle. This cause of suffering is the more difficult because it comes from those who should be protecting believers. The other causes stem from outside the community, from those who are enemies of God.

Forms of Suffering

Suffering of believers may occur in seven ways. First is shame, a sense of rejection by society (Heb. 10:33). Those who reject Christ and the worldview and value system he represents will cause believers to feel "reproach" (13:13). However, shame may also come to some believers at the return of Christ (1 John 2:28) if they fail to embrace his values and worldview.[5]

Second, suffering may entail poverty and loss of wealth (James 1:9–11; 5:4–5). As in Hebrews 10:34, many Christians throughout church history have been poor. They have faced all the struggles common to poverty worldwide. Persecuted Christians often lose their homes and livelihoods. Amazingly, James implicitly urges them to rejoice in that they are abased (James 1:10), knowing that life is transitory ("like a flower of the grass he will pass away").

Third, most Christians face illness at some time in life (James 5:13–15). Fourth, false accusation ("slander," v. 12, NASB) may confront God's people (1 Pet. 2:11–17). However, persevering in one's commitment to godliness will eventually give the lie to slanderers. Fifth, one's own conscience may cause suffering (1 John 3:19–20). The children of God are to love one another (vv. 17–18), but if they are lacking in love, their conscience will condemn them (v. 20).

---

[4]The conditional clause in v. 14 is a rare fourth-class conditional protasis. See Daniel B. Wallace, *Greek Grammar beyond the Basics: An Exegetical Syntax of the New Testament* (Grand Rapids: Zondervan, 1996), 484.
[5]On the important issue of shame and honor, see David de Silva, *Honor, Patronage, Kinship, and Purity: Unlocking New Testament Culture* (Downers Grove, IL: InterVarsity, 2000).

Sixth, suffering sometimes comes at the hands of wicked people. In James's day the rich sometimes hauled Christians into court (James 2:6–7). Christian slaves were vulnerable to unreasonable masters (2 Pet. 2:18–25). Godly people have even been murdered by the wicked as Abel was murdered by Cain (1 John 3:11–16). John explains that these sufferings come from those who are "of the world," that is, children of the Devil. Since they are of the world, they do not hear believers.

Seventh, Christians sometimes suffer from others in the Christian community. Even Christians sometimes treat the poor with disdain (James 2:1–7), and occasionally leaders, out of selfish ambition, cause difficulty for those committed to apostolic truth (3 John 9–10).

Attitudes toward Suffering

What attitudes should believers have toward their suffering? The General Epistles suggest six attitudes.

First, believers should recognize that suffering is sometimes God's judgment. Peter affirms that judgment will begin with God's household (1 Pet. 4:17). That judgment, in context, is persecution. "God allows persecutions as disciplinary judgment to purify the lives" of believers.[6]

Second, suffering should be viewed as brief (5:10). In God's providence he has set an end to suffering. However long it may last, it is not eternal. Believers may count on its ending when the purpose of God is complete.

Third, Christians must view their sufferings as shared by others (5:9). In difficult times, sufferers often think of themselves as being alone. Yet Peter reminds his readers that they share in the suffering of God's people wherever they are. Even more, the author of Hebrews commends the voluntary participation of his readers in the suffering of their community (Heb. 10:32–36) and commands Christians to care for prisoners "as though in prison with them" (13:3). Sufferers, then, are not alone, and those who are not facing difficulties at the present are encouraged to come to their aid. James 2:3–5 urges readers to identify with the poor rather than with the wealthy. James encourages the righteous poor laborers in the church with the certainty that the Lord will bring their oppressors to judgment. Therefore, they must practice patience in their sufferings (5:4–11) while waiting for the coming of the Lord. Most remarkably, when believers are suffering, they are joined with those who belong to Christ (1 Pet. 4:12–19). With such a perspective, they can rejoice "because the Spirit of glory and of God rests upon" them (v. 14).

Fourth, suffering must be embraced for the sake of Christ. This is the pattern of those of whom the world was not worthy (Heb. 11:35–38), and it is the

---

[6]Roger M. Raymer, "1 Peter," in *The Bible Knowledge Commentary: New Testament*, ed. John F. Walvoord and Roy B. Zuck (Wheaton, IL: Scripture Press, 1985; repr., Colorado Springs: Cook, 1996), 855.

command of Scripture (13:3). The epistle of James calls its readers to have a sober view of life, embracing mourning, weeping in place of laughter, and being humbled under God's powerful hand (James 4:7–10; cf. 1 Pet. 1:6–7).

Christians should not adopt a martyr complex that pursues persecution. On the other hand, they must recognize that suffering is inevitable. Thus 1 Peter 2:11–12 urges Christians to live "as sojourners and exiles," a status vulnerable to abuse. In such a condition "the Gentiles" will "speak against [believers] as evil-doers" (NASB). So Christians proceed with life, knowing something of the cost. Though pain awaits them, they know that the end result is worth the difficulty.

A fifth attitude is to view suffering in light of the return of Jesus. Whatever suffering one might experience, it will fall short of the glory of the resurrection (Heb. 11:35). With that greater end in view, James urges patience and long-suffering (James 5:7–11), citing farmers, the prophets, and Job as examples. They were considered blessed, especially in light of the outcomes of their patience. For all the grace received, Peter states that more grace will come when Jesus returns (1 Pet. 1:13, 21). As a kind of climax Peter teaches that one's good way of life will bring glory to God even from his opponents "on the day of visitation" (2:11–12).

Sixth, Christians should view suffering as a cause for joy. This was the response of the persecuted Christians in Hebrews 10:34. James 1:2–4 even commands it, as believers are aware of the outcome of their trials. Difficulty produces patience, and patience brings maturity,[7] and in time a glorious com-mendation from God (1:12). Even more, when Christians are persecuted for Christ's sake, they are joining in the sufferings of Jesus. This is a badge of honor, a mark of blessing, a reason for boasting in God (1 Pet. 4:12–16).

Benefits of Suffering
Four benefits come from suffering: reward, ceasing from sin, strengthening, and life with God.

A frequently mentioned benefit of suffering is the hope of reward. By per-severance in "faith and patience" believers "inherit the promises" (Heb. 6:12). By endurance they "receive what is promised," to the preserving of their souls (10:36, 39). Those who persevere under trials "receive the crown of life" from God (James 1:12). Trials, in which believers reveal the genuineness of their faith, bring "praise and glory and honor" when Jesus returns (1 Pet. 1:6–7).

As a second benefit, when believers bear hardship for Christ, they cease from sin (4:1–2), since they have determined to live "for the will of God." A third benefit is mentioned in 5:10. When Christians "have suffered a little

---

[7] This is based on translating the adjective *teleios* not as "perfect," as the NASB does, but as "mature."

while, the God of all grace . . . will himself restore, confirm, strengthen, and establish" them. This "rhetorical crescendo [refers] to the complete act of God."[8]

The most important passage in these books on the benefits of suffering is Hebrews 12:4–11. This is the longest passage on Christian discipline in the New Testament. Though divine discipline is not pleasant, four incomparable results flow from God's disciplining love (vv. 4–6). First, God demonstrates to believers that they are his sons (vv. 7–8). Second, much as children benefit from discipline by their parents, so Christians gain a meaningful life as they "submit to the Father of our spirits" (v. 9, NIV). Third, "He disciplines us for our good, that we may share his holiness" (v. 10). Fourth, being trained by discipline "yields the peaceful fruit of righteousness" (v. 11).

Strategies for Suffering

Hebrews, James, Peter, John, and Jude also detail strategies for suffering. These are techniques and approaches Scripture presents for dealing with suffering. The first of these, certainly the most important, is to adopt a mind-set of endurance (1 Pet. 1:13; 4:1). Such an attitude focuses on the promises of God and the as-yet-unseen future, staying centered on Christ much as Moses "endured as seeing him who is invisible" (Heb. 11:27). This involves being determined to endure God's discipline (12:7), viewing suffering as a blessing, an enviable way of life (James 1:12; 5:11). Only as believers view suffering as experiencing "favor with God" (1 Pet. 2:20, NASB) will they be able to endure, especially if the difficulties are prolonged (James 5:7–8). Followers of Christ are not running a sprint, which is finished in a matter of seconds. Nor are they in a marathon, which ends in a matter of hours. A mind-set of endurance is called for, because only at the "coming of the Lord" will the struggle be complete (v. 7). Such endurance is possible only as one exercises faith, trusting God's character, his Word, and his plan. God's promises are inherited only "through faith and patience" (Heb. 6:12). As believers endure, they realize that they have the company of the prophets (James 5:10). Endurance and long-suffering are essential in facing suffering.

A second strategy is to bless those who mistreat believers (1 Pet. 3:9). Called to be heirs of God's blessing, Christians are to be conduits of blessing to others, including even those who hate them. Jesus prayed even for those who crucified him. In imitation of the Savior, believers are to bless others.

A third approach is to refuse to return "evil for evil or reviling for reviling" to those who cause one's suffering (v. 9). In these circumstances their opposition must be viewed as a tool in God's hand for their good, even as they oppose believers.

---

[8]Karen H. Jobes, *1 Peter* (Grand Rapids: Baker, 2005), 316.

Fourth, Christians should not let suffering be a temptation to sin (James 1:13). It is wrong to think that because they have problems they have a license to sin, or that the problems mean they are "being tempted by God" to sin. Since God cannot be tempted, he does not tempt others.

Fifth, when suffering comes, believers are not automatically obliged to undergo it. If one has a headache, he should take an aspirin! This is the point in James 5:13–15, where the elders are to anoint the sick and pray for healing. The anointing probably does not refer to ritual anointing, for the Greek word is not used in ritual texts. In the New Testament this anointing "refers consistently to the physical action of anointing, performed exclusively on people for care of the body (Matt. 6:17), as a mark of honor for a guest (Luke 7:38), and to heal the sick (Mark 6:13; James 5:14)."[9]

When suffering comes, help should be sought from appropriate sources. If relief comes, one should thank God. If not, he should trust God. These ideas lead to the sixth strategy for suffering: "casting all your anxiety on him [God], because he cares for you" (1 Pet. 5:7). This humble attitude recognizes the goodness and love God has for believers as they are ready to receive from him all his providential care.

Seventh, Peter commands believers, "In your hearts honor Christ the Lord as holy, always being prepared to make a defense to anyone who asks you for a reason for the hope that is in you" (3:15). Verses 13–14 show that the context focuses on persecution. When believers suffer, they can be confident in the most trying times. As they are equipped (1 Pet. 4:1)[10] with God's perspective on trouble, they can be prepared to suffer and, in their suffering, to glorify God.

Eighth, believers can take hope in knowing that suffering will end (1 John 2:18–21). Trouble arose in the community John addressed because of false teachers. They had left by the time John wrote (v. 19), but problems remained among the people. If believers followed John's teachings and his encouragement, even the remaining doubts and anxieties would cease. One must not think that trouble is everlasting. Suffering will end. "The Lord knows how to rescue the godly from trials" (2 Pet. 2:9).

The Suffering of Non-Christians

Five passages address the suffering of non-Christians: Hebrews 10:26–31; 1 Peter 4:5; 2 Peter 2:8–9; Jude 5–7, 14–16.

---

[9]W. Brunotte, "Anoint," in *New International Dictionary of New Testament Theology*, ed. Colin Brown (Grand Rapids: Zondervan, 1975), 1:120.
[10]The verb in Greek is *hoplizō*, "to arm or equip oneself for battle."

Hebrews 10:26–31

Verses 26–31 of Hebrews 10 are among the most difficult in a difficult book. However, several clear points may be noted. First, some people will suffer a more severe punishment than physical death (vv. 28–29). Second, those who face such a fearful expectation of judgment are those who have trampled the Son of God under foot (v. 29), thus falling under the vengeance of God. These people face "a fearful expectation of judgment, and a fury of fire that will consume the adversaries" (v. 27), for "it is a fearful thing to fall into the hands of the living God" (v. 31).[11]

1 Peter 4:5

Verses 3–4 of 1 Peter 4 discuss the need to break with former sinful lifestyles. Old friends will find the believer's new pattern of life strange, since he has given up what they continue in. "But they will give account" to God (v. 5) and will be judged for their sin.

2 Peter 2:8–9; Jude 5–7

Peter assured his readers that the wicked will bring "upon themselves swift destruction" (2:1). One of his examples of sure judgment is the experience of Lot in Sodom, for "the Lord knows how . . . to keep the unrighteous under punishment until the day of judgment" (v. 9). Those who died in the fall of Sodom and Gomorrah are now "undergoing a punishment of eternal fire" (Jude 7).

Jude 14–16

Jude 14–15 announces the coming of the Lord "to execute judgment" against the ungodly. These people, Jude says, "are grumblers, malcontents, following their own sinful desires; they are loud-mouthed boasters, showing favoritism to gain advantage" (v. 16). It is, indeed, a fearful thing to fall into the hands of the living God.

Summary

The non-Pauline epistles clearly focus on the subject of suffering. A major issue is the place and role of Jesus's suffering and its application to believers' lives. In his temptations and death, Jesus set the model for the lives of his people. He who travailed deeply dispenses help from his throne of grace. He suffered, and so do his people. As his suffering led to glory, so his people may expect glory after they have suffered for a "little while" as they look to Jesus, "the founder and perfecter of our faith" (Heb. 12:2).

---

[11]Some commentators believe this passage refers not to unbelievers, but to believers who have renounced their profession of faith, throwing away their confidence in the Lord (v. 35) and shrinking back to Judaism.

Thomas L. Constable (ThM, ThD, Dallas Theological Seminary) is senior professor of Bible exposition at Dallas Seminary. He is the founder of the seminary's field education department and the Center for Biblical Studies. He maintains an active academic, pulpit-supply, and conference-speaking ministry around the world, having ministered in nearly three dozen countries.

Dr. Constable has written commentaries on every book of the Bible, including 1 and 2 Kings and 1 and 2 Thessalonians in *The Bible Knowledge Commentary*. His other published works include "The Gospel Message" in *Walvoord: A Tribute*, and *Talking to God: What the Bible Teaches about Prayer*.

14

SUFFERING IN THE BOOK OF REVELATION

Thomas L. Constable

What does the final book of the Bible reveal about suffering and the believer's response to it? This brief survey of the book of Revelation will highlight events that involve suffering, then apply lessons to the believer's outlook on suffering, whether in his own life or in the lives of those around him.

Instances of Suffering in Revelation

The Sufferings of Christ, the Apostle John, and the Churches
The apostle John, who wrote the book of Revelation, mentions several times that Jesus Christ suffered (Rev. 1:7; 5:6, 9, 12; 7:14). John does this partially to encourage people who are suffering and to remind readers that Jesus suffered for them and understands their sufferings.

John also refers to his own sufferings (1:9). He is believed to have been a leading elder in the church at Ephesus from about AD 40 until the Emperor Domitian exiled him to the Island of Patmos in the early 90s. John identifies himself as a "partner in the tribulation and the kingdom and the patient endurance that are in Jesus" (v. 9). John could write this book with an appreciation of suffering, having experienced it himself.

In the letters to the seven churches in Revelation, John writes that the Christians of his day were suffering persecution. He refers to this in four of the seven letters to the churches in Asia—in the letters to Ephesus (2:2–3), Smyrna (vv. 9–10), Pergamum (vv. 13, 16), and Thyatira (vv. 19, 22–23). In John's day many were suffering for their faith in Jesus Christ.

Suffering in the Tribulation

Following the letters to the seven churches, John relates what he saw in heaven "after this" (4:1; cf. 1:19). He saw a vision of God's throne room in heaven and those who were in heaven worshiping God (Revelation 4–5). No direct reference to persecution of humans is mentioned in these chapters. The angels and possibly humans were praising God in heaven for things he had done, specifically, creation and redemption.

Then in chapter 6 John begins to record the onset of the tribulation, a seven-year period in which people everywhere will experience the greatest persecution and trouble the world has ever seen (Jer. 30:7). In Revelation 3:10, in the letter to the church in Philadelphia, John writes of "the hour of trial" that is coming on "the whole world, to try those who dwell on the earth." He promises that the Christians in Philadelphia will not experience that. This is a reference to the coming tribulation that will be worldwide, and what follows in the book of Revelation, through chapter 19, describes that period of time.

The Seal Judgments

Revelation 6–19, which describes the tribulation period, begins with a series of judgments, introduced as seal judgments, depicted by the kind of seal that was put on a document in ancient times. When the first seal is broken, the scroll will be opened so that what is on the first section of the scroll can be read. Then the second seal will be opened, and a little more of the scroll can be read, and so on. These seal judgments show that much suffering will come on those living on the earth at this time (6:2, 4, 6, 8–17).

Believers Who Die in the Tribulation

The structure of Revelation 6–19 alternates between narration of unfolding events chronologically and material that is supplementary. This supplementary revelation gives more information about certain aspects of the tribulation. The first section of supplementary revelation concerns the saints who will die in the tribulation, the ones who will have come out of the great tribulation. Safe in the Lord's presence (7:14, 16–17; cf. 6:9–11), they will no longer be subject to the suffering that will take place on the earth at that time.

The Trumpet Judgments

Seven trumpet blasts will introduce the next series of judgments on the earth (chaps. 8–9). John saw an angel symbolically take a censer, a vessel used for worship, fill it with fire from the altar in heaven, and throw it to the earth. There followed peals of thunder and sounds and flashes of lightning and an earthquake, plus hail and fire mixed with blood. A third of the earth would be burned up.

Believers will be sealed during this time of tribulation (Rev. 9:4). They will be identifiable as God's people just as the followers of the Antichrist will have his seal and his number on them (cf. 13:16–18), and their salvation will be secure. Locusts, apparently demonic beings that will afflict people at this time, will target unbelievers. They will not kill anyone, but they will torment people for five months. The resulting pain will be so great that people will long for death, but they will not be able to take their own lives.

Two more woes will occur during this trumpet series of judgments. Four angels will be released from the Euphrates River so they can kill another third of humankind. What are these creatures? They are apparently angelic beings whom God will release on the earth to carry out this devastation. "The rest of mankind, who were not killed by these plagues, did not repent" (9:20). Great suffering does not always lead people to repentance, and it will not at this time.

The Two Witnesses

John gives another section of supplemental revelation that tells about two significant believers who will minister during the tribulation. These are the two witnesses described in chapter 11.

The kingdoms that the Antichrist is able to ally under his leadership will tread Jerusalem down for three and a half years, the second half of the tribulation. But God will protect these witnesses. They will have the power to shut up the sky so that rain may not fall during the days of their prophesying, and they will have power over the waters to turn them into blood and to smite the earth with every plague. Unbelievers will initiate some of the problems that will come on people during the tribulation. Satan, who is behind these unbelievers, will eventually kill the two witnesses, and their dead bodies will lie in a street in Jerusalem. Unbelievers will not permit the witnesses' dead bodies to be buried, which was a great indignity in John's day. Most people will be so happy that these two preachers are dead, they will celebrate all over the planet. The two prophets will have tormented unbelievers with their preaching.

Then there will be a great earthquake, a tenth of the city will fall, and seven thousand people will die in the quake. Here is another judgment in which thousands of people will lose their lives, this time as a result of the testimony of the two witnesses, who will have called on unbelievers to repent. But most unbelievers will refuse to repent, and the witnesses will die as martyrs. God will send judgment on earth dwellers for their deaths.

Israel

Revelation 12 gives supplementary revelation about Israel during the tribulation (vv. 2, 4–7, 9–17). John describes Israel as a woman clothed with the sun. She is with child and cries out in labor. This depicts how Israel brought forth the Messiah at Jesus's first coming. Satan tried to prevent the birth of the Messiah by moving Herod the Great to murder all the Jewish babies under his authority. Nevertheless Israel gave birth to a Son, Jesus. Next, John explains what Israel will experience in the future. Satan will again try to destroy the Jews, but God will again protect them. Jews who believe in Jesus will overcome Satan by continuing to live in spite of his hostility.

For part of the tribulation Satan will not have access to God's presence, as he does now, and as he has in the past (cf. Job. 1–2; 1 Pet. 5:8). But he will have freedom to influence the whole earth. Satan will persecute the woman, Israel, who gave birth to the male child, the Messiah. Nevertheless God will protect the Jews from extinction. Some Gentiles will give these persecuted Jews sanctuary. Because Satan will not be able to obliterate all the Jews, he will concentrate on messianic Jews, Jews who believe in Jesus. It will be particularly difficult for them during this period. Satan hates Israel and Jews who believe in Jesus because of the promises that God gave about how he would use Israel as his main channel of blessing to humanity.

The Beast and the False Prophet

The next individuals about whom God gives some special information are the beast and his false prophet (13:2–4, 7, 10, 14, 17; 17:8, 10–11; 19:20). In contrast to the two witnesses, these are unbelievers, followers of Satan. The dragon, Satan, gives the beast out of the sea, the first beast, his power and his throne (great authority). This "beast" will be Satan's right-hand man. As the world dictator, the Antichrist, this beast will kill many believers at this time. He will deceive people living on the earth and will require that his followers take his mark. Only in this way will they be allowed to buy and sell. However, God will eventually throw the beast and his false prophet, who will promote worship of the beast around the world, into the lake of fire.

Babylon

Babylon is the name of a city or an empire. But it is more. It represents all that Babel stood for, specifically salvation by works and self-exalting pride (Gen. 11:4). All that Babylon stands for will fall. It will be wiped off the face of the earth eventually. This will involve much suffering for multitudes of people (Rev. 14:8; 17:6, 16; 18:1, 4, 6–11, 14, 17–21, 24; 19:2–3).

Beast Worshipers

The beast worshipers—unbelievers living throughout the earth in the tribulation who are committed to following this world dictator—will experience judgment as well (14:7, 10–11). They will be tormented with fire and brimstone in the presence of the holy angels and of the Lamb. The smoke of their torment will go up forever and ever. Those who worship the beast will have no rest day or night.

Armageddon

Armageddon refers to the battle that will take place at the end of the tribulation, immediately before Jesus Christ returns to the earth (14:13–20; 17:14). Many people, Jews and Gentiles who oppose Israel's Messiah, will die in this battle. The enemies of Christ and of God will unite against Jesus under the leadership of ten kings, but the Lamb, Jesus Christ, will overcome them.

The Bowl Judgments

The third major series of judgments to occur in the tribulation, after the seal and trumpet judgments, is the bowl judgments (15:1, 7–8; 16:1–4, 6, 8–14, 17–21). These will be the worst of all the judgments. Every one of the verses noted above refers to suffering in some form. This will be the culminating and most intense series of judgments that will affect all people, all sea life, all fresh water sources, the sun, the beast, and demons.

Angels will be told to pour out the seven bowls of the wrath of God onto the earth.

> So the first angel went and poured out his bowl on the earth, and harmful and painful sores came upon the people who bore the mark of the beast and worshiped its image.
>
> The second angel poured out his bowl into the sea, and it became like the blood of a corpse, and every living thing died that was in the sea. (16:1–3)

In the other bowl judgments, rivers become blood, the sun becomes excessively hot, darkness and intense pain occur, the Euphrates River dries up, and lightning, a great earthquake, and hailstones occur.

Questions about Suffering in the Tribulation

Why will there be so much suffering in the tribulation? The Old Testament prophetic books report that God will send judgment on nations for several reasons: their pride and failure to acknowledge God's sovereignty, their violence to their fellow men, their treatment of the Jews, and their rejection of God's revelation. When Jesus Christ came the first time, most people rejected him, and many have rejected him since that time. Rejecting Jesus is not insignificant. It results in the most terrible consequences for unbelievers, namely, the outpouring of God's wrath. In today's pluralistic society many people think, *Well, if Christianity doesn't appeal to you, you can become a Hindu or a Muslim. It really doesn't matter that much because we're all going to the same place.* God does not look at it that way. He has sent to this planet his only Son, who gave up his life so people can enjoy eternity with him (cf. John 14:6). For a person to disregard or reject Jesus is the worst possible sin. And it results in the outpouring of God's wrath both in history and throughout eternity.

But why will the generation of people who will experience tribulation judgments have to suffer so greatly? For two reasons. First, they will be the worst generation in their rebellion against God since the day Christ died. The apostle Paul wrote that apostasy would increase and become worse and worse as time goes by (1 Tim. 4:1–3; 2 Tim. 3:1–5). Things are much worse morally, ethically, and spiritually than they were even fifty years ago. The tribulation generation will evidently be the worst of all, especially when the church is removed and its influence in the world ends at the rapture.

Second, the tribulation generation will bear the consequences, though not the guilt, of sins committed by previous generations of sinners. It is important to distinguish between consequences and guilt. When a person trusts in Christ for salvation, God removes the guilt of his sin forever (Rom. 8:1). But the sins that people continue to commit, even as believers, always have consequences. The consequences of generations of sinning accumulate, and eventually God will deal with them in the tribulation.

Another question is, who will suffer in the tribulation? These will include many groups and individuals, including all earth dwellers (i.e., beast worshipers), participants in Babylonianism, followers of the beast and the false prophet, Jews, believers in Jesus, and the two witnesses. Many, many people will experience great suffering.

Where will the suffering in the tribulation come from? Ultimately God himself will be the source of suffering, for he will send suffering through the seal, trumpet, and bowl judgments. Angels will mediate judgments from God. Satan (the dragon) and God's other angelic agents will also be his agents of judgment. Some of the suffering will come from the beast, the false prophet, and various hostile unbelievers and armies.

Suffering at Christ's Second Coming

When Jesus Christ returns to the earth, he will wage war against his enemies and judge them (Rev. 19:11, 13–15, 18–20; see also the above references to the battle of Armageddon). John saw Jesus clothed with a robe dipped in blood, probably an allusion to the blood of his enemies, including the beast and the false prophet, who will perish as Jesus intervenes and ends the battle of Armageddon. An army of angels (perhaps including immortal believers) will follow him. The sharp sword proceeding from Jesus's mouth probably refers to his ability to destroy his enemies with a word. Birds will feast on the flesh of those killed, since there will be so many of them that they cannot all be buried.

Suffering in the Millennium

Suffering during the millennial reign of Christ will be reduced because Satan will be bound during this long period of history. Even though people will still have sinful human natures, and society in general will not fully follow Christ's will, the elimination of Satan's opposition will result in better living conditions for everyone (20:2–3, 6, 8–10, 12, 14–15). However, God will release Satan at the end of the thousand years, and Satan will resume his wicked work Multitudes still inhabiting mortal bodies will be subject to pain and suffering then. God will judge Satan permanently at the end of the millennium and will cast him into the lake of fire, where he will suffer day and night forever. At this time death will cease, and those whose names are not found written in the book of life will be thrown into the lake of fire.

No Suffering in the Eternal State

When death ceases, the eternal state will begin (21:4, 8; 22:3). Then God will wipe away every tear from the eyes of the redeemed. "Death shall be no more, neither shall there be mourning, nor crying, nor pain anymore" (21:4). But the eternal fate of the ungodly will be quite different. "Their portion will be in the lake that burns with fire and sulfur, which is the second death" (v. 8). The effects of the curse placed on the creation at the fall will also cease.

Possible Suffering for the Readers of Revelation

One more indication of possible suffering is mentioned at the end of this book (22:18–19). John says that anyone who adds to or takes away from the words of the book of Revelation will experience suffering when they stand before God, if not before.

Application of This Revelation of Suffering
Since God gave this revelation of the culmination of suffering in history through an apostle who himself had suffered personally, its author, John, could empathize with those whose suffering he recorded. Typically people who have suffered much can empathize better with other sufferers than can people who have suffered little. And this suggests that believers who have suffered can have a special ministry of empathizing with others who are suffering (cf. 2 Cor. 1:3–7).

Suffering has ever been, is now, and always will be experienced by God's people. Therefore one should not be surprised or overly distressed when he encounters persecution and suffering. Suffering has resulted from the fall, but suffering is also something God uses to form godliness in his people (James 1:2–4, 12).

Since the time of greatest suffering the world has ever seen is on the horizon of history, Christians should help prepare as many people as possible to avoid it. Eschatology, the study of the future, should lead to evangelism (cf. 2 Cor. 5:11). Part of the task of God's children is to remind people that judgment is coming and that they can avoid it by trusting in Jesus Christ as their personal Savior.

Christians should also find comfort in the fact that they will escape this time of intense suffering, the tribulation (cf. 1 Thess. 4:18). Christians will not be on the earth for these judgments. That should be a comfort to every believer. Some Christians are afraid that the tribulation has already begun and that the Antichrist is already on the scene. But they need not worry about that. Christians will not be here for these events.

Perhaps the happiest lesson believers can learn from these facts about suffering in Revelation is that suffering will end. Believers who suffer now will not suffer forever. They will one day be free from all pain, tears, sorrow, and even sighing. And this wonderful condition will continue throughout eternity. So believers can look forward to the future with hope and enthusiasm. The end of suffering is part of the final aspect of salvation that God will provide for Christians, namely, their glorification. And as surely as he has declared believers righteous by faith in his Son in the past and delivers believers from present temptation in the present, God will complete his salvation and deliver them from all suffering and death in the future (Rev. 21:4; 22:3).

PART THREE

THEOLOGY, PASTORAL MINISTRY, AND MISSIONS

Two Brothers, by Dawn Waters Baker. These street children represent the plight of the poor around the world. They live without a bed or home but care for each other. Part of the answer to suffering is for each of us to care for others in a personal way. "If anyone has the world's goods and sees his brother in need, yet closes his heart against him, how does God's love abide in him?" (1 John 3:17).

Douglas K. Blount (MA, Baylor University; MA, PhD, University of Notre Dame) is professor of theological studies at Dallas Theological Seminary. He previously served on the faculties of Criswell College and Southwestern Baptist Theological Seminary. His passions include helping students to think Christianly and to grow in their commitment to the faith. Dr. Blount is a prolific author in the fields of theology and apologetics.

15

RECEIVING EVIL FROM GOD

Douglas K. Blount

*Not far from us, flames, huge flames, were rising from a ditch. Something was being
burned there. A truck drew close and unloaded its hold: small children. Babies!
Yes, I did see this, with my own eyes . . . children thrown into the flames. . . .
"Yisgadal, veyiskadash, shmey raba . . . May His name be celebrated
and sanctified . . ." whispered my father.
For the first time, I felt anger rising within me. Why should I sanctify His name?
The Almighty, the eternal and terrible Master of the Universe, chose to be silent.
What was there to thank Him for?* —ELIE WIESEL[1]

Shall we receive good from God, and shall we not receive evil? —JOB[2]

*Abba, Father, all things are possible for you. Remove this cup from me,
Yet not what I will, but what you will.* —JESUS[3]

Evil permeates this world; to live *is* to suffer. What follows takes these truths
for granted. So also it takes for granted God's sovereign and providential care

---

[1]*Night*, trans. Marion Wiesel, in *The Night Trilogy: Night, Dawn, Day* (New York: Hill and Wang,
2008), 50–51.
[2]Job 2:10.
[3]Mark 14:36.

for his creation. In so doing, it rests on solid ground as far as historic, orthodox Christianity goes. For whatever else the apostles' faith affirms, it surely affirms *both* the wretchedness of the human condition *and* the genuine, loving care of him who made all things.

In this chapter, I consider what seem to me the two most significant theological issues arising from the evil and suffering that surround us.[4] The second section discusses what may be the most vexing question facing humankind—namely, why does God allow evil and suffering?[5] Then, the third section considers a related and only slightly less troubling question—namely, how long must his creatures suffer before God sets things right? Before taking up these questions, however, I first consider whether awareness of evil makes belief in God untenable.

Does Evil Make Belief in God Untenable?

Critics of the biblical conception of God often maintain that in one way or another the existence of evil is incompatible with God's existence.[6] Thus, on their view, to ask why God allows evil is to ask an unanswerable question, unanswerable not simply because we cannot know its answer but rather because there is no such answer to be known. As stated above, I take the existence of both God and evil for granted. So I shall not argue for them here; I shall, however, respond briefly to the allegation that affirming the existence of one makes it irrational to affirm the existence of the other.

Some critics of the biblical conception of God claim that the existence of evil is *logically* inconsistent with God's existence.[7] In short, they claim that the following two propositions cannot both be true:

---

[4]Whether this world contains gratuitous evil—that is, whether it contains evil that serves no outweighing good—is not discussed in this chapter.

[5]This chapter deals with why God allows *any* evil and suffering at all. It does not discuss why he allows a particular evil or some specific instance of suffering. Henceforth, evil and suffering are referred to simply as "evil."

[6]See, for instance, David Hume, *Dialogues concerning Natural Religion and the Posthumous Essays Of the Immortality of the Soul, and Of Suicide, and Of Miracles*, ed. Richard H. Popkin, 2nd ed. (Indianapolis: Hackett, 1998), 58–66; J. L. Mackie, *The Miracle of Theism: Arguments for and against the Existence of God* (New York: Oxford University Press, 1982), 150–76; and Michael Martin, *Atheism: A Philosophical Justification* (Philadelphia: Temple University Press, 1990), 335–62. For a helpful introductory treatment of the so-called problem of evil, see Alvin Plantinga, *God, Freedom, and Evil* (Grand Rapids: Eerdmans, 1974). For a more recent discussion, see Daniel Howard-Snyder, "God, Evil, and Suffering," in *Reason for the Hope Within*, ed. Michael J. Murray (Grand Rapids: Eerdmans, 1999), 76–115.

[7]For discussion of what has come to be known as the logical problem of evil, see Alvin Plantinga, "The Free Will Defense," in *God and the Problem of Evil*, ed. William L. Rowe, Blackwell Readings in Philosophy (Malden, MA: Blackwell, 2001), 91–120.

(G) God, who is all-good, all-knowing, and all-powerful, exists.

(E) Evil exists.

Of course, E itself is undeniably true. So if G and E turn out to be logically inconsistent, G must be false. But why think G and E are in fact logically inconsistent?

Here the critic seems either simply to assume that G and E are inconsistent or to infer their inconsistency from something like the following:

(R) An all-good, all-knowing, and all-powerful being would have no good reason for allowing evil.

Of course, R's appearance in the argument simply raises another question: Why think R is true? Here the critic's reason seems simply to be that he cannot see what reason an all-good, all-knowing, and all-powerful being would have for allowing evil. Since he cannot see the reason, he concludes that no such reason exists. The fundamental assumption thus appears to be that if one cannot see what reason God would have for allowing evil, there must be no such reason.

Now in some situations one's inability to see a thing does indeed give one good reason to conclude that the thing in question does not exist. So, for instance, if one cannot see an elephant in one's bedroom, then—assuming that one's eyes are functioning properly, the room is properly lit, and so forth—it seems entirely appropriate to conclude that no such elephant exists. For, of course, an elephant is just the sort of thing one would expect to see if it were in one's bedroom. But what about divine reasons for allowing evil? Are they the sort of thing that—like elephants in bedrooms—one should expect to be able to see? No, they are not.[8] Or, at least, so the biblical portrayal of God indicates.[9]

If we take that portrayal seriously, we should expect *not* to understand God's reasons for acting as he does—unless of course he reveals those reasons to us. Thinking oneself capable of discerning God's reasons for acting as he does thus involves the stuff of which folly is made, namely, hubris. So, then, one's failure to see what reason God has for allowing evil seems to count not

---

[8]For elaboration on this point, see the discussion of "Noseeum arguments" in Daniel Howard-Snyder, Michael Bergmann, and William L. Rowe, "An Exchange on the Problem of Evil," in *God and the Problem of Evil*, 124–58, esp. 142–49.

[9]See Job 28:12–28; Isa. 55:8–9; Rom. 11:33–36; and 1 Cor. 2:11–16.

at all against the biblical conception of God. On the contrary, given that conception, it is precisely what one should expect. But then the charge that G and E are logically inconsistent, relying as it does on either a mere assumption or an unwarranted inference from one's own failure to see why God allows evil, should not trouble us.

Other critics of the biblical conception of God claim that E's truth makes the probability of G so low that one cannot reasonably affirm both G and E. These critics thus grant the logical consistency of G and E but nonetheless maintain that evil and suffering make belief in God irrational. After all, they argue, the fact that two propositions *might* both be true does not make it reasonable to believe them both true; for, they continue, whether one reasonably believes that two propositions are both true depends on the *probability* that they are both true. But, the critics claim, the probability of G given E is quite low.[10]

Even if that probability *were* quite low, however, that fact alone would *not* establish the irrationality of believing both G and E.[11] For, assuming E to be true, the rationality of believing that G is also true depends not on the probability of it given E but rather on the probability of it given *all* the available evidence. In other words, even if G were improbable given E alone, it would not follow that G is simply improbable. The critic correctly maintains that the rationality of believing two propositions both to be true depends on the probability that they are both true. But in that case, what is relevant is *not* the probability of G given E but rather the probability of G given *all* the available evidence, given *all* that one believes to be true.

Whether it is reasonable to believe a particular proposition depends not on its probability given one slice of the evidentiary pie, but rather on its probability given the whole pie. Needless to say, those who believe in God maintain that, even if the probability of God's existence is low when only evil is in view, it is nonetheless *not* low given the total evidentiary picture.[12] Those who believe otherwise need to establish their view by arguing for it rather than assuming

---

[10]For a more detailed discussion of this line of reasoning, see Daniel Howard-Snyder, ed., *The Evidential Argument from Evil*, The Indiana Series in the Philosophy of Religion (Bloomington, IN: Indiana University Press, 1996).

[11]Although I shall not press the issue, it remains far from obvious that the probability of G given E is in fact low. Critics who believe this probability *is* low thus need to do more than merely assert their view; if they wish their conclusions to be taken seriously, they need to argue for them.

[12]For a recent argument for God's existence, see J. P. Moreland, *Consciousness and the Existence of God: A Theistic Argument*, Routledge Studies in the Philosophy of Religion (New York: Routledge, 2008).

it. Until they do so, the claim that one cannot reasonably believe both G and E remains unconvincing.

Why Does God Allow Evil?

As stated above, the issues considered in this and the following sections arise from an awareness of evil in the world together with a commitment to divine sovereignty. By itself, such an awareness might lead to despair; it would not, however, lead to the questions discussed below. Were God less than sovereign—were he lacking in power or knowledge or goodness—our suffering might be no less acute, but it would not raise for us the issues discussed here. So commitment to an orthodox view of God's goodness, knowledge, and power—a view according to which that goodness, knowledge, and power are superlatively great—drives this discussion. In short, if we find the questions that this chapter addresses vexing, it is because we hold a high view of God.

We thus resemble Job. For when he cries out to God in the midst of his anguish, Job does so *not* because he has too low a view of God but rather because he has quite a high view of him. Surely, Job believes, he suffers only at God's pleasure; if God were so inclined, he could summarily end Job's misery. God's sovereignty is thus unquestioned; his motives for allowing one whom he allegedly loves to suffer, however, are not. For while Job recognizes God's sovereignty, he also recognizes his own innocence; he has done nothing worthy of his suffering. Indeed, according to the first verse of the book that bears his name, as Job's travails begin, he is "blameless and upright, one who feared God and turned away from evil" (Job 1:1; cf. v. 8).

So, as his story begins, Job *is* innocent. From there, however, things go quite badly for him; and they do not take a turn for the better until his story's final chapter. This, then, is the mystery that confounds Job. Not only could God summarily end—or, better still, have prevented—his misery, but Job has done nothing to deserve that misery. And this leaves Job with a legitimate question, namely, *Why?* Why does God allow one whom he loves—one who has done nothing to deserve misery—to suffer?

That Job's suffering cannot be explained in terms of his wickedness runs contrary to what his wife and friends think. Like the disciples who think a man's blindness must be punishment for someone's sin (John 9:1–5), Job's wife and friends see suffering as a manifestation of divine wrath.[13] Of course, one's suf-

---

[13]That Job's wife believes his suffering must be a result of his sin seems clear from her question: "Do you still hold fast your integrity?" (Job 2:9). She apparently encourages her husband to admit whatever he has done to incur God's wrath so that he might then be allowed to die.

fering does sometimes arise from one's sin. Suffering comes to Job, however, not because of his wickedness but rather because of his righteousness. When God initiates Job's ordeal by bringing him to Satan's attention, God emphasizes Job's righteousness: "Have you considered my servant Job, that there is none like him on the earth, *a blameless and upright man, who fears God and turns away from evil*?" (Job 1:8). As rain falls on the unjust as well as the just, so also suffering comes to the righteous as well as the unrighteous.

That Job's suffering cannot be explained in terms of his wickedness is thus clear. How it *can* be explained, however, is not clear. And, as much as one wants to offer a satisfying explanation for that suffering—and thus provide a compelling answer to the question of why God allows Job to suffer as he does—one seeks such an explanation in vain.[14] For if Job's story shows nothing else, it shows that God declines to give his reasons for allowing evil.[15] In short, God *refuses* to explain himself.

In the midst of his suffering, Job protests his innocence. Underlying that protest is the question, Why? And God responds to Job's query with questions of his own.

> Then the LORD answered Job out of the whirlwind and said:
>
> "Who is this that darkens counsel by words without knowledge?
> Dress for action like a man;
>> I will question you, and you make it known to me.
>
> "Where were you when I laid the foundation of the earth?
>> Tell me, if you have understanding." (Job 38:1–4)

Later, God's response continues.

> Then the LORD answered Job out of the whirlwind and said:
>
> "Dress for action like a man;
>> I will question you, and you make it known to me.

---

[14]Of course, many have nonetheless tried to answer Job's question. Attempts to provide God's reasons for allowing evil, either generally or in particular instances, are known as theodicies. A theodicy, then, seeks to justify God to humans by explaining why he allows evil. For reasons discussed below, such attempts are invariably presumptuous. For the moment, however, I simply note that, when his story ends, it is not Job with whom God is angry but rather those who foolishly presumed to justify God to Job (Job 42:7–10).

[15]As mentioned above, God initiates Job's suffering; it thus seems a gross understatement to describe God's role in that suffering as simply "allowing" it. But I will not pursue this point here.

> Will you even put me in the wrong?
>> Will you condemn me that you may be in the right?
> Have you an arm like God,
>> and can you thunder with a voice like his?
>
> "Adorn yourself with majesty and dignity;
>> clothe yourself with glory and splendor.
> Pour out the overflowings of your anger,
>> and look on everyone who is proud and abase him.
> Look on everyone who is proud and bring him low
>> and tread down the wicked where they stand.
> Hide them all in the dust together;
>> bind their faces in the world below.
> Then will I also acknowledge to you
>> that your own right hand can save you." (Job 40:6–16)

The point of this response seems clear: one who understands neither the laying of the earth's foundations (38:4) nor the humbling of the proud (40:11–14) cannot rightly expect to fathom God's reasons for allowing evil; in short, one who lacks wisdom is in no position to understand why God allows the suffering we see around us. To expect God to explain himself to us not only presumes a right—namely, the right to hold God accountable—we do not have, but it also presumes a wisdom—namely, the wisdom to understand his reasons—we do not have. Such an expectation is thus doubly foolish. Job's reaction makes it clear that the point of God's response is not obscure to him.

> Therefore I have uttered what I did not understand,
>> things too wonderful for me, which I did not know. (42:3)

Since all mere humans lack the wisdom to understand the mind of God—for, as Scripture asks, "Who has known the mind of the Lord?" (Rom. 11:34; cf. 1 Cor. 2:16)—no such human is in a position to understand the reasons God providentially governs the world as he does.

So God refuses to explain himself to us. And as long as he remains silent about his reasons for allowing evil, we cannot hope to understand those reasons. Still, though he declines to give Job an explanation of his providential governance of the world, God does not leave him without hope. Job may seek a reason from God, but he receives from him something far better—namely, a relationship. In response to the man's query, God reveals himself in an extraordinary way; and as Job's reaction shows, he doesn't miss the point. "I had heard of you by the hearing of the ear," Job says, "but now my eye sees you" (Job 42:5). So rather than respond to the man's suffering by explaining himself, God manifests his presence—and, in a manner of speaking, gives Job a glimpse of himself—in the midst of that suffering. And Job finds that satisfying.

So also God declines to explain himself to us. But he nonetheless manifests his presence to us in the midst of our suffering. Whether, like Job, we find that manifestation sufficient is up to us. And the extent to which we come to know God and his Word *prior* to our suffering will determine the extent to which we are troubled by having no explanation of that suffering.

Suppose I happen to see my father driving wildly along a dangerous stretch of highway. He weaves in and out of traffic, causing other cars to swerve to one side or the other to avoid being hit. His speed makes the cars around him appear to be standing still. What do I conclude? Do I conclude that my father is a reckless maniac who cares nothing about anyone else? No. For even if I don't know my father's reason for driving as he does, I know that he has one—and, moreover, that it is a good one—*because I know him.* Of course, others who see him driving in ways that appear reckless might well conclude that he *is* a maniac; since they do not know him, that might be the most reasonable conclusion from their point of view. But I know him; consequently, I *know* he has a good reason for driving as he does *even if I do not know what that reason is.*

So also it might be reasonable for those who do not know God to conclude from the evil surrounding them that he is a cosmic maniac. But we who are his people—we who know him—*know* that he has good reasons for providentially governing his creation as he does *even if we do not know what those reasons are.* We cannot explain God's reasons in a way that satisfies an unbelieving world, in a way that assuages the critic who thinks the evil surrounding us makes belief in God untenable. But we who have been redeemed by Christ's sufferings know that, regardless of whether he shares his counsel with us, God has his reasons; and, though we may never understand *how* our sufferings work together for our good, we know that they ultimately will do so (Rom. 8:28).

How Long Must God's Creatures Suffer?

While Job wrestles with the question of *why* God permits him to suffer as he does, the psalmist confronts a different but only slightly less troubling question:

How long will God permit his people to suffer as they do? "How long, O LORD?" he asks.

> Will you forget me forever?
> How long will you hide your face from me?
> How long must I take counsel in my soul
> and have sorrow in my heart all the day?
> How long shall my enemy be exalted over me?
> Consider and answer me, O LORD my God;
> light up my eyes, lest I sleep the sleep of death,
> lest my enemy say, "I have prevailed over him,"
> lest my foes rejoice because I am shaken. (Ps. 13:1–4)[16]

Of course, the prophets anticipate a great and awesome day of the Lord, a day when all things will be made right, when justice will be established, when the proud will be humbled, and the humble exalted. On that day, Malachi tells us, "the sun of righteousness shall rise with healing in its wings" (Mal. 4:2). The blind shall see, the deaf hear, the lame leap, the mute sing (Isa. 35:5–6). Those whom God has redeemed

> shall return
> and come to Zion with singing;
> everlasting joy shall be upon their heads;
> they shall obtain gladness and joy,
> and sorrow and sighing shall flee away. (v. 10)

Elsewhere Isaiah anticipates the coming of the Lord's anointed, one sent

> to bring good news to the poor;
> . . . to bind up the brokenhearted,
> to proclaim liberty to the captives,
> and the opening of the prison to those who are bound. (Isa. 61:1)

God loves justice and promises one day to establish it (vv. 8–11).

So the psalmist's expectation that the Lord will not forget him, but will rather consider and alleviate his suffering, rests on the promises of God himself. Like Job, the psalmist cries to God out of belief rather than unbelief. Despite his cries, however, God refuses to tell the psalmist—or anyone else—how long

---

[16]Cf. Psalms 6, 35, 89, 94, and 119.

he must wait for the coming of that great and awesome day. "But concerning that day and hour no one knows," Christ himself says, "not even the angels of heaven, nor the Son, but the Father only" (Matt. 24:36).

So God *will* make all things right, but he will do so according to his own timetable, and he shares that timetable with no one. Until he does make things right, moreover, suffering continues to multiply. And this leads many to take offense, to question God's love for them, to doubt his goodness. So, for instance, Elie Wiesel suffered horribly during the Holocaust. And his experiences, such as the one recounted in the quotation that begins this essay, led him to take offense. Of the flames in Birkenau, flames in which he saw children consumed, Wiesel writes, "Never shall I forget those flames that consumed my faith forever. . . . Never shall I forget those moments that murdered my God and my soul and turned my dreams to ashes."[17] He finds repulsive the suggestion that he worship a God who allows such suffering, a God who offends him.

> "Blessed be the Almighty . . ."
> The voice of the officiating inmate had just become audible. At first I thought it was the wind.
> "Blessed be God's name . . ."
> Thousands of lips repeated the benediction, bent over like trees in a storm. Blessed be God's name?
> Why, but why would I bless Him? Every fiber in me rebelled. Because He caused thousands of children to burn in His mass graves? Because He kept six crematoria working day and night, including Sabbath and the Holy Days? Because in His great might, He had created Auschwitz, Birkenau, Buna, and so many other factories of death? How could I say to Him: Blessed be Thou, Almighty, Master of the Universe, who chose us among all nations to be tortured day and night, to watch as our fathers, our mothers, our brothers end up in the furnaces? Praised be Thy Holy Name, for having chosen us to be slaughtered on Thine altar?[18]

Perhaps the greatest tragedy of Wiesel's horror-filled experiences—the worst of all the crimes his Nazi tormentors subjected him to—is that they robbed him of his faith. When his story begins, he sees himself as a devout follower of his father's God. By his own account, however, his suffering drives him away from that God. Wiesel thus finds himself alienated from him.

[17]Wiesel, *Night*, 52.
[18]Ibid., 85.

I was the accuser, God the accused. My eyes had opened and I was alone, terribly alone in a world without God, without man. Without love or mercy, I was nothing but ashes now, but I felt myself to be stronger than this Almighty to whom my life had been bound for so long. In the midst of these men assembled for prayer, I felt like an observer, a stranger.[19]

Wiesel expects God to deliver those caught up in the Holocaust, but God does not act according to the man's expectations; instead, he delays. And Wiesel—not to mention untold others—suffers horribly because of it. This tempts the man to take offense at God; and Wiesel succumbs to that temptation.

In the Gospel accounts, John the Baptist faces a similar temptation. He finds himself languishing in prison. Like Job, who suffered not despite his righteousness but because of it, John in his faithfulness is brought to grief. He has prepared the Lord's way before him, heralding his coming, the coming of God's anointed. As John himself understands, Christ's increase means his own decrease; Jesus rising means John declining (John 3:30). But Jesus is the Christ, the Messiah; he will rule forever on David's throne. So his coming signals the coming of the kingdom, the coming of the great and awesome day of the Lord. John's own decline is a price he would gladly pay to see all things made right. But there he is, suffering in prison. And Christ does not proceed according to the timetable that John has set for him.

So John sends two of his disciples to Jesus with a question: "Are you the one who is to come, or shall we look for another?" (Luke 7:20). John thus makes it clear that Jesus is not doing what John thinks the Messiah should do. And John suffers because of it. By his lights, then, Jesus has taken too long to assume the messianic role of conqueror. If, as John believes, Jesus is the Messiah, he needs to act in accord with John's expectations; in short, Christ needs to pick up the pace and work according to John's timetable.

Jesus's response to John's query is twofold. First, he instructs the messengers to tell John what they see happening—"the blind receive their sight, the lame walk, lepers are cleansed, and the deaf hear, the dead are raised up, the poor have good news preached to them" (Luke 7:22). To their account of Jesus's ministry, he also instructs the messengers to add this: "And blessed is the one who is not offended by me" (Luke 7:23). So Christ responds to John first by pointing out that, as anyone familiar with the prophets' writings should understand, he *is* doing the Messiah's work. While he may not be doing that work according to John's expectations or timetable, he *is* doing it nonetheless. Second, he

[19]Ibid., 86.

encourages John *not* to take offense at him. So Jesus acknowledges that, as far as John—for whom he has very high regard (Luke 7:24–28)—is concerned, he is not proceeding according to expectations. But, he says, blessed are those who are not offended by that fact. Blessed is he who, with the psalmist, can respond to the delay in the kingdom's coming—and the suffering that attends that delay—in faith.

> But I have trusted in your steadfast love;
>> my heart shall rejoice in your salvation.
> I will sing to the Lord,
>> because he has dealt bountifully with me. (Ps. 13:5–6)

God *will* keep his promises, but he will do so according to his timetable, not ours. Our task is to resist the temptation to take offense at him for doing so; our task is to trust him.

Conclusion

Despite claims to the contrary, the existence of evil does not make belief in God irrational. Critics who say otherwise typically do so on the basis of either a mere assumption or an unwarranted inference. In neither case, however, do their claims constitute a serious threat to the rationality of belief in God. Critics inclined simply to assume that God and evil are somehow inconsistent may do as they choose; such is the privilege of living in a free society. But they can hardly complain when Christians refuse to be cowed by their cavalier assertions. Other critics infer such inconsistency from their own inability to see why God permits evil; in doing so, they presume that, were God to have reasons for allowing evil, they would see what those reasons were. But such hubris on the part of unbelievers presents no serious challenge to historic, orthodox Christianity.

Since God does not disclose to us his reasons for allowing evil, the vexing question of why he does so remains unanswered. So also he declines to tell us when the promised day of the Lord will come and thus leaves unanswered the question of how long his people must suffer. Instead of providing us with explanations and timetables, God calls us to trust him. In response to the questions of Job and the psalmist, then, God gives us not the answers we seek but rather the invitation we need—the invitation to follow after him, to find no offense in him, to *trust* him.

Of course he has also given us promises—promises that one day all things *will* be made right, that every tear *will* be wiped away, that pain and suffering *will* be no more. When that day will come, we do not know; why he allows pain and suffering in the interim, we do not know. But he promises that one day he will make all things right. Until then, we are invited to trust him. And, until that great and awesome day, the question for us is whether we will receive evil from God as well as good.

Victor D. Anderson (ThM, Dallas Theological Seminary; PhD, School of Intercultural Studies at Biola University) is department chair and an associate professor of pastoral ministries for Dallas Seminary. When not in Dallas, Vic is often found serving the people of Ethiopia through a wide variety of ministries with SIM. During his fifteen years as a full-time missionary in Ethiopia, he served in several theological education ministries, ranging from vernacular-level training programs to graduate-level schools. His pastoral ministry work has been equally varied, ranging from a large multiethnic setting at an international church to small Bible churches in the United States. Across these varied settings, he has experienced firsthand the challenges of providing pastoral care to people faced by disabilities or suffering through crises.

16

PASTORAL CARE AND DISABILITY

Victor D. Anderson

In reading the previous chapters your heart has likely been stirred by the biblical passages that touch on suffering. Amazing, isn't it? Like a quilt sewn with ragged patches of cloth, the biblical record portrays life as innumerable episodes of suffering stitched together by God's inscrutable craftsmanship. With such a wonderful cloth, some may be tempted to engage in endless study, mesmerized by the wonder of God's work in and through the realities of suffering. Yet simply staring at this beautiful cloth may fail to catapult individuals into pastoral care for hurting people. Something more may be needed to motivate us to action.

The remaining chapters of this book delve deeply into practical issues related to providing care. Specific needs of people who suffer in various disabilities are discussed. Techniques for moving alongside them and being a channel of God's blessing in their lives are presented. Valuable ministry insights are given for providing pastoral care for disabled people. Yet the complexity of needs and the challenges of skill development may deter some from action. To motivate to action, something more may be needed.

Sitting between the foundational building blocks of biblical theology and the nuts-and-bolts skills of practical care, this chapter seeks to provide that motivation for action. This chapter steps up to the plate to engage in real pastoral care.

The term *pastoral care* does not mean *professional care*. While professional caregivers and clergy may benefit from this chapter, its intended audience is much wider. *Pastoral care* simply means tending to the needs of another person with a motivation and manner that are rooted in biblical theology and love for the Lord Jesus. Pastoral care may be performed by any believer, regardless of office.

Since pastoral care is founded on biblical theology, this chapter begins with a brief look back at major concepts touched on in earlier sections of the book. This chapter examines major ideas of biblical theology that impact pastoral care, then looks at the core needs of people who are disabled in an attempt to sensitize readers to the many challenges of those who are suffering. Then having looked back at the biblical record and outward to the needs of the disabled, this chapter looks inward, examining obstacles that inhibit people from activating pastoral care. Hopefully this chapter, like a springboard, will catapult believers into active ministry for someone who is suffering or disabled.

Four Major Biblical Concepts

The preceding chapters provide a vast, rich survey of biblical data, and its breadth may be overwhelming. Countless observations have been noted. Amid this sea of data, some ideas recur in chapter after chapter, and some of these carry exceptional potential to impact how one engages in pastoral care. Four concepts rooted in biblical theology provide a base for ministry to the disabled and suffering.

Suffering Is Universal and Inescapable

The biblical writers never set out to prove that suffering is ubiquitous; they simply assumed it. Suffering is part of life; it is an inescapable reality. Beginning in Genesis 3 and ending in the final chapters of Revelation, the biblical record pummels readers with pervasive agony. Men, women, children, and the earth itself suffer. God's people suffer, as do those who are not his own. Indeed, suffering typifies life in a broken world. Although there are occasional respites from the otherwise constant forces of decay, life generally moves incessantly in a disabling direction.

While suffering does not grasp every person uniformly, its tentacles extend to all members of the world. After the fall (Genesis 3) and before the re-creation of the last day, normal life is suffering. Stephanie Hubach, an author and a mother of a son with Down syndrome, writes, "Disability is essentially a more noticeable form of the brokenness that is common to the human experience—a normal part of life in an abnormal world. It is just a difference of degree along a spectrum that contains difficulty all along its length."[1]

---

[1]Stephanie O. Hubach, *Same Lake, Different Boat: Coming alongside People Touched by Disability* (Phillipsburg, NJ: P&R, 2006), 29.

This universality of suffering carries implications for providers of pastoral care. One ought never be surprised that persons suffering with disabling conditions are always nearby. Ministry to such people in need is not an exception to life; it is the norm. One must not be surprised by the call to help suffering people; rather, it should be expected. For suffering is bound up with earthly life itself.

Further, the universality of suffering connects the provider of care with the receiver of care through common experience at some level. Many people tend to see the obviously disabled person as different or unusual. Such a viewpoint creates distance between the provider and the recipient of pastoral care. But when one truly grasps that the suffering experiences of a disabled individual are more a matter of degree than of difference, one is more likely to see a common connection to them. In Hubach's words, people find themselves in the same lake but in different boats.[2] With such a viewpoint, initiating pastoral care is a little less daunting. One can therefore envision himself extending care to someone who is not so different from him.

Causes of Suffering Are Complex

Scripture often links suffering to direct personal sin, but not always. Suffering may come from sin within a family (e.g., Achan) or within a nation (e.g., Israel) or within the world (e.g., the world's condition at the time of the flood). Yet a man could be born blind with no direct link to sin (John 9). The unrighteous suffer, and, much to the consternation of the righteous, God-followers like Job also go through undeserved, intense suffering. Suffering may come at the initiation of demons, through persecution by evildoers, or from self-infliction. Frequently, the biblical records do not state the cause of suffering, and one is left wondering about its cause. In the end, the complexity of causes leaves people mystified and at times frustrated.

The disturbing *why* question is haunting, wherever suffering and disability rear their heads. "Why did this happen to me?" "Why doesn't God heal me?" "Why didn't God protect me from this?" In light of the Bible's presentation of the complexity of the causes of suffering, pastoral caregivers need not be frustrated by their inability to provide authoritative answers about causes. As in the case of biblical events, answers to the *why* question may remain buried in the unrevealed wisdom of God. As a result, caregivers would do well to anticipate a ministry of listening to unending questions without giving answers that are completely satisfying. Appreciation of the mystery of God's work in and through suffering brings with it a humility of service and a proper pause in providing answers.

---

[2]Ibid., 37.

Suffering Has the Potential to Draw People Closer to God

Scripture repeatedly shows suffering people calling out to God. Suffering and deprivation (as opposed to comfort and wealth) would keep Israel close to their God, acknowledging their dependence on him. Naaman, afflicted with leprosy, proved to be soft toward the God of Israel. Lament psalms picture an agonizing individual laying bare his humbled, ravaged soul to the Lord. In the New Testament, people disabled with blindness, diseases, and other physical handicaps were often the ones seeking out Jesus. The apostle Paul, afflicted with a thorn in his flesh, related how he was thereby sensitized to the grace of God. The overwhelming sense from Scripture is that suffering heightens—or at least has exceptional potential to heighten—spiritual sensitivity.

What are the implications for initiating pastoral care? Engaging in ministry with those who suffer may well be an investment with extraordinary potential for spiritual impact. Suffering softens hard hearts and weakens spiritual barriers. Suffering often presses humility into places where pride has ruled. By moving alongside one who is disabled, a caregiver may be perfectly positioned to be a tool in God's hands. While drawing close to a disabled individual or family may initially seem unappealing or even repulsive, recognition of potential for spiritual impact ought to motivate individuals to engage often and deeply in pastoral care.

Full Relief from Suffering Will Occur Only in the Life to Come

Suffering finds its ultimate solution only in the last day. Creation groans for it, and Christians long for their suffering-free inheritance. The idyllic pictures of the millennial kingdom, the new heavens, and the new earth evoke in readers of Scripture a wonderful hope for resolution beyond this life. How much more for those who suffer intensely! Anticipation of the Messiah's coming burns more brightly when suffering is fueling the fire.

In the early stages of a disability, people may more likely seek present relief over future restoration. With the passage of time, however, these individuals are positioned to develop a faith that looks intensely for future restoration. Every day they are reminded directly of their brokenness. And every day their faith must be stimulated to look to the future. What a privilege to minister to and learn from such individuals. Initially caregivers may be put off by feelings of anger, bitterness, or depression from suffering individuals. Ministry with such individuals is laborious and draining. But when the caregiver looks beyond the negative emotions, he can see the immense potential for faith development in a disabled believer. A caregiver who sees beyond the initial ministry challenges appreciates this capacity for exceptional faith development, initiates soul care, and sticks with it for a longer period. The result of this cultivated faith may be great spiritual blessing to the disabled person, to the caregiver, and to all who are touched by the life of the one intensely anticipating future restoration.

This brief survey of suffering in the Bible is not intended to replace the more careful examination of previous chapters. Rather, it provides a summation of key concepts that helps motivate people to provide care. These motivations can include recognizing one's connections with others in this broken world, acknowledging the mystery of suffering, and being spiritually sensitive to the one in need.

Core Needs of the Suffering and Disabled

Needs of the suffering fall into three categories: relational challenges, practical challenges, and psychological/emotional challenges. Not every disabled person struggles with all these challenges. Some will struggle simultaneously with all three categories, and others will sense that these difficulties come and go and recur in waves.

Relational Challenges

My wife and I spent many years living and working in East Africa. One of the great challenges we encountered was relational stress caused by being different from everyone else. We spoke English, and almost everyone else preferred a different language. We were white, and they were black. We initially had no children, and they all valued large families. We valued our privacy, and they valued constant contact. We felt the stares of people everywhere we went, even when we tried to get away for an anniversary dinner at a nice secluded restaurant. Like a dark cloud that casts a shadow over the day, a looming sense of isolation and nonacceptance often brought gloominess to our days. At times, though surrounded by people, we felt the stress of being alone.

People suffering with disabilities often face similar though intensified feelings of being misfits. They are misunderstood and isolated, even to the point of being oppressed. Joni Eareckson Tada describes her own experience in these same terms.

> Thirty years of moving in this wheelchair among pews, rehab centers, dirt villages, and government villages had taught me that people with disabilities often get set aside. In some cases they have become an oppressed minority. They have had to adjust to a world system that is not designed with them in mind. Laws, cultural norms, business transactions, and underlying attitudes can make them feel like second-class citizens.[3]

---

[3]Joni Eareckson Tada, *Barrier-Free Friendships: Bridging the Distance between You and Friends with Disabilities* (Grand Rapids: Zondervan, 1997), 22.

This sounds like someone living outside his own country! While the missionary does it by choice and has a place to retreat when he boards a plane, the disabled arrives without choice and without a path for escape.

Deep within every person resides the longing to be understood and accepted. It is a desire to have real friends with enduring relationships. Everyone has experienced the distress of having that core need unmet. For those who suffer with disabilities, that distress is heightened and prolonged. Walkers, wheelchairs, crutches, and physical impairments increase the barriers that inhibit the building of relationships. Friendships are difficult to initiate because of the heightened sense of difference. Friendships are difficult to keep because of the physical and emotional investments that must be made. As a result, most people do not befriend someone with a disability, some will become a friend for a short time, and only a few will establish an enduring friendship.

For many who suffer with disabilities, their source for friendship begins and ends with family. Yet here again relational challenges may become unbearable. Families undergo tremendous strain when caring for a member with a disability. Families caring for the disabled have a higher divorce rate than the norm.[4] Many disabled people are not able to marry, and if they do, they are at a higher risk for divorce.[5] Families who have little assistance with care for a disabled member find themselves stressed to the point of fragmentation. Jackie Sullivan, a chaplain in a long-term-care facility, enumerates some of the relational challenges surrounding family life: "Marriages seldom last, siblings become distanced, children of these young and midlife adults with disAbling [sic] conditions become strangers, and families all too frequently become burned out."[6]

These relational challenges experienced by disabled persons point to a deep need for friendship and companionship. By developing understanding of and loyalty to a disabled individual, a true friend provides meaningful pastoral ministry. Such a ministry likely will differ from the services provided by a professional therapist, doctor, nurse, lawyer, dietician, or attendant, for it stems from loving character and patient commitment rather than an employment obligation. Further, a ministry of friendship does not depend on a vast biblical knowledge or refined pastoral technique. Rather it displays loyal love to an individual and a family, modeled after the love God has shown to his broken people.

Relational needs are seldom met with an occasional contact. Family fragmentation may be irreparable, and feelings of aloneness that are controlled in

---

[4]Tada reports that families with a disabled member experience a divorce rate of approximately 80 percent (ibid., 24).

[5]Jackie Sullivan, *Pastoral Care with Young and Midlife Adults in Long-Term Care* (New York: Haworth Pastoral Press, 2007), 7.

[6]Ibid., 6.

one hour may be ferociously unleashed in the next. Yet true friendship serves as a balm repeatedly applied and rubbed deep into the soul.

Of the core needs for people who are suffering with disabilities, relational challenges, though not immediately obvious, present significant needs to be met primarily through friendship.

Practical Challenges

Over the last few decades I have experienced multiple minor ailments that have impaired otherwise normal ways of living. As a young teen, I daily strapped on my ugly full-length leg braces and orthopedic shoes that pressured my legs and ankles to grow in a better direction. A little later in life, orthodontic braces pressured my teeth to move into better locations. As a parent, I have been challenged on two occasions to care for a daughter immobilized by a body cast. And my annual struggles with allergies impair my breathing and my work.

While such personal afflictions have been relatively minor, their impairing effects on my physical performance were painfully and continuously obvious to me. When challenged by their own "in-your-face" disabling conditions, even on a temporary basis, people are acutely aware of the restrictions placed on their normal lives. People are highly sensitized to their limitations.

But most people tend to be less sensitive to the impairments of others. The following paragraphs may help believers be more sensitive to the plethora of practical needs experienced by disabled persons. While the following list is neither comprehensive in scope nor uniform in its applicability to all persons with disabilities, it may serve to heighten awareness of practical needs. Three types of practical challenges are examined briefly: mobility, personal care, and family care.

Mobility

Many disabilities make movement difficult. Injuries and diseases that impact the skeletal, muscular, and/or neurological systems of the body may impair walking. Blindness and deafness impair one's ability to move, particularly in places of less familiarity. While wheelchairs, crutches, and specially equipped automobiles may improve mobility for some, these devices certainly do not remove all impairments related to mobility. Not all buildings and houses are wheelchair accessible. At the very least, disabled persons must expend much effort to get from point A to point B. Movement may require arrangement of transportation assistance, additional physical exertion to move, anxiety over accessibility, increased time to move, and an inordinate amount of fatigue from the whole process. For many, these mobility challenges bring such fatigue that they may simply forego the event altogether, choosing to remain home.

With a bit of imagination people who are not mobility impaired can become aware of the needs of those who are. By imagining a wheelchair-bound person unable to attend a meeting because of lack of access, one is more likely to offer a ride, change the venue, or modify the meeting room (widening doors, adding a ramp, etc.) when events are viewed from that perspective. One can invest a little additional energy to lend guidance to a visually impaired person or hold the door a little longer for someone who is walking with crutches. For someone confined to a nursing home or other institution where unassisted contact with the outside world is impossible, offering him or her a drive in the country, a trip to a park, or a stop at a store can be a great help. The key is envisioning the world from the perspective of the mobility-impaired individual and moving to provide a proper level of assistance.

Personal Care

Other disabled persons need assistance with personal care. One of my good friends is wheelchair bound, her body ravaged by multiple sclerosis. Once an active young woman with exceptional abilities on the tennis court, she now is unable to use arms or legs. When she needs a drink, someone must help her. She is unable to lift a fork or spoon to her mouth. When a wisp of hair strays over her face, someone else must brush it away. When her skin starts to dry, a helper must sense it for her and apply lotion. I marvel at the sensitive care provided by her husband. He seems always ready to lift her cup or her fork. He senses when to provide a tissue and when to nudge her motorized wheelchair into a new position. In short, this woman's husband has developed a whole set of sensitivities to the needs of his disabled wife. He gives care consistently and without being prompted.

While most readers will not reach this level of sensitivity toward the needs of others, one certainly can seek to perceive those needs and act accordingly. Of course in the area of personal care a good foundation of friendship must first be established, and caregivers should still ask before taking action. They must see the need and ask permission to help. Perhaps there is an opportunity to turn the pages in a book or magazine that someone is reading. It could be helping others accomplish a project (but not doing it all for them), so that they feel a sense of fulfillment in the work completed. A caregiver might learn from a therapist and then provide therapeutic assistance between visits to the professional. The opportunities are countless. The point here is that one must develop the ability to see these personal care challenges faced by people with disabilities, and having seen the need, to ask permission to assist in some way.

Family Care

Alongside challenges of mobility and personal care, disabilities often bring practical challenges for the family. This third area of practical challenges takes different forms, depending on the nature of the disability and the family member carrying it. However, regardless of the exact configuration of disability, if family members are involved, there will be needs for practical care at a family level.

Healthy parents agree that raising children is a lot of work. How much more challenging when one or both parents suffer with a disability! Disabled parents likely will have their own mobility challenges and personal care obstacles that accelerate fatigue. Add the challenge of raising children, and fatigue levels may become unbearable. Here is a great opportunity for a sensitive caregiver to step in with parental assistance. In this case the assistance may be rendered to the disabled parent by spending time with a healthy child. Helping with homework, taking a child into one's home or to the park, or bringing the child to spend time with one's own children are simple but significant acts of assistance.

Perhaps the more common situation involves parents caring for a disabled child. Depending on the disability, the demands of parenting rise exponentially when one of the children suffers with an impairment. Basic tasks such as housecleaning, cooking, shopping, and laundry cannot be completed without multiple interruptions since a parent's attention cannot be long removed from a disabled son or daughter. While all children at times mess their pants, spill their milk, and knock over the planter, children with some disabilities will have such accidents more frequently, and parents in these situations must spend larger portions of their days in cleanup and repair. When multiple children are in the family, healthy children may be neglected or given unreasonable levels of responsibility while the parents focus more attention on the disabled child. The strains of child care in turn place stress on the marriage relationship, with each partner feeling abandoned by the other.

> That children have two parents when they start life is a biological fact. Mothers of impaired children, however, frequently find themselves in a one-parent role in which they are nurse, physical therapist, purchasing agent, cook, cleaning lady, chauffeur, and fill-in for all types of emergencies. In this type of situation the wife feels that she doesn't have a husband, for he never helps with the feeding, bathroom duties, putting on of braces, therapy, and other responsibilities with the impaired child. On the other hand, the husband may complain that

his wife doesn't want to go any place with him and that she is too tired or too tense to be affectionate.[7]

An individual sensitized to these needs will see many opportunities to provide care. In these situations pastoral care may take the form of helping with grocery shopping, transportation, and housecleaning. Care may come in the form of helping the healthy children with homework or recreation. It may be in the form of caring for the kids while Mom and Dad get a night out to fortify their own relationship. These practical kinds of assistance for a family become important acts of pastoral care when they are done out of Christian love and passion.

Emotional Challenges

Volumes could be written on the emotional needs of people suffering through disabilities. The purpose here is not to be comprehensive. Rather, a few of the frequently occurring emotions to which a caregiver should be sensitized are discussed. By being aware of emotional upheavals within a disabled person, one is more likely to provide care that is empathetic and affirming rather than pitying, condescending, and condemning. Three kinds of emotions will likely exist in the people for whom pastoral care is provided.

Helplessness

As a pastoral caregiver, one must expect that those suffering with disabilities will at times struggle with feelings of utter helplessness. The disabled may develop an overwhelming sense of not being able to accomplish what he wants to do, a feeling of hyperdependence on others. Such feelings of futility will affect most disabled people and will be particularly problematic for those who are institutionalized and for their families.[8] Loss of motor control, loss of strength, loss of sight, loss of mental capacity—all bring with them a loss of ability to control basic elements of life. Loss of options extracts decision making from the world of the disabled. This sense of loss may be particularly acute for those who are disabled through trauma or who experience degenerative conditions. They have known life with fuller capacity and production, and like an unwanted thief, a disability steals away control, resulting in a feeling of helplessness. As they lose ability to control some aspect of their lives, disabled persons lose a sense of self-worth, seeing themselves as more of a liability than an asset to family, friends, and society.[9] In response, a caregiver must be prepared to be patient

---

[7]Lorraine Guild-Smith, "Toward an Understanding of Parents with an Impaired Child," in *Pastoral Care of the Handicapped*, ed. Roy E. Hartbauer (Berrien Springs, MI: Andrews University Press, 1983), 163.

[8]R. H. Ferris, "Pastoring the Family of the Institutionalized," in *Pastoral Care of the Handicapped*.

[9]Sullivan, *Pastoral Care with Young and Midlife Adults in Long-Term Care*, 49.

and affirming. The caregiver who helps a disabled person achieve control over some area of life will help that individual have a greater sense of self-worth and will help decrease the frustrations that come with helplessness.

Anger

Loss of control often leads to anger. R. H. Ferris explains the connection of anger with helplessness: "Externally, anger may be presented as a response to being deprived of 'normal' social contact, but deeper examination demonstrates it to be a response to the erosion of self-image exacerbated by the helplessness that is present."[10] This anger may be directed toward family, institution, self, God, and caregiver. The anger may stew inside or erupt on others with a violence that may surprise even the ones who are suffering.[11]

Givers of pastoral care must prepare for angry outbursts from the people they are trying to help. Without preparation, a caregiver may be caught off guard by angry words hurled from the one receiving care. Surprised by the intensity of the outburst and the apparent lack of appreciation, the caregiver will be tempted to lash back in defense or reprimand. However, in the face of such displays of anger, the caregiver will often provide the best ministry by listening and quietly absorbing the blows. While anger should not be encouraged, a suffering person should not be condemned for raw emotions that at times will be uncontrollable. A caregiver may be tempted to lecture or correct (even in a sentence or two). Such urges for reprimand must be controlled. How much better to listen quietly, always keeping in mind the biblical wisdom that a soft answer turns away wrath (Prov. 15:1).

Grief

Emotions of helplessness and anger may eventually give way to a profound sense of grief. As pointed out above, a disabled person often lives with a distinct sense of loss. Grief enters with the realization that life in its former state is gone. Then grief swells with a growing awareness that a disability will not likely be removed. At its worst, grief escalates into hopelessness and despair. Hubach explains how grief begins and then progresses through various stages.

> When a personality-altering disability occurs, such as a dementia, a family will likely grieve over the *loss of the "person" whom they once knew*, but who is rapidly slipping relationally from their grasp. Other forms of loss exist in the *crushing of hopes and dreams* or the *wrenching of a perception of control*

[10]Ferris, "Pastoring the Family of the Institutionalized," 50.
[11]Joe Fornear, *My Stronghold: A Pastor's Battle with Cancer and Doubts* (Longwood, FL: Xulon, 2009), 58.

over one's life. Families need the opportunity to work through the stages of healthy grief, which may include periods of denial, isolation, anger, bargaining, depression and acceptance.[12]

While givers of pastoral care might quickly realize the importance of the grieving process for those dealing with death in a family, they may be less sensitized to this need in situations involving a disability. A caregiver will do well to maintain the perspective of one who shepherds people through a healthy grieving process, infusing hope along the way. "Hope is that belief that somehow God is very present in times of pain and will bring us through to a moment of life and resurrection. Hope is the ability to remember how God has been present and loving in the past and trust that it is also true in the present moment and will be true in the future."[13]

Personal Obstacles to Providing Care

Two internal obstacles may impede one's willingness to provide pastoral care. Faced with the opportunity to provide pastoral care to disabled individuals, some people may be fearful about moving forward.[14] They fear that they will say the wrong thing or not have anything to say at all. They fear that they will help too much or not enough. Or perhaps they even fear that they will physically hurt the individual they are trying to help. In some instances one's fears may rise over uncertainty regarding a commitment to provide care. Will provision of care become a never-ending commitment? In the midst of busy schedules one may fear that he may not be able to complete the care he desires to give. Perhaps most threatening is a sense that one may become emotionally overwhelmed if he enters into a commitment to provide care. C. W. Brister's words point out how fear prevents some people from initiating care: "Our human tendency is to view wounded spirits from a safe distance. . . . Prejudice closes doors to understanding, and fear of the 'other' dictates a policy of caution, a defensive lifestyle, rather than acceptant attitudes of helpfulness."[15]

A person needs to locate and overcome such fears within himself if he hopes to move into pastoral care for disabled people. While some of the fears may be well founded, they must be evaluated in light of the provision of God's Spirit to equip people for ministry.

A second personal obstacle that may hinder one's giving pastoral care is the sense of a minimal return on his investment of hard work. Ministry to a disabled

[12]Hubach, *Same Lake, Different Boat,* 85 (italics hers).
[13]Michael F. Friesen, *Spiritual Care for Children Living in Specialized Settings: Breathing Underwater* (Binghamton, UK: Haworth Pastoral Press, 2000), 79.
[14]Hubach, *Same Lake, Different Boat,* 36.
[15]C. W. Brister, *Pastoral Care in the Church,* 3rd ed. (San Francisco: Harper, 1972), 19.

individual may seem like pouring limited resources of strength, energy, and money into a bottomless pit. Some may fear being sucked dry by an individual or a family who could drain them of all they have. This is a tough ministry, and little benefit or affirmation may be received. This sense of wasted effort is particularly common when one engages in extended ministry for someone in an institution. As Sullivan notes, even family members grow weary of these situations and find it difficult to continue visiting someone who is unresponsive.

> So, visits become fewer and farther between, and families become distanced, not because they don't love that family member, but because it is so difficult, as that love for them makes them hurt too much to see them in their condition. Many, many family members have told me that they wished they had allowed their loved one to die at the time of the critical medical event that disAbled [*sic*] them because this type of life is so completely contrary to all their hopes and dreams.[16]

If a caregiver hopes to see tangible benefits from giving care to a disabled person, he may not get deeply involved in such a ministry. The prospects of minimal return may be too discouraging. With ministry to the disabled, fixes and solutions often cannot be manufactured. One's efforts will not bring healing, and he may go home with a sense of moral frustration over the injustice of suffering. Under such ministry conditions, it is difficult to move forward with giving care.

Yet a successful caregiver is one who can see with eyes of faith beyond immediate rewards, working from the satisfaction that God is well pleased with such acts of kindness. And God's pleasure is sufficient to initiate the provision of care and to persevere in it.

Conclusion

Great is the challenge of providing pastoral care to those who suffer with disabilities. In fact the immensity of the challenge causes many to forego ministry here, seeking instead to provide care within their own safety zones. While the challenges are significant, God would have believers move forward in ministry. Armed with the principles of Scripture, knowing the core needs of those who suffer, and being willing to fight through their own internal fears, Christians must move forward to provide pastoral care. Frustration and fatigue may occur. One may wonder if there is any measurable benefit. Yet, engaged in this type of ministry, caregivers recognize that Christians image the God who gives himself for broken people.

---

[16]Sullivan, *Pastoral Care with Young and Midlife Adults in Long-Term Care*, 47.

James A. Neathery (ThM, DMin, Dallas Theological Seminary; MA, Fletcher School of Law and Diplomacy) was diagnosed with the neurological disease CIDP (chronic inflammatory demyelinating polyneuropathy) in 2001 while on the mission field. Forced to leave the field, he now serves as the stateside director of the Center for Christian Leadership in Albania (EastWest Ministries International) and is adjunct professor in world missions and intercultural studies at Dallas Theological Seminary.

Dr. Neathery's experience includes working with gangs through Young Life and serving as a think-tank facilitator with STEP (Strategies to Elevate People) and as spiritual formation coach at the Center for Christian Leadership at Dallas Seminary. He is a coauthor of the Transforming Life series on spiritual formation.

17

GLOBAL SUFFERING

James A. Neathery

Besieged with the media matrix, our consciences are affected by the residual memories of horrific photographs, testimonies, and video clips of those who have suffered, are currently suffering, or anticipate suffering. The types of suffering are as varied as the multitudes who suffer. Natural causes and human evil are factors in this global equation. Where there are wars, famine, and pestilence, human suffering can be found. Where there are human beings, there will be suffering.

This chapter does not speak for everyone, nor does it catalog all the suffering in the world. Instead of seeing global suffering as an embarrassment for God, for which he must apologize, Christians can be equipped with the truth that God has revealed about global suffering in the Bible. Knowing the truth helps the church today mobilize for maximum influence. It equips the church to be transformed into the character of Christ, the Suffering Servant. Instead of wringing its hands, the church can march into a suffering world with eyes wide open to the many opportunities to alleviate suffering, present the gospel, and glorify God.

Global suffering is not an exclusively twenty-first-century reality. Consider the Black Death (also known as the bubonic plague), which swept Europe in the 1340s; the An Shi rebellion in China, which resulted in the deaths of thirty-six million people in the 760s; or the Great Irish Famine of the later eighteenth century, which took a million lives. Then consider all the obscure tragedies that history has not recorded. Each moment in history has its own peculiar expression of evil resulting in human suffering.

Christians should not be surprised by these realities. The Bible thoroughly discusses the profound consequences of sin in the world. Sin expresses itself through the actions of human beings, like, for example, the genocide in Rwanda. Sin expresses itself in a convulsive wave when fallen creation heaves itself on Banda Aceh, Indonesia, on December 26, 2004. Then too there are subtler manifestations of sin in human behavior when clever groups of people form corporate, governmental, or institutional identities to protect themselves from the consequences of their actions on others, like the victims of black lung and asbestos. God's people too have been and are a part of the landscape of human suffering as they stand for Jesus Christ in places that are hostile to Christians and that conspire to silence or exterminate them.

With Eyes Wide Open: The Consequences of the Fall
Though Jesus Christ said, "In the world you have tribulation" (John 16:33), many believers avoid this truth by insulating themselves from the world through the pursuit of comfort or by ignoring the world by not engaging it. Understandably Christians may be overwhelmed by the complexity of global suffering and how best to respond to people's needs. But it is a dereliction of duty for Christian leaders to cower at the task of equipping their people to bring the power of the gospel to bear on the world's most complex, heinous, and despicable causes of human suffering. The suffering of others is the church's entry point for humble service. Global suffering testifies to the veracity of the Bible's message when it says, "The Scripture has shut up everyone under sin" (Gal. 3:22, NASB), "All these are but the beginning of the birth pains" (Matt. 24:8), and "Do not be surprised at the fiery trial when it comes upon you" (1 Pet. 4:12). Therefore the actions of believers must testify to the suffering world that the risen Christ is taking action to address global suffering through the church. David Livingstone, missionary to Africa, phrased it well: "Sympathy is no substitute for action."

Christians Familiar with Suffering
To be familiar with suffering in the twenty-first century one must grasp the fact that the world's population is genuinely entwined and variously miserable with suffering. C. T. Studd, nineteenth-century missionary, described poetically the mind-set necessary to engage suffering: "Some want to live within the sound of church and chapel bell; I want to run a rescue shop within a yard of hell." This quotation describes a dilemma in the church: to enjoy the relative safety

of huddling close to other believers, or to move out together with those same believers into a suffering world with the good news of Jesus Christ. Moving toward those who are suffering is unusual for most people. People tend to avoid uncomfortable situations. But for Christians, who are destined to be transformed into the likeness of Christ (2 Cor. 3:18), this familiarity with suffering is not an option. In Isaiah 53:3 the prophet spoke of Christ's sufferings.

> He was despised and rejected by men;
>   a man of sorrows, and acquainted with grief;
> and as one from whom men hide their faces
>   he was despised, and we esteemed him not.

Jesus is familiar with suffering. He knows distress, trouble, and emotional torment—not just in the abstract but in the experiences of life. He is steeped in the experiential knowledge of what it means to be a human being. He knows what it is like to be afflicted. And as the Savior of the world, he is well aware of the global consequences that the fall of man brings to the earth and its inhabitants. In an instant he can see the entire world's personal and corporate sin, calamity, and death. He is familiar with all kinds of violent rancor and bodily pain.

To be familiar with something means to be acquainted with it. Familiarity means that there is a well-worn path of use, like an old friend or the back roads of one's hometown. Whatever it is, it has been encountered before and is very common. Old men give knowing looks when certain familiar events begin to unfold. Fishermen and farmers are linked to ocean tides and weather patterns. But to be familiar with suffering is a different matter.

To be so intimate with suffering that it is regarded as an old friend is an uncommon personal trait in any culture. Instead of being familiar with suffering, people are at odds with it, averse to it, and astonished by it. The body of Christ has theological difficulties with the reality of suffering. Some say that suffering is incompatible with the teaching of Scripture. Some see it as a consequence of sin. Some unwittingly endorse a "do everything right so that God will protect you" philosophy. But those who doggedly follow Christ are destined to become like him (Rom. 8:29). Those who follow Christ yearn to know him in the camaraderie of his suffering. They know that death will make them like Christ (Phil. 3:10). Christians who radically identify with Christ become people of sorrow and are familiar with suffering. When believers live out the life of Christ in this way, they are a power to be reckoned with. Therefore, to be a person familiar with suffering means that one does not mistake abstraction for experience. A greater familiarization with global suffering will help prepare believers to aid the victims of suffering.

The Global Context

What does the term *global suffering* mean? Is suffering limited to mankind or does it include all creation wheezing its collective groan (Rom. 8:22)? Could it be that global suffering can be calculated by taking the number of people in the world and multiplying that figure by some individual suffering metric?

Through technology the population of the world is interrelated by a network of communication and exchange. The term that describes this is *globalization*. The syllables *-ization* are a suffix denoting the process or result of doing something. Globalization affects many lives. As David Smick describes in his book, *The World Is Curved*, "We live in a globalized world where we have to care much more about one another's problems, while simultaneously solving our own."[1] Missiologist Richard Tiplady agrees: "Globalization impacts every part of human life, including our cultural and religious existences. Since we are whole human beings embedded in communities, globalization has an effect on every aspect of our lives."[2] Darren Marks adds this about globalization:

> It has become almost too trite to speak of living in a global world. As in many other slogans of the *Zeitgeist*, the meaning is both clear and unclear. It is clear that living in a global world means that persons, things and ideas are now easily mobile and thus one is aware of analogues with, differences from, and so forth in places other than "here."[3]

Although suffering existed in the past, the consequences of that suffering were often limited to a specific location. Now severe acute respiratory syndrome (SARS) can spread from the Guangdong province of China to rapidly infect individuals in some thirty-seven countries around the world in only three weeks.

Comparative Suffering

Some people suffer at the hands of oppressive despots. Some suffer as victims of natural disasters. Some suffer because of their own foolish choices. To the people who are suffering, their troubles are immediate and affective,

---

[1]David M. Smick, *The World Is Curved: Hidden Dangers to the Global Economy* (New York: Penguin, 2008), 305.
[2]Richard Tiplady, ed., *One World or Many? The Impact of Globalisation on Mission* (Pasadena, CA: William Carey Library, 2003), 276.
[3]Darren C. Marks, ed., *Shaping a Global Theological Mind* (Hampshire, UK: Ashgate, 2008), 198.

essentially eclipsing an awareness of the suffering of others. However, do some people suffer more than others? Robert Seiple, former president of World Vision, addresses this question based on his encounter with a woman from Chad.

> A woman in the country of Chad gave birth to twins in the midst of a severe African famine. She immediately realized that she did not have the resources to keep both alive, so she made a choice. When World Vision got there, her choice was already made, and it was irreparable. One baby was lively, bouncy, smiley, and obviously going to make it. The second was weak, sallow, pale, and vomiting. Within a couple of days, the second baby died.[4]

As Seiple states, some people do suffer more than others, especially children, women, and the poor (all encapsulated in that short episode above). Every day thirty-two thousand children under the age of five die of diseases long eradicated in the West. That is "like a hundred 747s chock full of children crashing and burning outside a major airport, without survivors, each and every day."[5] This statistic does not include the suffering families who witness these deaths, nor does it tell of the other consequences these deaths have on society. This does not mean that the misery that results from affliction in suburban Toronto or Marseilles, for example, is unimportant, but it may help the church see the suffering world objectively so that it may respond with triage priorities.

The Peculiar Sufferings of the Church

A sobering fact is that the church, which seeks to reach the suffering world with the gospel of Jesus Christ, suffers as well. The sufferings of believers are unique in comparison to those of the world because their sufferings are related to their faith in Jesus Christ. As Seiple observes:

> Today more than 200 million Christians are being persecuted because of their faith. The vast majority of this persecution, in which Christians are being kidnapped, driven from their homes, raped, beaten, tortured and murdered, takes place outside the United States. However, it is persecution occurring inside the divine circle drawn for the body of Christ.[6]

---

[4]Robert A. Seiple, "The Hidden Faces of Suffering," *Review of Faith and International Affairs* 3 (Winter 2004–2005): 1.
[5]Ibid., 7.
[6]Robert A. Seiple, *Ambassadors of Hope: How Christians Can Respond to the World's Toughest Problems* (Downers Grove, IL: InterVarsity, 2004), 222.

Lamin Sanneh writes of these realities:

> The statistics of martyrdom in the 20th century make grim reading. The *World Christian Encyclopedia* gives the figure as 160,000 as the annual martyrdom rate for all Christian denominations. "Martyrdom" here describes Christians who die as an explicit consequence of their faith, though complex issues are often involved.[7]

Inasmuch as the church's sufferings are related to preaching the gospel and run cross-grain to the aims of the state, one can be assured that his sufferings are part of being a follower of Christ. Tentative and self-inhibited action by the worldwide church in response to crises like the genocide of Christians in Rwanda reveals ecclesiastical cowardice. If "the blood of the martyrs is the seed of the church," when is it advisable to intervene and rescue the body of Christ from slaughter?

The distant suffering of others and especially those of the global body of Christ should be "up front and center" among Christians in these days of globalization. The needs of those who endure misery with joy because they are persecuted for spreading the gospel should be in the prayers of every Christian.

An Enduring Christian Response
The church is God's instrument to call a suffering world to himself. With all its foibles and imprecise misfires of action the church is God's pliant responder to the needs of the world. The thought of responding to global suffering is overwhelming. The needs seem limitless. But this perceived limitless list of ills and suffering is matched and outdone by the manifest grace of God in the lives of gifted believers. The church is a cosufferer in this world. Its task is not to eradicate all suffering, but by sacrificial care of those who suffer, the task is to so "adorn" the gospel of God that unbelievers might better understand their need for Jesus Christ. All other efforts sustained by anything other than Christ will fade when the appeal and the applause wane.

Leaders Who See
A good friend often asks, "What do you see?" He does not want a literal response of what is in one's line of vision. Instead he wants to know the leadership vision. That is, what is the leader seeing in the disparate parts of his world, or are parts missing from one's visualization of the world? Many Christian leaders

---

[7]Lamin Sanneh, "Persecuted Post-Western Christianity and the Post-Christian West," *Review of Faith and International Affairs* 7 (2009): 21.

have vision statements that indicate they do not sense that they are living in a globalized society, much less that they live amid suffering millions. The emphasis for many of these leaders is provincial. They are seeking to take care of their own "backyards" before helping someone else overseas. But the truth about globalization is that when one helps someone at a distance, he is helping take care of his own local needs as well. And the truth about one's own "backyard" is that it is no longer insular and monoethnic. David Livermore writes about this phenomenon.

> Cultural intelligence isn't something needed only by those with a heart for the so-called mission field. It is needed by ministry leaders all across the United States. Eddie Gibbs, senior professor of church growth at Fuller Seminary, writes, "local church leaders are trained to be teachers and pastors of their flock rather than cross-cultural missionaries to their broader contexts." We must learn to live alongside sincere followers of other faiths, engage in ongoing conversations, and work together on issues of mutual concern while faithfully witnessing to the reign of God. Otherwise, we'll be left behind by this unavoidable new reality.[8]

Also, it is important for local church leaders to "see" and connect to the global church and its mission. The complexities of global suffering and the church's response provide challenges for today's church leaders and mission leaders. The kind of leader needed to see this big picture is called a synthesizer. Deborah Nutter, assistant dean of the Fletcher School of Law and Diplomacy, Tufts University, Medford, Massachusetts, describes this type of person as "someone who can perceive and understand the cultural, economic, and political forces behind an issue."[9] Howard Gardner reports a similar finding.

> The synthesizing mind takes information from disparate sources, understands and evaluates that information objectively, and puts it together in ways that make sense to the synthesizer and to other persons. Valuable in the past, the capacity to synthesize becomes ever more crucial as information continues to mount at dizzying rates.[10]

A brilliant example of the synthesizing mind is development economist Jeffrey D. Sachs. In his book *The End of Poverty: Economic Possibilities for*

---

[8]David A. Livermore, *Cultural Intelligence: Improving Your CQ to Engage Our Multicultural World* (Grand Rapids: Baker, 2009), 287.
[9]Deborah Nutter, "Message from the Director," accessed November 18, 2009, http://fletcher.tufts.edu/gmap/overview.shtml.
[10]Howard Gardner, *Five Minds for the Future* (Boston: Harvard Business School, 2006), 196.

Our Time Sachs looks at how developing countries can escape extreme poverty. Poverty, as noted earlier, is a chief indicator of suffering. Sachs has worked as a consultant in Bolivia, Russia, Poland, China, and various countries in Africa. He struggled to understand the complexities of extreme poverty. Then, inspired by his pediatrician wife, he adopted a framework found in clinical medicine called "differential diagnosis," which he applied to development economics. Essentially he would engage suffering (poverty) in a developing nation much the same way as a doctor would engage a patient in clinical diagnosis. Some of the complexities of these various situations became less muddled, and Sachs was able to see connections he could not see before. The lessons Sachs learned from clinical medicine and applied to development economics are these: (1) The human body is a complex system. (2) Complexity requires a differential diagnosis. (3) All medicine is family medicine. (4) Monitoring and evaluation are essential. (5) Medicine is a profession.[11] These points gleaned from clinical medicine can help leaders deal with a complex aspect of global suffering, such as poverty. These principles can help leaders diagnose the causes and symptoms of global suffering and apply them to specific areas that are of biblical concern (e.g., hunger, oppression, disease, and injustice).

A valid Christian response to global suffering should not be thought to compete with evangelism. The gospel message must often be given in the context of global suffering. To ignore this fact diminishes the relevance of the gospel to those who suffer. Believers continue making disciples while imitating the risen Christ in caring for the suffering. The most effective response to a world in need is to multiply disciples whose hearts burn with compassion for the lost world—disciples whose lives will take them, for example, into ethics discussions at multinational companies, grassroots implementation of state department foreign policy, and wheelchair distribution in South Waziristan.

People Who Take Action

Most Christians want to help those who are in legitimate need. Some who are reading this chapter may be thinking, *Yes, but what can I do?* People are inundated with images, news, stories, and statistics from the media. Many requests for money are in the mail. On street corners poor people ask for food and change. All of this can lead to compassion fatigue, which occurs when caregivers are engaged in situations where life, death, and trauma occur.

---

[11]Jeffrey D. Sachs, *The End of Poverty: Economic Possibilities of Our Time* (New York: Penguin, 2005), 75–78.

This term [*compassion fatigue*] has replaced the more familiar term burn-out. It refers to a physical, emotional and spiritual fatigue or exhaustion that takes over a person and causes a decline in his or her ability to experience joy or to feel and care for others. Compassion fatigue is a one-way street, in which individuals are giving out a great deal of energy and compassion to others over a period of time, yet aren't able to get enough back to reassure themselves that the world is a hopeful place. It's this constant outputting of compassion and caring over time that can lead to these feelings.[12]

Applied to the subject of global suffering, compassion fatigue can occur even if a person does not work every day in an environment mentioned above. Access to Internet news, constant guilt about not being able to help the starving masses, and trying to respond meaningfully to prayer and financial requests can bring on feelings of inadequacy and frustration.

In addition to compassion fatigue is the rather recent phenomenon of the moral and political implications of the distant suffering of others seen in the media. Luc Boltanski discusses these issues in his book *Distant Suffering: Morality, Media and Politics.*[13] What can a person do when he witnesses the distant suffering of others on television? Lilie Chouliaraki, a colleague of Boltanski's, comments,

> Confronting ourselves with the limits of the ethical and political legitimacy of modernity, distant suffering on our screens was then, and still is now, a reminder of a world divided in zones of prosperity and poverty, safety and danger—persistently raising the question of "what to do," only for us to keep evading it in our everyday lives.[14]

She continues:

> The argument now has it, we are now more connected with and closer to distant others than ever before—and this brings with it an awareness of just how interdependent our lives and fates are on this planet as well as a new sense of responsibility for those distant others. But what kind of awareness? What kind of responsibility?[15]

---

[12]"Compassion Fatigue," accessed April 22, 2009, http://www.pspinformation.com/caregiving/thecaregiver/compassion.shtml.
[13]Luc Boltanski, *Distant Suffering: Morality, Media and Politics* (Cambridge, UK: Cambridge University Press, 1999).
[14]Lilie Chouliaraki, "Distant Suffering in Media," accessed October 13, 2009, http://www2.lse.ac.uk/home.aspx, 2.
[15]Ibid., 3.

Watching the suffering of others a world away, many Western Christians are asking, "What can I do? What should I do?" One answer is to have a "world affairs club" in one's church. In these "club" meetings, findings from different parts of the world can be reported, members can pray, and plans of action can be developed. Or the group could watch and discuss Fareed Zakaria, *Global Public Square* on CNN Sunday afternoons. Events like these can familiarize believers with global suffering, which is often the first step toward action.

Every person can take action to help those who are suffering both near and far. Because of globalization, the refugees and immigrants living in the West can have enormous influence on their family members and friends who live in the developing world. Those who live in the West can send money, clothes, and ideas back home. These transfers are called remittances. From the Remittance Prices Worldwide website comes this report:

> The World Bank estimates that remittances totaled $443 billion in 2008, of which $338 billion went to developing countries, involving some 192 million migrants or 3.0% of the world population. The money received is an important source of family (and national) income in many developing economies, representing in some cases a very relevant percentage of the GDP of the receiving countries.[16]

Imagine the influence that a family of four can have on a refugee family from Somalia. Consider the impact a Christian business owner can have on the lives of his newly immigrated employees from Kurdistan. News of righteous and honest behavior travels quickly and far. Then, too, consider with joy the "spiritual remittances" that will be sent back home to Uganda by friends with whom the gospel is shared. Then there is the unseen fruit of giving money faithfully over time to perennial and often intractable crises. One can sponsor an AIDS orphan in Burundi for thirty-five dollars a month, which will provide health care, education, and nutritious food. And the entire community benefits from access to things like clean water, agricultural assistance, medical care, and more.[17]

Prayer
Christians can participate in the mission of God as they pray by the power of the Holy Spirit. Though believers are in the world and know what is occurring locally and globally, the primary input into their lives comes not from the media

---

[16]"Remittance Prices Worldwide," accessed November 30, 2009, http://remittanceprices.worldbank.org.
[17]"Sponsor a Child Now," accessed November 30, 2009, http://www.worldvision.org/content.nsf/pages/search-for-a-child?open&campaign=1193512&cmp=KNC-1193512.

with its images of distant suffering, but from God. He has opened the door of honest communication called prayer.

Compassion fatigue and the dilemma of being a spectator to distant suffering tend to make Westerners anxious about the world they live in. The very fact that there is suffering in the world may cause some to live in a continual emergency mode. But the apostle Peter counters with these words: "The end of all things is at hand; therefore be self-controlled and sober-minded for the sake of your prayers" (1 Pet. 4:7). In the general overload of needs and evocative images, believers are commanded to be clear minded and self-controlled, so that they can pray effectively. Second Timothy 4:5 has a similar emphasis. Paul instructed Timothy, "As for you, always be sober-minded, endure suffering, do the work of an evangelist, fulfill your ministry." Keeping a cool head in the midst of suffering is important for maintaining a focus on God in prayer.

Praying for people associated with global suffering is not an alternative to action; it is action. Though saying, "I'll pray for you," may be a polite exit from an awkward conversation with someone who is afflicted and suffering, it does not have to be that cowardly. Personally, I am limited by the neurological disease called chronic inflammatory demyelinating polyneuropathy. I am impressed by the limitless applications of prayer to distant lands where I am unable to travel. Though millions of Christians are moored to their communities and jobs and cannot be physically present in other lands, they, like me, can pray.

How can one consider any sustained sacrifice without complete dependency on God in prayer? Christians should not be so daft that they fail to realize that unseen spiritual battles are being fought for the souls of men. If believers enter the battle spiritually unarmed, they will fall victim to compassion fatigue and the paralysis of witnessing distant suffering. Christians ought not abdicate their unique, comprehensive means of global power and influence, namely, prayer. In this way they participate meaningfully in the mission of God.

Partnerships

The worldwide body of Christ is meant to work together. Globalization makes colaboring more feasible than ever before because of speedy travel, world phones, e-mail, and the predominance of English. Samuel Escobar makes this point about partnerships: "Global partnership of churches will be indispensible for mission in the twenty-first century. Among evangelicals this conviction grew in the last quarter of the twentieth century."[18]

---

[18]Samuel Escobar, *The New Global Mission: The Gospel from Everywhere to Everyone* (Downers Grove, IL: InterVarsity, 2003), 164.

National believers are key points of influence for the alleviation of global suffering. The resources of the developed world as well as the indigenous points of contact around the world can be helpful. A modest-sized church in the West can partner with a church in Indonesia, for example, to help the homeless in Banda Aceh put life back together. Also a church in Manipur can help a church in Chicago embrace the entire Lausanne Covenant, including difficult parts like this: "Those of us who live in affluent circumstances accept our duty to develop a simple life-style in order to contribute more generously to both relief and evangelism."[19]

Partnerships among and between various parts of the church are strategic choices for helping fulfill the Great Commission in a suffering world. The idea of partnership has been God's intention for the church since the beginning.

Conclusion

The Bible explains that global suffering is the context in which the church carries out its mandate. And for individual Christians, the Bible is clear in stating that they are destined to become like Jesus Christ and therefore will be familiar with suffering. In a world replete with suffering, it is understandable that many will experience compassion fatigue and a certain volitional paralysis when viewing distant suffering. But the follower of Christ is replenished in spirit in the midst of his or her own suffering to care for others. The obedient path will be difficult. But where suffering abounds, the manifest grace of God superabounds. Gifted believers can spring into the world empowered by the Spirit of God and wielding a sanctified moral imagination and a predilection for action.

---

[19]Ibid., 165.

PART FOUR

COUNSELING AND
PROFESSIONAL SERVICES

Tree in the Mist, by Dawn Waters Baker. A tree can be a symbol of strength, such as the strength gained in support groups in which people grow. The father with the child alludes to the span of life in which the disabilities of children may place added responsibilities on parents. This tree, larger than life and about to be drenched by the oncoming rain, symbolizes how believers can draw strength from above in the body of Christ. The small birds and small people suggest the fragility of life amid storms of the unknown.

Amy J. Wilson, MD, is the chief of physical medicine and rehabilitation for the Baylor Health Care System and medical director for Baylor Institute for Rehabilitation. She graduated from medical school at the University of Texas, Houston. As an inpatient physician, Dr. Wilson has a primary interest in amputee care.

18

Dealing with Disabilities in Adults

Amy J. Wilson

Understanding the Concept of Disability

According to the United States census in 2000, nearly one in five individuals in the United States lives with a disability. The Americans with Disabilities Act (ADA) of 1990, signed into law by George H. W. Bush, is the original resource document offering clarification on questions of disability. The ADA was an expansion of the first attempts to prevent discrimination that were originally written in the 1970s. This act was meant to protect those with disabilities, to eliminate discrimination, and to provide consistent standards when questions about persons with disabilities arise.

The ADA states, "The term 'disability' means, with respect to an individual:

- a physical or mental impairment that substantially limits one or more of the major life activities of such individual;
- a record of such an impairment; or
- being regarded as having such an impairment."

The major life activities as defined in the 1990 act include but are not limited to caring for oneself, performing manual tasks, seeing, hearing, eating, sleeping, walking, standing, lifting, bending, speaking, breathing, learning, reading, concentrating, thinking, communicating, and working. More recently in the updated ADA Amendments Act signed in 2008 by George W. Bush, the list was expanded to include major bodily functions, including but not limited to functions of the immune system, normal cell growth, and conditions related to digestive, bowel, bladder, neurological, brain, respiratory, endocrine, and reproductive systems. Also episodic or transitory conditions or conditions in remission are included if they would substantially limit a major life activity. The list of major life activities is certainly not exhaustive and continues to be interpreted by the law, including activities such as driving, sexual activity, and using a computer.

The word *impairment* also must be understood in relation to disability. Impairment is considered the condition itself or the deviation from "normal." *Disability*, then, is the functional consequence of the impairment. *Handicap* is the inability to accomplish a task that most people are able to accomplish. As an example, if a person has had a stroke and is paralyzed on one side, his or her impairment is the paralysis, the disability is the inability to walk, and the handicap is the inability to ascend the steps at the old office building at which he or she works.

Understanding the Impact of the Aging Population

With an aging population, an increasing number of adults are experiencing disabilities. Innovations in medicine over the past one hundred years, particularly the past twenty or thirty years, have enabled persons with illnesses and injuries to survive much longer than ever before. For example, heart transplants and hip or knee replacement surgeries were just being pioneered in the late 1960s, but are commonplace now. Also, one's ability to accommodate for the disabilities arising from impairments is improving. In view of the aging population, current survival rates, and life expectancy, we must be prepared to support even more persons with disabilities in our communities.

In 1900 only 4 percent of the population lived beyond age sixty-five, which was approximately three million people. In the 2000 US census, 12.4 percent of the population were older than sixty-five years old, amounting to approximately thirty-five million people. Currently, it is estimated that forty million people are over sixty-five years old. By 2050, nearly ninety million people will be older than sixty-five.

According to the US Census Bureau, life expectancy for a baby born in 2010 is just over seventy-eight years, an overall gain of almost eight years compared to a baby born in 1970. A person born in the United States who is sixty-five years old today can on average expect to live another eighteen years. People born in the United States who are eighty-five years old today can on average expect to live another six or seven years. Surprisingly, the United States does not rank at the top with life-expectancy rates. For example, a baby born in China in 2010 has a life expectancy of eighty-four years, a full six years more than the US baby, according to the *CIA World Factbook 2007*. The United States currently ranks fiftieth in the world for overall life expectancy.

Who Cares for Adults with Disabilities?

The community support system to assist in caring for adults with disabilities is quite large and includes a variety of health-care professionals, social agencies, friends, families, and of course the church. Of special mention is the rehabilitation community, including the physicians, therapists, and other professionals who assist in their care. A medical specialty exists specifically to address those patients with disabilities.

Physiatry, or physical medicine and rehabilitation (PM&R), is the medical specialty dedicated to caring for patients with disabilities. The concept of this field was first being considered between World War I and World War II, a time when trauma associated with war had escalated because of weaponry advancements, and survival of such injuries improved because of modest improvements in medical care. For the first time in history larger numbers of patients not only were surviving multiple trauma, but also were living out their lives with the resultant disabilities. Physiatry became a specialty in 1947.

Physiatry as a whole is focused more on the management of the impairment or subsequent disability than on the disease or injury itself. The general philosophy of the specialty is to restore maximum function and quality of life lost through illness, injury, or other disabling conditions. The physiatrist's emphasis is on the optimization of function through a combined use of medications, modalities, therapeutic exercise, movement, adaptive equipment (e.g., a walker), assistive devices (e.g., a reacher), braces, artificial limbs, restorative surgeries, and various research approaches. A physiatrist typically uses a holistic approach with the patient, developing a comprehensive program for putting the pieces of a person's life back together medically, socially, emotionally, vocationally, and spiritually.

The physiatrist typically relies on other health-care professionals and community individuals to assist with helping the patient achieve his or her maximum potential. For example a hospitalized stroke patient with paralysis and difficulty speaking might need the services of a rehabilitation nurse, social worker, insurance case manager, physical therapist, occupational therapist, speech-language pathologist, hospital chaplain, and community pastor, as well as church members and other lay persons and professionals, to assist in a team effort on the rehabilitation journey. The physiatrist leads and coordinates this comprehensive rehabilitation effort.

Four Common Conditions Leading to Disabilities in Adults
The list of medical conditions, diseases, or injuries causing impairments and leading to disabilities in adults is too exhaustive to discuss in an introductory book. For this reason four conditions are selected for this discussion because of the frequency with which they are seen in the community and the residual deficits they can cause. If the basic concepts of the conditions and the resultant disabilities are understood by the reader, he then is better able to understand the overall impact to the patient when he suffers other conditions that cause the same disabilities. For example, although stroke and multiple sclerosis are very different diseases from an etiologic standpoint, they can cause identical disabilities (i.e., inability to walk and the need to use a wheelchair for mobility).

Stroke
A stroke is any event that stops or limits blood flow to the brain. Brain-cell death begins within minutes of the event, so getting to a hospital emergency department as quickly as possible offers the best chance of preserving healthy brain tissue and thus limiting the impact of a stroke. Early medical intervention in certain types of strokes is a time-restricted process, so in these cases intervention must occur within the first three hours after onset. Sadly, an estimated 5 percent or fewer of stroke victims get to the emergency department on time to qualify for the earliest intervention.

Strokes are of two types. In an ischemic stroke, blood supply to the brain tissue is blocked. In a hemorrhagic stroke, direct bleeding occurs in brain tissue. Both types of stroke damage healthy brain tissue and can cause identical deficits. An ischemic stroke is by far the more common type. A hemorrhagic stroke has a better ultimate prognosis, but is also more dangerous in the early stages, with up to 30 percent of patients dying.

Strokes can occur in four parts of the brain—the left hemisphere, the right hemisphere, the cerebellum, and the brain stem. The location of the event helps determine roughly the resultant neurologic impairment. A left-hemispheric stroke results in right-sided weakness, aphasia (trouble with expression or comprehension of language), apraxia (trouble with motor planning), memory difficulty, emotional disturbance, dysphagia (trouble with swallowing), dysarthria (slurred speech), visual trouble, and incontinence.

A right hemispheric stroke results in left-sided weakness, trouble with cognition or reasoning, emotional disturbance, dysphagia, dysarthria, visual trouble, neglect of the left side, and incontinence.

A cerebellar stroke leads to loss of balance, ataxia (loss of coordination), incoordination, weakness in arms and/or legs, headache, nausea, vomiting, vertigo, extreme dizziness, dysarthria.

A brain-stem stroke causes breathing trouble, dysphagia, dysarthria, weakness of all four extremities, and trouble with cranial nerves (the nerves that control much of the face muscles, mouth, and eyes).

Stroke is the third leading cause of death in the United States, according to the American Heart Association. The World Health Organization recognizes stroke as the second leading cause of death in the world. The lifetime risk for stroke for any individual is one in six. Of all stroke patients, between 20 and 30 percent of them die within a few weeks. After five years 50 percent of stroke patients are still alive. Of the survivors, 10 percent recover completely, 25 percent recover with minor disabilities, 40 percent recover with moderate to severe disabilities needing help from another person, and 10 percent need long-term care of some type.

Many patients who have suffered a stroke require rehabilitation, but this depends on the severity of the stroke. Some may need inpatient rehabilitation, others outpatient; still others may need home-health, vocational, or a variety of other methods of rehabilitation to address their deficits. By far the greatest recovery for a stroke patient occurs within the first few weeks or months after a stroke, but some patients make slow changes a year or more after the stroke has occurred.

Spinal-Cord Injury

A spinal-cord injury (SCI) is an insult to the spinal cord, whether traumatic or otherwise, that results in neurologic weakness or paralysis (essentially the loss of motion and sensation to the limbs). In the United States alone, nearly twelve thousand cases are diagnosed each year, according to the National Spinal Cord Injury Statistical Center. Currently at least a quarter million people are living in the United States with SCI. Males suffer this injury most often, approximately 80 percent of the time. The average age of onset is between thirty-five and forty years old. A growing segment of the population living with SCI is people over sixty who have sustained a fall; this now amounts to 10 percent of all cases. The causes in order of frequency are motor vehicle accident, falls, violence, and sporting activities. In the United States these injuries happen most frequently to Caucasians, followed by African Americans, Hispanics, and Asians.

Once past the acute phase of SCI, 80 percent of people with this condition are able to live in a community setting, for example, a private residence, and not in an institution like a nursing home. People living with SCI are more susceptible to divorce and have an overall lower probability of marriage after their injury. Half of the people who have sustained SCI are employed at the time of injury, but only 10 percent of these people remain employed after the first year following the injury. People living with SCI are more apt to gain employment after SCI if they are already educated, have increased community mobility, have increased functional independence, have a low incidence of medical complications, are Caucasian, and were working before the injury.

Caregivers of patients with SCI need to remember that medical technology has allowed patients with this diagnosis to live much longer than before. Fifty years ago the most common cause of death was kidney failure. However, medical care is more adept at dealing with kidney function, so that now the most common cause of death is related to pneumonia or respiratory failure. These patients are now living long enough to succumb to conditions similar to the noninjured population, such as cancer and cardiovascular disease. The life expectancy of a person with SCI has improved, no matter what the level of injury, but it is not yet the same as for noninjured persons. A person with SCI may have a life expectancy anywhere between ten to thirty years less than a noninjured person. Depending on the person's age and the spinal level at which one is injured, the cost associated with lifetime care can run into the millions of dollars.

The spinal column can be divided into four segments from top to bottom: cervical spine, thoracic spine, lumbar spine, and sacrum/coccyx. The spinal cord travels down from the brain to the middle of the lumbar spine to carry the nerve impulses to the rest of the body. The spinal cord is protectively encased by the cervical, thoracic, and lumbar spine. An injury of the spinal cord disrupts the nerve signal to the rest of the body. The main point to understand is that the higher the level of injury in the spinal column and subsequently the spinal cord, the more difficult and severe is the patient's functional loss.

A spinal-cord injury in the cervical spine, or neck, is the most devastating of the spinal-cord injuries. These injuries are the ones in which the person is said to be "paralyzed from the neck down." The predictable functional outcomes of persons with cervical injury depends on the specific level.

- Very-high-cervical level: The patient needs breathing assistance full- or part-time (i.e., by a ventilator), has little or no movement in arms or legs, needs someone to feed him, needs help with *all* activities of daily living, cannot walk, uses a power chair, and needs full assistance with bowel and bladder management. This injury requires full-time caregiving.
- High-cervical level: The injured person has a small amount of movement of the arms but none of the legs, may be able to feed himself,

can help put on his shirt, may be able to push a wheelchair a very short distance but probably still needs a power chair, can perform some oral hygiene, and needs assistance with bowel and bladder management, transfers, and lower body dressing. He still needs attendant care.

- Mid-cervical level: The patient has improved movement of the arms; is increasingly independent with dressing, bowel and bladder management, and self-care; can help transfer himself; is more independent in a manual wheelchair; and has more hope of independent living with some attendant care.
- Low-cervical level: The person has movement in most parts of the arms, including hands, and is much less dependent on others; many can live without attendant help.

Injuries that occur in the thoracic or lumbar spine are the ones characterized as "paralyzed from the waist down." Persons with this injury should have normal arm and hand function, but most do not have functional leg movement. Injuries in the thoracic level present challenges with holding oneself up by means of trunk muscles in sitting positions. However, most patients with this level of injury have the ability to achieve more independence than patients with cervical injury, and many achieve complete independence in all areas at a wheelchair level.

As a general rule the older a person is when he or she suffers SCI, the poorer the functional outcome is for a number of reasons. And as patients live longer with SCI, they may feel more financial stress and experience more medical issues. However, as a person with SCI ages, he still reports overall satisfaction with his life when questioned directly about it.

Traumatic Brain Injury (TBI)

The brain is like gelatin floating in a pool of water. Considering this, one can imagine that it is easily injured. Acquired brain injury is trauma of any kind that causes damage to the brain. It can result when the head hits an object of any type or when an object pierces the skull and enters the brain (i.e., penetrating). Something as simple as a fall from a standing height is sufficient to cause a brain injury of severe proportions.

The Centers for Disease Control note that in the United States alone, 1.7 million persons sustain a traumatic brain injury each year. Of these, at least fifty thousand die and a quarter million are hospitalized. Approximately one million of these injuries may never get any medical care for their injuries.

The leading causes of TBI are falls, motor vehicle accidents, and assaults. Alcohol seems to be involved as a very important factor in at least 50 percent of the cases. Males are almost twice as likely to sustain a TBI as are females.

Nonhelmeted motorcycle and bicycle riders are more likely to die of their brain injuries than are helmeted riders. Helmet use has been shown to reduce the degree of brain injuries significantly.

A mild TBI is often called a concussion. In such a case, brain imaging, such as a computed topography (CT) scan, or a magnetic resonance imaging (MRI) may look normal. However, the person may have suffered loss of consciousness, loss of memory immediately before or after the injury, alteration of his mental state at the time of the accident, or focal neurological deficits. He may have trouble afterward with headaches, dizziness, or concentration. A moderate-to-severe TBI is often associated with an unconscious state at the time of the injury and may involve coma. More often, the brain damage is easily seen on a CT scan or especially an MRI in more severe cases. These more severe injuries often have a wide range of neurologic presentations.

The changes in a person who has suffered a TBI can be many, but for the purposes of this discussion the changes are divided into three categories. *Cognitive changes* (changes in thinking) include shortened attention span, memory problems, problem-solving difficulties, poor judgment, partial or complete loss of reading and writing skills, language problems including communication deficits and loss of vocabulary, inability to understand abstract concepts, and difficulty learning new things.

Physical changes that can follow brain injury include weakness, muscle coordination problems, full or partial paralysis, changes in sexual functioning, changes in one's senses (hearing, sight, touch, etc.), seizures (also called traumatic epilepsy), sleep problems, speech difficulties, and headaches.

Personality and behavioral changes may be subtle or severe and may include difficulty with social skills, disinhibition, inability to empathize with others, tendency to be more self-centered, inability to control one's emotions, increases in irritability and frustration, inappropriate and/or aggressive behavior, extreme mood swings, and depression (common with TBI).

The difficulty with persons with TBI is that they often appear to be "normal," but they have residual emotional, behavioral, or psychiatric problems up to 90 percent of the time. This can occur with people who have suffered any brain injury, whether mild, moderate, or severe, and these residual problems can last many years after the initial injury. Such problems present challenges in all areas of life and are primary reasons for marital discord, difficulties with social relationships, family strife, and problems at school or the workplace. Rehabilitation professionals can help guide families and clergy through these problems, but community resources are seriously lacking.

Dementia

Dementia is a "loss of the mind," a group of symptoms but not a disease itself. Dementia is a loss of mental function in more than one area, such as memory and language. Alzheimer's dementia accounts for 50 percent of the cases, but there are many other types such as stroke/atherosclerosis/vascular disease (about 30 percent), alcohol/substance abuse, hormone imbalance, vitamin deficiency, other medical conditions (e.g., kidney failure), hydrocephalus, brain tumor, Parkinson's disease, Pick's disease, Lewy-body disease, and Huntington's disease.

Only 10 percent or less of patients with dementia symptoms have a reversible cause, one that can be helped with treatment.

The characteristics of dementia include two or more of the following: memory loss, decreased attention, loss of motor skills, difficulty performing familiar tasks, problems with language, disorientation to time and place, poor judgment or change in judgment, misplacing things, trouble keeping track of things, changes in mood/behavior/personality, and loss of initiation.

The overall lifetime risk of developing Alzheimer's disease is one in six for women and one in ten for men, according to the Alzheimer's Association and its 2010 Alzheimer's Disease Facts and Figures. For people who reach age fifty-five and beyond, the remaining lifetime risk for developing Alzheimer's disease is 17 percent for women and 9 percent for men, and for any dementia it is 21 percent for women and 14 percent for men. For the millions of baby boomers born between 1946 and 1964, approximately ten to fourteen million men and women may develop some type of dementia. Once a person is diagnosed with dementia, the overall life expectancy is about four and a half years for women and about four years for men. If the onset of dementia is before age seventy, the person may live ten years or more.

Caring for Someone with Disabilities

The community support system that assists families in caring for disabled family members needs to be acutely aware of the caregiver. The caregiver is typically addressing key losses of the patient and managing behaviors and personal care issues. However, the caregiver frequently gets lost in the process. Caregivers are often unaware of their own stress and depression, but many of them are depressed 50 percent of the time. Not only is the day-to-day caregiving difficult and challenging, but the financial impact on caring for the disabled can also be overwhelming.

Patricia Evans, MD, FAAN, FAAP, serves at the University of Texas Southwestern Medical Center and is an associate professor of pediatrics and neurology, medical director of the Traumatic Brain Injury Clinic, medical director of the Attention and Learning Disorders Clinic, medical director of the Autism Spectrum Disorders Clinic, medical director of the Cognitive Delay Disorders Clinic, and director of Neurodevelopmental Disabilities Residency. Dr. Evans received her MD degree from Texas Tech University and is a PhD candidate in Research Psychology at Walden University.

19

Children with Disabilities

Patricia Evans

Lana and Charlotte

Lana was a stunningly beautiful child. Soft golden rings of hair framed her perfectly symmetrical face and large brown eyes. She loved detail. And she loved books. But other children really confused her, and because of this she preferred isolation to the overwhelming demands and sounds of even a few other children. She did not know that it was the least bit unusual to feel this way, although it worried her mother, Charlotte. Subsequently Lana's beautiful face and sweet personality belied her difficulties socially—difficulties that made other children and, later, teens and adults a confusing set of variables that took all her energies to decipher.

Unfortunately, her hometown prized just the sorts of social skills she lacked. The small West Texas city thrived on sock-hops, rock and roll, cowboys, and football. So, with no real concern on Lana's part one bright Saturday morning in 1952, she was completely absorbed in the process of a lovely, fat, shiny beetle slowly wobbling its careful way across the wooden parsonage floor.

Above the heads of both untroubled child and beetle, however, a particularly cruel joke was being played on her. Though the joke was instigated by a couple of other eight-year-old girls, the pastor's wife and friends struggled to suppress near-hysterical laughter during an entire sleepover at the parsonage, while finding ways to help all ten second-grade girls avoid Lana for the entire thirty-six hours. The children were completely confused by Lana. The adults had no excuse.

Some weeks earlier Lana's mother was surprised and delighted to hear announced in church what sounded like a perfect social opportunity for her shy and slightly odd child: an overnight at the parsonage with cookies and stories and play, just for the second-grade girls. In due course Lana, with pressed clothes and perfect hair, had been dropped off with her spotlessly made overnight bag, items lovingly and carefully packed. As the Friday evening rolled into Saturday morning, Lana was given activities to do but never once even saw another child, much less was she aware of the energy being used to perpetrate such a hoax. In such a large and lovely old parsonage, full of nooks and crannies, it was especially easy to hide giggling little girls, particularly with the aid of Christian women who were unable or unwilling to see the meanness of it all. It became a game for all but Lana.

Late Saturday morning Lana was waiting for her mother to be the first mother to come and pick up her child. What became one of the most searingly hurtful memories of this young girl's life was no more than a passing amusement to the rest. Presumably good Christian grown-ups had taught ten little girls how to practice rejection in the name of Christ. And at least a year later she finally understood that she would never be truly accepted in her family church, the one place that should have been a truly safe haven.

What happened might never have been known, as cleverly carried out as it was. However, as her mother, Charlotte, waved good-bye to the pastor's wife and friends, and helped Lana into the car, she asked the lovely little girl with the large questioning eyes if she had had a good time. In her innocence and incomprehension Lana said, "Yes, but where were all the children?" Some days later, in giggles and unapologetic language, the pastor's wife, an otherwise mature and sensible woman in her forties, finally admitted the prank to Lana's mother.

It is difficult even now, decades later, for Charlotte, now in her nineties, to discuss this incident with equanimity. Forgiveness certainly came from both Charlotte and Lana without the other parties ever requesting it or even realizing it was needed. Nevertheless, both mother and daughter paid a high price for the church's blessing of such casual and practiced rejection. Charlotte, at age thirty-six, recently widowed and raising five young children alone, knew then and always that acceptance—even in one's home church—for herself and all her children was not necessarily going to happen. Lana would take many more years to realize not only that she was significantly different, but that she was different in an invisible way—no wheelchair, no speech defect, no obvious defect would ever be seen. And so this seemed to make it socially acceptable for church leaders, teachers, and peers to practice rejection based on her social awkwardness. Such attitudes led Lana on an amazing, often tortuous, sometimes dangerous, and certainly lonely path to seek answers to many questions.

When asked many years later why she became so deeply attracted to the study of Hebrew and Jewish writings, she spoke very clearly. She said she felt that she had been sent on her own Diaspora by the Christian church itself.

We will return to Charlotte and Lana at the end of this chapter. There were many heroes along the way for both women, of many religious traditions and different faiths. And they themselves were their own best advocates. Nevertheless, Charlotte and Lana's experiences illustrate that it matters profoundly, now and always, that churches must take the lead in the community in caring for all people, regardless of differences, whether visible or invisible; regardless of severity, whether mild, moderate, or severe; regardless of an individual church's budget or personnel resources. Simple kindness is always free.

Responding to Differences, Delays, and Disorders

How can ministers and laity serve all of our children and adolescents and their families? How can we recognize common differences? What additional resources are available?

Cognitive Delays

The terms *intellectual disability* or *cognitive disability* are gradually replacing the older term *mental retardation*, although the latter is still frequently used in many settings. The diagnosis of intellectual disability is made when a child has some degree of cognitive delay, with impaired adaptive behavior, occurring before age eighteen. Intellectual delay can be mild or severe and may be present in either subtle or clearly apparent ways.

Individuals with intellectual delay in the absence of autism or other emotional difficulties typically are socially engaging, but may struggle with comprehending complex stories, jokes, or other pieces of conversation that are not necessarily information driven and concrete. Care must be taken to include these individuals in activities and fun without being overly concerned with trying to explain jokes or otherwise highlighting differences in a public or overt manner.

Additionally, some individuals with intellectual delay do not always demonstrate adequate boundaries, either socially or physically, but may not be aware that they are speaking over others, touching too much, or otherwise being socially intrusive. Speaking clearly, kindly, and if possible privately to the child's parents to seek the best ways to redirect him or her is important. Then once a strategy is devised, it should be implemented kindly and quietly.

Developmental Delays

In early childhood it is sometimes unclear whether a child who is delayed in speech, play, or motor skills will eventually become involved with other children. However, a diagnosis of developmental delay implies just that; the delay suggests that with inclusion, therapy, and time a child's delays may be remedied.

Children with delay may present any number of challenges, including play that is delayed for age, not being able to keep up physically with other children of the same age, or not being able to speak or comprehend spoken language as well as other children. The capacity to understand the child's special needs should again be dictated by the parents. Ideally a parent will volunteer such concerns; however, this is not always the case, especially if the parent is not aware of the difficulties. When children are not able to keep up with other activities of the Sunday school classroom, a sensitive teacher ideally will avoid removing the child from the other children, but will modify the tasks at hand. For instance, if a child is not able to handle crayons well enough to color, it may be sufficient for the child to simply sit with the teacher and turn pages of a book and point to interesting pictures. The key again is being alert for children who are too embarrassed or shy to acknowledge their inability to do the same tasks as other children, and having backup plans for them.

Motor Delays

Much has been written about the condition that was originally coined Little's disease in the nineteenth century, now more commonly referred to as cerebral palsy (CP). CP is a disorder of movement and posture that results from an insult to or anomaly of the immature central nervous system happening between the age of conception to the first few months of life outside the womb. While CP typically presents increased stiffness most commonly involving the lower extremities, it may involve only one, two, or three limbs, or all four. Also, CP may have a wide and diverse set of related concerns, including epilepsy, intellectual delay, and emotional problems.

While all children with CP have at least some use of their muscles, the CP may be so minimal as to be virtually undetectable at a glance. Such a child may seem unaffected until asked to run, climb, or otherwise keep up with other active children. The child himself may not be aware of the difference. Visiting with parents about any concerns the pastor or educator may have about a child's needs must come before discussing them with the child.

Muscular Dystrophies

Though far more rare than cerebral palsy, muscular dystrophy in children presents special concerns that a pastor and church staff would want to know. While some forms of muscular dystrophy can be very severe and even fatal, many other forms are not. These children are particularly self-conscious and are often eager to be included in as many activities as possible, since intellectual impairment is rarely a concern. Being as independent as possible, especially for older children and teens, is particularly important. A creative and sensitive educator or pastor will promote inclusion while preserving a child's independence as much as possible, and thus will greatly enhance a child's sense of belonging.

Wheelchairs can be scary to other children; having the parent or, with the parent's permission, even the child himself talk to the other children about what the wheelchair does can go a long way toward reducing the strangeness of it.

Motor Coordination Delay

Having one of the less visible syndromes, the "clumsy" child may struggle with not only hand-eye coordination but also body-in-space issues. The problem may not be obvious until he or she attempts fine motor tasks. For instance a teacher whose lesson plan includes cutting out pictures may not realize that the bright, beautiful little boy who is so athletic cannot keep up because of subtle hand-coordination issues. Also, a child may suddenly seem oppositional or very shy and may need the creative involvement of other "cool" things to do.

Autism Spectrum Disorders

Because autism is in epidemic proportions in this country, pastoral-care teams can expect to see a child with an autism diagnosis for every ninety-two children that enter their front door. The parents themselves may sense that it is nothing more than idiosyncratic behavior. But educators and pastors alike must be aware of those individuals who seem exceptionally shy, socially awkward, or able to talk about only one or two rather unusual topics at great lengths.

The spectrum of autistic disorders is broad enough to range from very verbal and highly intelligent children and teens, to nonverbal, exceptionally anxious individuals who simply cannot tolerate being with other people except family members. Regardless of the level of functioning, all but the most impaired will be fully aware of whether an environment is accepting or hostile to him or her. In the case of a highly functioning individual who needs help with social skills, simply being welcomed into a group committed to inclusivity is one of the best approaches. For individuals who need more space, speaking to family members about what is best tolerated will be essential. This may mean simply that a child is allowed to be in the classroom with other children, or to listen to earphones, or to play preferred games or videos until he or she exhibits enough confidence to participate more. In such cases, inclusivity may need to be approached as an option until the individual is able to tolerate more social interaction.

Emotional Disorders

Children and teens are experiencing increasing degrees of mood and emotional disorders. The increase is thought to come from many factors. But if a church cannot "fix" all the ills a child may have, the first and most important step is to provide a safe haven for a child who is in emotional distress. Any child or teen who comes to a pastoral team in acute need, particularly in emotional crisis, needs immediate assistance with mental-health counselors or facilities.

Those children who are not acutely in crisis may still struggle with the daily burden of depression, bipolar disorder, or anxiety-based problems. The open and inclusive atmosphere of the church may be the single most important area of an individual's life. Teachers and pastors who are aware and accommodating can make enormous differences in the lives of such children and teens. Many adolescents have wide mood swings as a normal part of their development; however, when the swings are disruptive to a class or to themselves, it is important to visit with the teen and the family privately, and ideally with more than one staff person.

Children who have rage events may also be very disruptive to a class. Finding ways to have families instruct the pastoral-care team on what is most helpful at home is critically important. Typically removing a child from overstimulation can be helpful. Again, as always, safety comes first. Anytime a child puts himself or herself at risk, pastoral-team intervention with the family may be necessary.

The onset of unusual movements, such as jerking or sudden motions, seizures, or sudden change in the child's orientation, may represent a change in the disorder or a possible side effect of medication. The emergence of these behaviors must be clarified with parents, with written instructions from the caring physician for the church staff on how to proceed for everyone's safety. Having cell phone numbers for the parents for immediate contact will also be necessary.

If written releases are not provided, then a pastoral-team approach may be needed as an intervention with the family to see how best to serve but at the same time provide "best practices" so that everyone is safe.

Safety, Privacy, and Restraint

Many incidents needlessly put a staff person, a parent, or the child in harm's way. The best intention does not necessarily provide the best measures for a child. If a low-functioning teen or child is out of control, the pastor and his team must be in agreement with the family on how best to respond to the teen's or child's needs. Such discussions should happen before a child is enrolled in a program at the church. Ideally such understandings are kept in a written format that is protected for privacy.

Although churches have typically enjoyed privilege in the context of private information, if written records are to be kept, the pastor must be aware of whatever church policies exist for privacy of records. Ideally any such written releases or specific information should be stored in a locked system, where only a few individuals have access to the data. Though beyond the scope of this chapter, being aware of what legal and ethical obligations a church staff has regarding record management is critical to the care of children with special needs.

Attempts to restrain a visibly or invisibly disabled child or teen through corporal punishment can escalate adverse behaviors. If a child cannot be adequately and safely restrained, he or she must be managed in a safer environment. To practice inclusivity may mean removing a dangerous situation from other children and staff, and finding the best and safest place for the child or teen in question. If a church is not equipped to handle aggressive children or teens, then pastoral counseling may still be needed if available.

Communication, Family Involvement, and General Safeguards

Jesus instructed his disciples, "Let the little children come to me," not ever worrying that some of those little ones might have visible or invisible disabilities that would exclude them from the rest of society. Likewise, Christians are called to serve all "children," regardless of how old in years they may be.

Communication is essential but can be a challenge as we approach a special-needs child. If communication is impaired cognitively, motorically, or emotionally, a variety of strategies may be needed:

- When communication is nonverbal, find ways to show care, using nonlinguistic means.
- When communication is aggressive, find ways to lovingly but safely place boundaries.
- When communication is limited to a few basic concepts, love is always understood by all of God's children, regardless of age.

Everyone working with children must keep the individual's privacy, dignity, and safety as priorities. Knowing how the family works with the individual will be critical to the success of the pastoral team. Ideally more than one staffer initially meets with a family to discuss the best ways to implement care for the individual, both during services and in classroom instruction. The following are some final points to bear in mind:

- *Never* attempt to help either learning, emotionally, or physically different individuals without adequate safeguards in place for yourself, your staff, your church, and most importantly, the individual.
- Involvement of the family is critical to the success of inclusive pastoral care. With that in mind, have the family communicate to you as pastor or teacher what is needed and what has worked best.
- Ideally an atmosphere of inclusivity will encourage the most reticent and anxious of families to privately volunteer their concerns. However, a family member or the child should not be asked about it in front of others, and only in private if the family seems to indicate a willingness to share.
- When a family is not forthcoming about specifics, but a child's and/ or staff's welfare is of concern, finding ways to ask a family how they best handle such situations at home will be important.
- If a child's safety is of concern, either at home or in a church setting, clear boundaries must be established with the family, and ideally this should be done by a pastoral team.

The Rest of Lana and Charlotte's Story

Eventually Lana was licensed to drive. A dedicated believer in Christ, she became fluent in Hebrew and several other languages. She finished her formal training and earned master's degrees in library science as well as theology. She married a wonderful Christian man, a seminary librarian. When she discovered a lump in her breast in the mid-1980s, she began translating the Pentateuch by hand—the Lana Translation she called it. To her family's great grief, in April 1988 she passed on to the God who knew her, loved her, and had so wondrously knit her from the beginning.[1]

At the time of her death, her desk was covered with various snippets of poetry, Scripture, and prose, scattered about in not less than seventeen languages, including Norwegian, Aramaic, Latin, and German. In her forty-two years on this earth, she traveled the world, usually alone, to Israel, Morocco, Spain, Egypt, Mexico, and Europe. She profoundly influenced this writer, her sister, to "never stop asking questions," making clear that the highest faith was trusting that God enjoyed the dialogue. Her funeral was attended by what resembled something from a central casting of an epic movie: Orthodox rabbis, Franciscan monks, stately Episcopal priests, and Methodists from her hometown, whom she had loved and embraced throughout her adult life. Her mother, very healthy and chatty in her tenth decade of life, and the rest of her family all miss her daily. We all remain grateful for the gift of Lana, the young woman who never stopped asking why, and found great peace in the process.

May God grant that we all love and treasure our Lanas of the world.

Resources[2]

Autism Spectrum Disorders

Akins, Karla. *How Churches Can Support Families Living with the Autism Spectrum/ Pervasive Development Disorders or Other Disabilities.*

Bass, Simon. *Special Children, Special Needs: Integrating Children with Disabilities and Special Needs into Your Church.*

Newman, Barbara J. *Autism and Your Church: Nurturing the Spiritual Growth of People with Autism Spectrum Disorders.*

---

[1] Although a formal diagnosis was never determined, Lana most likely suffered from Asperger's syndrome. She had a mixture of absence seizures ("petit mal") and a diagnosis somewhere along the autistic spectrum.

[2] A more comprehensive list of resources dealing with the various disorders discussed in this chapter is available from the author.

Websites

Autism Society. One of the oldest organizations in the country, it has a wealth of free information for support groups, ongoing research, and how to participate in fund-raising. http://www.autism-society.org.

Autism Speaks. Their goal is "to change the future for all who struggle with autism spectrum disorders." http://www.autismspeaks.org.

Finding God in Autism. Aims to give parents of children with special needs strength, inspiration, and encouragement, and to teach them how to pray effectively. http://www.findinggodinautism.com.

National Autistic Society (UK). "Religion: Going to a Place of Worship." Strategies to use when taking children with autism spectrum disorder to a place of worship. http://www.autism.org.uk.

Cerebral Palsy

4MyChild. An excellent source for both national and state-by-state listings of resources. http://www.cerebralpalsy.org/cerebral-palsy-assistance.

United Cerebral Palsy. One of the oldest organizations in the country and supported by national and regional funding. http://www.ucp.org.

Muscular Dystrophies

Muscular Dystrophy Association. Instrumental in funding research and community support for a wide range of muscle diseases, including muscular dystrophy, but many other disorders as well. http://www.mda.org.

Intellectual Disabilities

American Association for Mental Retardation. One of the most comprehensive websites for persons with intellectual disabilities, they provide the following exhaustive list of resources for not just individuals with intellectual disabilities, but also many of the associated conditions. Many of those are provided here, but the reader is encouraged to go to the parent website for updated lists. http://www.aamr.org.

Epilepsy Foundation. Dedicated to the welfare of people with epilepsy. www.epilepsy foundation.org.

National Disabilities Rights Network. An association that represents federally mandated programs that protect the rights of persons with disabilities. http://www.napas.org.

National Down Syndrome Society. National advocate for the value, acceptance, and inclusion of people with Down syndrome. http://www.ndss.org.

National Mental Health Association. Addresses all aspects of mental health and mental illness. http://www.nmha.org.

US Department of Health and Human Services. Provides a centralized source for research, evaluation, and policy information concerning managed care and people with disabilities. http://www.hhs.gov.

Emotional Disabilities

American Academy of Child and Adolescent Psychiatry. Has not only excellent written materials, but also lists of services, often by state and region. http://www.aacap.org.

National Institute of Mental Health. Provides excellent resources for church staffs and families alike for a wide variety of emotional disorders in children. http://www .nimh.nih.gov/index.shtml.

Richard L. Voet (MD, University of Cincinnati
College of Medicine; MA, Dallas Theological
Seminary; MA, Trinity Graduate School) is chairman
of the pathology department and chairman of the
bioethics committee at Texas Health Presbyterian
Hospital Dallas. He is also an associate clinical
professor at the University of Texas Southwestern
Medical School and an adjunct professor in pastoral
ministries at Dallas Seminary, where he teaches
bioethics. Dr. Voet is a member of the ethics
committee of the Christian Medical Association.

20

BIOETHICS AND SUFFERING

Richard L. Voet

Bioethics is becoming increasingly important as medicine becomes more complex. The availability of advanced technology such as hemodialysis, respirators, cardiopulmonary resuscitation (CPR), intensive care units (ICU), and organ transplantation introduces decision-making dilemmas that previously did not exist in the field of medical ethics. Bioethics examines ethical issues relating to biomedical technology, medical research, and the provision of health care from both individual and social perspectives.

Since history has demonstrated that these decisions have the potential to marginalize the most vulnerable members of society, Christians need to evaluate how bioethical decisions are made. This chapter explores historical aspects in the development of bioethics and important legal decisions that have shaped the application of ethical decision making in medicine. A crucial aspect of Christian ministry involves helping those who are suffering and disabled. Requests for prayer often center on needs for those who are sick.

Understanding the current environment of medicine and recent trends in medical ethics will help facilitate complex and difficult decisions when the need arises. Christians should be known as thoughtful and reliable sources of information and advice for bioethical issues. All who are involved in the care of patients need a Christian view of life, suffering, and death. Christianity has always been known for its ministry to the sick. The eminent Jewish medical historian H. E. Sigerist made the following observation:

The most important and decisive development in the special status assigned to the sick was introduced by Christianity. This new teaching, in contrast to the other religions for the healthy and just man, appealed to the sick, to the weak and to the crippled. It spoke of spiritual healing, but it also spoke of bodily healing.[1]

For over two thousand years the medical profession used the Hippocratic Oath as the basis for medical ethics. It viewed the doctor-patient relationship as a covenant with prohibitions against abortion and assisted suicide. Margaret Mead, well-known cultural anthropologist, made the following statement about the Hippocratic Oath:

> For the first time in our tradition there was a complete separation between killing and curing. . . . One profession . . . dedicated completely to life under all circumstances, regardless of rank, age, or intellect—the life of a slave, the life of the Emperor, the life of a foreign man, the life of a defective child. . . . But society is always attempting to make the physician into a killer—to kill the defective child at birth, to leave the sleeping pills beside the bed of the cancer patient.[2]

Ethical Theory

During the Enlightenment, secular philosophy began to marginalize religion, and various ethical theories developed. Ethical theory is broadly divided into normative and descriptive systems.[3] Normative ethical theories describe how people should determine what is right and wrong. Descriptive ethical theories describe what different populations actually believe to be right and wrong.

Normative ethical theories are divided into three general areas. First, if the person making the decision is considered the primary factor in the decision process, the system is referred to as *virtue ethics*. Second, if the action of the decision is the primary focus, it is referred to as *deontological ethics* (*deon* referring to a duty, rule, principle, or law). Third, if the outcome of the decision is considered the primary factor (where the end justifies the means), it is referred to as *teleological ethics* (*telos* referring to an end or goal). The most common teleological system is *utilitarianism*.

The concept of virtue ethics goes back to the Greek philosophers, particularly Aristotle (384–322 BC). It was the dominant moral theory in ethics until the Enlightenment. From the Enlightenment until the mid-twentieth century, it was not as popular. In 1958, Elizabeth Anscombe published a paper titled "Modern

[1]H. E. Sigerist, quoted in J. T. Aitken, H. W. C. Fuller, and D. Johnson, *The Influence of Christians in Medicine* (Downers Grove, IL: InterVarsity, 1984), 8.
[2]Margaret Mead, quoted in M. Levine, *Psychiatry and Ethics* (New York: G. Braziller, 1972), 324–25.
[3]L. P. Pojman and J. Fieser, *Ethics: Discovering Right and Wrong*, 6th ed. (Belmont, CA: Wadsworth Cengage Learning, 2008).

Moral Philosophy,"[4] which was critical of utilitarian and deontological ethical theories and proposed a return to a system based on the concept of character and virtue. In 1984, Alistair MacIntyre published *After Virtue*,[5] which, like Anscombe's position, was critical of the Enlightenment theories and advocated a return to virtue ethics. MacIntyre looked at developing character qualities (virtue) that can be nurtured in everyday life. These are social forms of activity that seek to realize goods that are internal to that activity. These activities are to be habitually practiced and taught in order to develop this character quality as a way of life. Education therefore becomes an important way of developing character.

Aristotle emphasized the external goods of virtues that are related to the overall end or goal for proper moral behavior. The end or *telos* for Aristotle was *eudaimonia*, "happiness." Aristotle recognized that actions are not pointless; they have a specific aim or goal. Each aim or goal eventually points to the greater end or the greatest good of all, *eudaimonia*. MacIntyre, on the other hand, looks more toward the internal goal of each virtue that has worth in and of itself in an unfolding narrative, and he places less emphasis on the greater end of happiness. Virtue ethics enables agents to have guidance in situations even where rules do not exist or might seem to be useless. It permits individual rationality to supplement rules. A virtuous person of high character would comply with the general community of laws and rules but would also have the wisdom and discernment to make judicial decisions applicable to each individual situation.

Immanuel Kant (1724–1804) developed a deontological ethical system based on reason alone in which moral duties do not vary based on circumstances. His theory is based on the moral obligation known as the "categorical imperative." Categorical imperatives are principles that are intrinsically good and must be obeyed in all circumstances. He postulated three formulations. The first is the formula of universal law in which one is to "act only according to that maxim by which you can at the same time will that it would become a universal law." The second is the formula of humanity in which one is to "act as to treat humanity, whether in your own person or in that of any other, in every case as an end and never as merely a means." And the third is the formula of autonomy in which "every rational being is able to regard oneself as a maker of universal law." Kant is known as a champion of intrinsic human dignity, and his philosophy has had a profound influence on Western thought.[6]

---

[4]G. E. M. Anscombe, "Modern Moral Philosophy," *Philosophy* 33 (1958): 1–19.
[5]A. MacIntyre, *After Virtue: A Study in Moral Theory* (Notre Dame, IN: University of Notre Dame Press, 1984).
[6]Immanuel Kant, *Fundamental Principles of the Metaphysics of Ethics*, trans. T. K. Abbott (London: Longman's, 1965), quoted in Louis P. Pogman and James Fieser, *Ethics: Discovering Right and Wrong*, 6th ed. (n.p.: Cengage Learning, 2008), 129.

Utilitarianism is a teleological ethical system in which the morality of a decision is based on the consequences of the act (the end justifies the means). This view argues that the proper decision is one that produces the greatest good for the greatest number of people. Jeremy Bentham (1748–1832) and John Stuart Mill (1806–1873) were two of the primary proponents of this philosophical position. Bentham was an English social reformer who felt that "nature has placed mankind under the governance of two sovereign masters, pain and pleasure."[7] His position is called hedonistic utilitarianism. Mill distinguished happiness from mere pleasure. He defined happiness (*eudaimonia*) in terms of higher-order pleasures such as intellectual, aesthetic, and social. His position is called eudaimonistic utilitarianism.

Peter Singer, professor of bioethics at Princeton University, is a well-known, modern-day utilitarian philosopher. He holds the view that personhood is dependent on levels of consciousness and awareness. This shapes his opinion on abortion, euthanasia, and infanticide. Singer is an outspoken critic of the sanctity of human life, as illustrated by the following quotation:

> During the next 35 years, the traditional view of the sanctity of human life will collapse under pressure from scientific, technological and demographic developments. By 2040, it may be that only a rump of hard-core, know-nothing religious fundamentalists will defend the view that every human life, from conception to death, is sacrosanct.[8]

Descriptive ethical theories are relativistic and describe how different population groups actually make moral decisions. Cultural relativism acknowledges that different cultures have differing standards of right and wrong—"When in Rome, do as the Romans do." Ethical subjectivism leaves moral decisions up to individual preferences (something may be right for one person but not for another). Conventionalism is the view that cultural acceptance determines morality. Society determines what is right and wrong. In essence, morality evolves and society evolves. These views fail to account for the sin nature of mankind, and history has shown the failure of such thinking. This was displayed in the atrocities of World War II.

History of Bioethics

A significant contributing factor that led to the Holocaust in Nazi Germany was the concept of eugenics. Eugenics was first introduced by Sir Francis Dalton,[9]

---

[7] Jeremy Bentham, chap. 1 of *An Introduction to the Principles of Morals and Legislation* (1789), quoted in Pojman and Fieser, *Ethics: Discovering Right and Wrong*, 103.
[8] P. Singer, quoted in H. Cox, *Dallas Morning News*, November 27, 2005, p. 1P.
[9] N. W. Gillham, *A Life of Sir Francis Galton: From African Exploration to the Birth of Eugenics* (Oxford: Oxford University Press, 2001).

a cousin of Charles Darwin. It is based on the concept of selective breeding in humans. Positive eugenics promotes the reproduction of those couples who have desirable or "superior" traits that would be transmitted to their offspring. Negative eugenics advocates preventing reproduction of those who have undesirable or "inferior" traits. Eventually this line of reasoning led to forced sterilization and ultimately euthanasia. It was in essence "a war against the weak." The physically and mentally disabled were targeted, as well as groups that were thought of as socially undesirable. Unfortunately, some American religious leaders were also involved in the early stages of this movement.[10]

Although the Nuremberg Trials condemned the Nazi eugenic practices as war crimes, there continues to be controversy regarding the treatment of the handicapped. In 1963 an infant with trisomy 21 (Down syndrome) and duodenal atresia (a blockage in the intestines) was admitted to the Johns Hopkins Hospital.[11] The usual treatment would be a surgical repair of the blockage. The parents and physicians requested that it not be performed because of the developmental handicap of the child. The physicians assumed the parents had a right to make this decision, and the court was never asked to intervene. The child was not treated, and so the child died.

In 1973 physicians at the Yale New Haven Hospital reported on a series of forty-three patients who were allowed to die without treatment. The infants had a variety of medical conditions, including congenital anomalies, chromosomal abnormalities, cardiopulmonary disorders, and central-nervous-system disorders. The physicians indicated in their report that some of the infants had a "right to die" and some needed to escape a "wrongful life" that would have involved institutional care. This would also spare the families the burden of caring for children who had little or no possibility of a meaningful life. The Johns Hopkins case and the Yale series became the focus of numerous commentaries and debates about the role of parental decision and the rights of infants who had developmental handicaps.

One of the best-known cases was that of Baby Doe in 1982 in Bloomington, Indiana.[12] The baby was born with trisomy 21 and a tracheoesophageal fistula. The obstetrician recommended to the family that they not have the defect repaired. The pediatricians at the hospital and at the regional referral facility disagreed and petitioned the court. Three courts, including the Indiana Supreme Court, ruled in the family's favor, and the infant died without surgery. This case drew significant public attention, especially from right-to-life advocates and advocacy

---

[10]C. Rosen, *Preaching Eugenics: Religious Leaders and the American Eugenics Movement* (Oxford: Oxford University Press, 2004).
[11]J. B. Boyle, "Paradigm Cases in Decision Making for Neonates," *NeoReviews* 5 (2004): e477-e83.
[12]State ex rel. Infant Doe v. Baker, No 482 S 140 (Ind., May 27, 1982).

groups for disability. The US Department of Health and Human Services quickly developed regulations to prohibit hospitals from withholding care from imperiled newborns.[13] These regulations became known as the Baby Doe rules and are summarized as follows:

1. All such disabled infants must under all circumstances receive appropriate nutrition, hydration, and medication.
2. All such disabled infants must be given medically indicated treatment.
3. There are three exceptions to the requirements that all disabled infants must receive treatment or, in other terms, three circumstances in which treatment is not considered "medically indicated." These circumstances are:
   a. If the infant is chronically and irreversibly comatose.
   b. If the provision of such treatment would merely prolong dying, not be effective in ameliorating or correcting all of the infant's life-threatening conditions, or otherwise be futile in terms of the survival of the infant.
   c. If the provision of such treatment would be virtually futile in terms of the survival of the infant, and the treatment itself under such circumstances would be inhumane.
4. The physician's "reasonable medical judgment" concerning the medically indicated treatment must be one that would be made by a reasonably prudent physician, knowledgeable about the case and the treatment possibilities with respect to the medical conditions involved. It is not to be based on subjective "quality of life" or other abstract concepts.

The rules did acknowledge that aggressive care was not required for infants who had anencephaly or for extremely premature infants. They also identified a crucial role for parents in decision making with regard to making choices among various medical treatments and rehabilitative services. The regulations were challenged in the courts and were overturned on a procedural issue. However, Congress amended the Child Abuse Protection Act to include a category of "medical neglect" and placed enforcement of the rules in the hands of each state's child protection unit. One of the elements of the amendment was the establishment of "infant

---

[13]United States Department of Health and Human Services, Nondiscrimination on the basis of handicaps: procedures and guidelines relating to health care for handicapped infants, Fed. Reg. 49 (1984): 622–54.

care review committees," which became the foundation for ethics committees in many institutions.

Current Secular Bioethics

T. L. Beauchamp and J. F. Childress popularized the approach to bioethics known as the four-principles method.[14] The guidelines grew out of a consensus statement known as the Belmont Report, which addressed the ethics of using human subjects in research experiments. One of the foundational principals was *respect for persons*. This concept eventually became known as autonomy or self-determination. The principle is related to the concept of informed consent and of truth telling. Every individual is entitled to have full disclosure as to the risk and benefits of the proposed treatment options. Initially this was for experimental research; however, it has been expanded into clinical practice for treatment decisions. Respect for autonomy does not end when a patient no longer has decision-making capacity. This principle is important in end-of-life decisions since the patient's prior wishes should be honored when he or she no longer has the ability to express them.

The principle of autonomy became a dominant principle in the 1970s and 1980s, when society was focusing on individual rights. One should remember that this is a principle and not a right. In addition to patient autonomy, physician autonomy is an important concept that also deserves respect. The role of autonomy in a pluralistic society is important since there will be a great variety of values and traditions that stem from cultural and religious traditions. When used appropriately and reasonably with common sense, respect for autonomy is an important principle that should be honored whenever possible.

The second of the four principles is *beneficence*, which, simply stated, is "doing good." Treatment decisions and research should be designed for the benefit of the patient. These principles were designed for a patient-centered philosophy; the benefit that results from a treatment or experiment should be primarily for the patient. The benefit to society and to humanity as a whole is a worthwhile endeavor; however, it must be tempered by precautions against potential harm to the patient involved. Beneficence sometimes conflicts with autonomy when the patient or the patient's surrogate requests a treatment that the physician believes will not provide a beneficial effect.

The third principle is *nonmaleficence*. This is the reverse of beneficence and implies "doing no harm." This is one of the primary principles that go back to the writings of Hippocrates. It is often quoted as *primum non nocere* ("first do no

---

[14]T. L. Beauchamp and J. F. Childress, *Principles of Biomedical Ethics*, 6th ed. (Oxford: Oxford University Press, 2009).

harm"). Some treatments may be questionable as to whether they are beneficial, but they certainly should not cause more harm than good to the patient. This concept is often referred to in a clinical context as the risk-benefit ratio or weighing the benefits versus the burdens of treatment options.

The fourth principle is *justice*. Justice encompasses the concept of fairness and equal treatment for all patients. This broad concept extends into public policy bioethics in addition to individual clinical bioethics. Discrimination against the elderly, the mentally impaired, racial minorities, and the poor typically raises questions of justice. As new and expensive treatment options become available, the concept of distributive justice will become increasingly a pressing bioethical principle.

The four-principles method is sometimes known as the secular approach to bioethics. It tries to incorporate principles that cross religious and philosophical boundaries and are common to all patients. If applied reasonably and as general principles, there is no reason why this method cannot be an underlying guideline for bioethics for people with a broad background of religious and ethnic traditions. The four-principles method has been criticized in that it evolved from a research environment and was primarily designed for experimental protocols. The application of these principles in the practice of medicine is somewhat limited. It has conceptual and philosophical implications more than practical bedside-ethics applications. Bernard Lo, a physician ethicist, has written a clinically oriented book on medical ethics used in many medical schools.[15]

End-of-Life Issues

The concept of futility has become a controversial topic in end-of-life decisions.[16] Since the term *futility* is frequently invoked during discussions of withholding or withdrawing life-sustaining treatment in terminally ill patients, a thorough understanding of the topic is essential. The word *futile* comes from the Latin *futilis*, which means a vessel easily emptied, leaky, hence untrustworthy or useless. The origin of this word lies in Greek mythology regarding the daughters of Danaus, king of Argos. The daughters were forced to marry the sons of Aegyptus, and in an act of rebellion they murdered their husbands on their wedding night. As a punishment, the daughters were condemned to the endless task of filling water in a bath that had no bottom. Since filling the bath would be impossible, continued attempts at adding water were then considered "futile." The *Oxford English Dictionary* defines *futility* as "inadequacy to produce a result or bring about a desired end

---

[15]Bernard Lo, *Resolving Ethical Dilemmas: A Guide for Clinicians*, 4th ed. (New York: Lippincott, Williams, and Wilkins, 2009).
[16]Wesley Smith, *Culture of Death* (San Francisco, CA: Encounter, 2000).

or ineffectiveness or uselessness." When applied to medicine, futility is one of the oldest concepts in medical ethics. Hippocrates states that physicians may "refuse to treat those who are overmastered by their diseases, realizing that in such cases medicine is powerless."[17]

Ethical issues regarding refusal of treatment were originally centered on a patient's or a family's refusal of therapy recommended by a physician. Many cases revolved around religious beliefs.[18] Some religious traditions refuse only certain treatments, such as blood products, refused by the Jehovah's Witnesses. Some refuse immunizations, and others limit medical interventions. Other traditions refuse all treatment, the most well-known of which is Christian Science.

A series of court cases beginning in 1976 focused on patients' rights, usually expressed by the family in refusing life-sustaining treatment. The first and best known of these decisions was the case of Karen Ann Quinlan.[19] She was a twenty-two-year-old woman who suffered severe brain damage when she intermittently stopped breathing after ingesting drugs and alcohol. She subsequently lapsed into a persistent vegetative state and was placed on a ventilator. Her parents wanted to withdraw ventilator support, and the request was supported by their local Roman Catholic priest and the bishop. The physicians refused to withdraw the treatment, stating that it was contrary to the standard of care. The court ruled in favor of the parents, and the ventilator was removed. However, she unexpectedly continued to breathe on her own. She continued to live for ten more years in a vegetative state and then died from pneumonia. The publicity in this case generated widespread interest in medical ethics. The legal decision supported the concept of shared decision making between physicians and families. Previously, most treatment decisions were made unilaterally by physicians. The court recommended that these cases be kept out of the legal process, and it encouraged the formation of hospital ethics committees to help resolve such conflicts.

Another important decision was the Nancy Cruzan[20] case in 1990. At thirty-three years old she was in a permanent vegetative state after an automobile accident.

---

[17]Hippocrates, *On the Art*, in *Hippocrates*, vol. 2, trans. W. H. S. Jones (Cambridge: Harvard University Press, 1981).

[18]R. D. Orr and L. B. Genesen, "Requests for 'Inappropriate' Treatment Based on Religious Beliefs," *Journal of Medical Ethics* 23 (1977): 142–47.

[19]In re Quinlan, 70 N.J. 10, 355 A.2d 647 (1976). This was the first major judicial decision to hold that life-sustaining medical treatments may be discontinued in appropriate circumstances, even if the patient is unable or incompetent to make the decision. The New Jersey Supreme Court's decision has been followed by nearly every state appellate court to consider the issue. In addition to establishing a patient's right to refuse life-sustaining medical treatments, the *Quinlan* decision also made clear that a decision to remove or withhold life-support systems from an incompetent patient would not constitute homicide or medical malpractice.

[20]Cruzan v. Harmon, 760 S.W.2d 408 (Missouri Supreme Court, 1988); Cruzan v. Director, Missouri Dept. of Health, no. 88–1503, cert. granted, 109 Supreme Court 3240 (1989).

After three years her parents requested that the feeding tube be discontinued. The hospital insisted on a court order before removing the tube. Of interest is that approximately one year before the accident, she allegedly indicated to her housemate that she would not want to live as a "vegetable." The local court granted the request to remove the feeding tube, but it was overturned by the Missouri Supreme Court and the United States Supreme Court. The latter ruled that her prior conversation did not meet the standard of "clear and convincing evidence" that the State of Missouri required to remove life-sustaining medical treatment. The court recommended that states develop procedural requirements for advance directives regarding end-of-life treatment decisions. This led to the Patient Self-Determination Act in 1991, which requires hospitals to give information regarding advance directives to all patients at the time of admission. The role of artificial nutrition and hydration continues to be a controversial issue. The Ethics Committee of the Christian Medical and Dental Society examined this issue in 1998 and offered the following opinion:

> While artificially administered nutrition and hydration may be considered an artificial support to life, food and water by mouth should be offered to all patients. Sincere Christians differ about the morality of withholding or withdrawing artificially administered nutrition and hydration from patients in a permanent vegetative state. There are compelling arguments on both sides. Since we hold that withdrawal of nutrition or hydration for the specific purpose of taking a patient's life is impermissible, we suggest that anyone (either patients and surrogates or physicians) faced with such a decision weigh both sides of the issue prayerfully and seek God's will in reaching a decision.[21]

In an article published in *First Things*, R. D. Orr and G. Meilaender, both pro-life evangelical Christians, discuss different views regarding artificial nutrition and hydration.[22]

In 1997 two cases were brought before the US Supreme Court regarding physician-assisted suicide.[23] Both cases argued that there is a constitutional right for physician-assisted suicide. The US Supreme Court ruled unanimously (nine to zero) that there is no constitutional right to physician-assisted suicide. The ruling stated that states have an interest in preserving human life, preventing suicide, protecting vulnerable groups, protecting the integrity of the medical profession, and avoiding the slippery slope to euthanasia. It acknowledged

---

[21] Http://www.cmda.org/AM/Template.cfm?Section=Home&TEMPLATE=/CM/ContentDisplay.cfm&CONTENTID=3990.
[22] R. D. Orr and G. Meilaender, "Ethics and Life's Ending: An Exchange," *First Things* 145 (2004): 31–37.
[23] Vacco v. Quill, 521 U.S. 793 (1997).

that withdrawal of treatment is distinct from physician-assisted suicide. The court encouraged palliative care with adequate pain control and supported the principle of double effect.

The principle of double effect dates back to Thomas Aquinas's view of homicidal self-defense.[24] The principle states that it is morally permissible to perform an act that results in both good and bad effects if the following conditions are met: (1) The act must be good in itself or at least indifferent; (2) the good effect must not be obtained by means of the bad effect; (3) the bad effect must not be intended, only permitted; (4) there must be a proportionately grave reason for permitting the bad effect; and (5) there must be no other way to achieve the good. The application of this principle in medicine is usually to permit aggressive pain management in patients suffering from terminal cancer.[25]

The principle of autonomy is a recent development in bioethical literature. This important concept recognizes informed consent that protects individuals from powerful others. However, there are some restrictions to autonomy. One is when there is harm to a third party. Another is when the decision that the patient is requesting would violate a deep moral conviction of the physician (such as abortion or physician-assisted suicide). A third restriction is when it violates good medical practice. This third restriction to autonomy is the central component in much of the debate today regarding futility. Since patients have a right to refuse medical treatment, do they also have a right to demand treatment or insist on continuation of treatment that the physicians consider futile?

Definitions of medical futility have been fraught with frustration and controversy. Medical futility has often been described in three categories.[26] First is physiologic futility, in which the treatment will not work. As an extreme example, transfusing a patient who has been decapitated would represent this type of futility. Second, quantitative futility describes the situation in which a treatment will probably not work. Most interventions in medicine have some chance of success even if extremely unlikely. The third category of medical futility is qualitative futility. In this type of futility the treatment will not have a beneficial outcome. The problem with this type of futility is in the definition of a beneficial outcome. In the mind of the patient or the family, just sustaining biologic life may be beneficial.

[24]Thomas Aquinas, *Summa Theologiae*, 2b.64.7.

[25]D. P. Sulmasy, "The Rule of Double Effect: Clearing Up the Double Talk," *Archives of Internal Medicine* 159 (2005): 545–50.

[26]L. J. Schneiderman, N. S. Jecker, and A. R. Jonsen, "Medical Futility: Its Meaning and Ethical Implications," *Annals of Internal Medicine* 112 (1990): 949–53.

The concept of quality of life is a part of this category and becomes controversial as to who defines quality and how it is measured.

E. D. Pellegrino has sought to define the concept of medical futility as the relationship among the effectiveness, benefit, and burden of the treatment in question.[27] He says that this is not a quantitative relationship but a judicious balancing of each factor against the others. Effectiveness is an assessment of the capacity of the procedure to alter the natural history of the disease. This is an objective determination, which is in the province of the physician's clinical knowledge. It is based on as much evidence, outcome studies, and prognoses as possible. The benefit is determined by the patient's assessment of the value or desirability of the treatment's result. This is the province of the patient, with the assistance of factual input from the physician. It covers a wide range of things desired or sought by the patient. The burdens include the cost, discomfort, pain, and inconvenience of the treatment in question. It is determined by both the physician and the patient, or the surrogate, acting together.

Sulmasy proposes two standards of futility.[28] One is biomedical futility, in which the treatment will not work (physiologic futility) or there will be a repeated or continual need for treatment over a short period of time before death (clinical futility). His other is subjective futility, in which the treatment might work and the patient might make it out of the hospital, but there may be significant limitations. Sulmasy states that there is no moral obligation to provide treatments that are biomedically futile. His opinion is based on the internal rationality and morality of medicine and on the claims of conscience of the practitioner. This is also the opinion of the American Medical Association: "Physicians are not ethically obligated to deliver care that, in their best professional judgment, will not have a reasonable chance of benefiting their patients. Patients should not be given treatments simply because they demand them."[29]

The distinction between biomedical and subjective futility is an important one. Protecting the right of conscience for all health-care professionals is a critical issue that must be maintained. Christians should oppose legislation that requires physicians to provide services that they feel are morally or professionally inappropriate. However, the concept of subjective futility leads to much of the controversy. Physicians should take care not to abuse the concept of futility as their "trump card" to overrule a family's decision when the primary issue is a subjective assess-

[27]E. D. Pellegrino, "Decisions to Withdraw Life-Sustaining Treatment," *Journal of the American Medical Association* 283 (2000): 1065–67.
[28]D. P. Sulmasy, "Futility and the Varieties of Medical Judgment," *Theoretical Medical Bioethics* 18 (1997): 63–78.
[29]*AMA Code of Ethics*, Opinion 2.035 Report, June 1994.

ment of the quality of life. Although Pellegrino supports the concept of medical futility, he identifies three moral dangers with its misuse.

> First, is the danger of eroding the fundamental moral obligation of those who profess to be healers. The aim of healing is always to relieve pain and suffering and provide care, comfort, and emotional support. Care is never futile. Indeed, to recognize the dimensions of futility greatly magnifies the obligation to provide care. Second, is the extreme vulnerability of certain patients to personal agendas involving social and economic values. A diagnosis of futility must never justify deprivation of any human being of his or her inherent dignity as a human person. A third moral danger is the temptation to use futility, out of a distorted notion of compassion, to justify physician-assisted suicide, or euthanasia, voluntary and involuntary, even in infants.[30]

Although medical interventions may be futile in some situations, there is no such thing as "futile care." It is inappropriate to say that nothing else can be done. Comfort care with adequate pain control can and should always be provided to every patient. A classic aphorism in medicine is "to cure sometimes, to relieve often, to comfort always." In a lecture to Harvard Medical School students in 1927, Francis Peabody stated that "the secret of the care of the patient is in caring for the patient."[31] The proper role of hospital ethics committees and ethics consultations is to help facilitate appropriate patient care.

> When conflict between patients and physicians about the best course of action cannot be resolved, it is in the best interest of the patient to involve individuals with expertise in medical ethics to aid in reaching a decision that is ethically sound and, ideally, acceptable to both parties. This is the role of the ethics consultation. The ethics consult is not to be construed as a means by which to persuade the family to agree with the physicians or to make a final ruling on how the dilemma should be settled. Rather, ethics consultants serve as mediators. Mediators are trained to be impartial and independent; they are equally concerned with the rights of all parties involved in the dispute. Their role is to ensure that the views of all involved parties, both family and caretakers, are expressed and reconciled.[32]

Serving on hospital ethics committees is an excellent opportunity for Christians.

---

[30]E. D. Pellegrino, "Futility in Medical Decisions: The Word and the Concept," *HEC Forum* 17 (2005): 308–18.

[31]F. W. Peabody, "The Care of the Patient," *Journal of the American Medical Association* 88 (1927): 877–82.

[32]N. K. Yamada, I. J. Kodner, and D. E. Brown, "When Operating Is Considered Futile: Difficult Decisions in the Neonatal Intensive Care Unit," *Surgery* 146 (2009): 122–25.

An individual's religious faith in medical decisions should always be taken into consideration. A few years ago an interesting study was made regarding cancer treatment in which patients with advanced lung cancer had to choose between aggressive treatment and comfort care.[33] Patients were asked to rank the importance of seven factors regarding the decision, one of which was their faith in God. The patients and their caregivers all ranked faith in God as number two after the cancer doctor's recommendation in their decision process. The oncologists uniformly ranked faith in God as the last factor. Physicians need to understand which factors are most important to patients in their decision-making process. The concept of involving a "religious interpreter" is quite useful in ethics consultation.[34] This person should be a trusted member from the same religious and cultural background as the patient and family. He or she can be used as a liaison between the physician and the family. Decisions regarding life support are difficult for any family, and establishing trust is important.

Death is often viewed as a failure within the medical profession. Patients and their families may have unrealistic expectations based on television shows and movies that include fictional portrayals of medicine. A hundred years ago it was easier to appreciate the fact that death is inevitable. At that time most people died at home, so the death was observed by the family and community. Norman Geisler states that "protecting life is a moral obligation, but resisting natural death is not necessarily a moral duty."[35] Having more open discussions regarding the use of medical technology and the role of advance directives would provide useful information for decision making about end-of-life care.

Advance directives are of two types. The first is known as a *directive to physicians* or a *living will*. This is a document in which patients express what treatment options they would prefer if they were to become terminally or irreversibly ill and could no longer communicate their preferences. The second is known as a *medical power of attorney*. This document designates a surrogate decision maker who is empowered to make treatment decisions when someone lacks decision-making capacity. The medical power of attorney is a very important document, and everyone should have one. It is important to select a person who understands one's values and preferences for treatment. In addition, that person should agree to act in this capacity, which is often stressful. Since it is difficult to anticipate every possible

---

[33]G. E. Silvestri et al., "Importance of Faith on Medical Decisions regarding Cancer Care," *Journal of Clinical Oncology* 21 (2003): 1379–82.
[34]R. D. Orr, P. A. Marshall, and J. Osborn, "Cross-cultural Considerations in Clinical Ethics Consultations," *Archives of Family Medicine* 42 (1995): 159–64.
[35]Norman L. Geisler, *Christian Ethics: Options and Issues* (Grand Rapids: Baker, 1989), 153.

scenario, a general statement of one's personal values sometimes is helpful. The Christian Medical and Dental Association has provided an example of such a statement.

> I consider physical life a blessing from God. It is in my physical life that he has led me to faith in Jesus and that assures my eternal life in Heaven with God. I believe he has left me on earth to do his work in serving others. If there is a reasonable chance that I will be able to provide spiritual service to others, I desire medical technology to preserve that function. However, if by reason of spiritual, emotional, mental, or physical infirmity I am no longer able to serve others, I do not want my life prolonged. At no time do I want anything done that would actively terminate my physical life. If there is uncertainty as to whether I will recover sufficiently to serve others, and if it is elected to use some technology to prolong my life [and], after a reasonable period, I have not recovered, I want that technology discontinued.[36]

Christian Bioethics Resources: A Challenge

Christian bioethics is Hippocratic in orientation and views medicine as a covenant relationship. Human dignity is respected from conception to natural death. Science is viewed as a sacred trust, and technology must be directed in morally responsible paths. There are a number of excellent resources regarding Christian bioethics.[37] The Christian Medical and Dental Association (CMDA) hosts a website (www.cmda.org) with a wealth of information. The CMDA Ethics Committee has issued a number of statements on a variety of topics. The Center for Bioethics and Human Dignity (CBHD) hosts a website (www.cbhd.org) with abundant useful resources. The CBHD also hosts an annual conference on bioethics. William Cutrer and Sandra Glahn have written very informative books for Christians regarding contraception[38] and infertility.[39] Christians are encouraged to become active in ministries that support and affirm the sanctity and dignity of human life. Examples include disability ministries, crisis pregnancy centers, hospice services, and hospital ethics committees.

---

[36]Http://www.cmda.org/AM/Template.cfm?Section=Home&Template=/CM/ContentDisplay. cfm&ContentFileID=296.

[37]S. Rae, *Moral Choices: An Introduction to Ethics*, 3rd ed. (Grand Rapids: Zondervan, 2009); G. Meilaender, *Bioethics: A Primer for Christians*, 2nd ed. (Grand Rapids: Eerdmans, 2005); D. VanDrunen, *Bioethics and the Christian Life: A Guide to Making Difficult Decisions* (Wheaton, IL: Crossway, 2009); and R. D. Orr, *Medical Ethics and the Faith Factor: A Handbook for Clergy and Health Care Professionals* (Grand Rapids: Eerdmans, 2009).

[38]William R. Cutrer and Sandra L. Glahn, *The Contraception Guidebook: Options, Risks, and Answers for Christian Couples* (Grand Rapids: Zondervan, 2005).

[39]Sandra L. Glahn and William R. Cutrer, *The Infertility Companion: Hope and Help for Couples Facing Infertility* (Grand Rapids: Zondervan, 2004).

Linda M. Marten (MA, University of Northern Iowa; PhD, University of North Texas) is assistant professor of biblical counseling at Dallas Theological Seminary. She helped begin the Dallas Christian Counseling Services when the integration of psychology and theology was a new and growing issue. With over thirty years of client interactions, she specializes in trauma and dissociation. Dr. Marten is a licensed professional counselor and supervisor, a member of the Christian Association of Psychological Studies, and a clinical member of the American Association of Marriage and Family Therapy.

21

DEATH AND DYING

Linda M. Marten

Intense emotions, people weeping, anger at God, anxious children, major frightening changes, death. These are components of real life, real loss, and real pain. These are also ministry opportunities in which people feel most awkward and ill prepared. How friends respond can add comfort or hurt. By learning more about the needs of the dying, the issues intertwined with grief, and the different styles of mourning, comforters can become more sensitive and effective.

Elisabeth Kübler-Ross is credited as the first person to study the emotions of the dying. As a medical doctor and instructor, she would bring her patients on stage at her lectures and interview them before the medical and health-care students. From her extensive listening she identified five stages of dying that patients described. Kübler-Ross wrote a book titled *On Death and Dying.*[1] She originally labeled the process "the Five Stages of Catastrophic Loss," which applied mainly to unexpected loss. These stages, however, became commonly known as the five stages of grief.

Stages of Grief

Stage 1: Denial, Shock, and Isolation
The initial reaction to a sudden loss, such as a serious diagnosis or a sudden death, may take the form of not believing the results of the medical tests or of

[1]New York: Macmillan, 1969.

asking for a second opinion. Denial and isolation can function as a buffer that allows the patient to collect himself and, with time, to mobilize other defenses and resources.

It is helpful at this stage to join the person in his reaction by saying something like, "I can't believe it either. Everything was going so well!" or "It is hard to get my mind around it."

Stage 2: Anger

After the initial shock comes the "Why me?" question. Anger might be directed at anyone and everyone—family, doctors, God. The person may also get mad at healthy people, or happy people, or those for whom life seems to go on without interruption. This stage is more difficult for family and friends to cope with.

Do not take this anger personally or blame the person. He or she is trying to deal with unwanted changes and loss of control. The grieving person might say, "It's hard to see others doing what I can't do any more."

Stage 3: Bargaining

In the third stage the person bargains with God, trying to "bribe" him for escape from the situation. The person may promise to change his career and serve God if . . . or to donate large sums of money if . . . or never to ask him for anything else, or . . .

Most of this stage will be done internally and privately. If it is voiced, just listen. One could add, "I, too, pray God changes this for you."

Stage 4: Depression

Depression sets in when the grieving individual is past the denial and when making bargains with God has not worked. Kübler-Ross identifies two forms of depression: "reactive depression" is about the new demands, financial issues, and illness-related problems; "preparatory depression" takes into account all the activities the person will never do again or future events he will not be a part of.

Do not try to cheer up the individual. It will offend and imply that, as counselor, you know more about the situation than the grieving individual knows. Let him talk and express his own sorrow. Support should be shown by nonjudgmental listening and being present.

Stage 5: Acceptance

Acceptance occurs when the individual has made peace with his or her circumstances. It can be a good time to put one's affairs in order, to say good-byes to loved ones (for the dying), and to begin to look at life in a new way (for the grievers).

Follow the grieving person's lead. Conversations can be about the hope to come, reunion with saved loved ones, prayer for the salvation and care of remaining loved ones. One can also show kindness by doing errands to help the sufferer get affairs in order.

These stages are not confined to death losses. They are relevant to all significant losses, such as the news of a lost job, infidelity, financial crisis, natural disasters, and others. The stages are also not always sequential. A person can move into a new stage and then later return to the issues in a previous stage.

As soon as a serious illness begins, life changes, both for the person now called the patient and for family and caregivers. The first realization of change is that the patient's schedule is controlled by doctor's appointments, blood tests, CT scans, X-rays, EKGs, and more tests. Added to this are piles of paperwork to fill out, insurance forms and questions, and later, confusing bills. Another discouraging change is all the waiting—waiting for appointments and tests, and then waiting for the results and treatment decisions to be made and authorization by an insurance company. Some wait to figure out how to pay for help or how to qualify for free treatment. This waiting often adds to a person's suffering and anxiety. The patient has a sense of feeling out of control.

Doctors and medical providers can help minimize patients' anxiety or can intensify their emotional pain. It is easy for a professional to be only "a body of knowledge" talking to "a disease." The personhood is lost; human compassion is missing.[2] Symbolically the individual (the patient) has ceased to be there. This form of suffering, coming from the professional, is called iatrogenic suffering. This should not exist, but too often it does. If a patient's speaking up about the lack of sensitivity and kindness does not result in improvement, at least the patient can be sure a supportive person is present with him or her at all appointments as a buffer to provide the care and encouragement lacking from the medical staff.

The following list was compiled over a span of twenty-five years by hospice physicians, nurses, social workers, and aids who were involved with and spoke directly to the dying. It is not complete, nor does it deal with individual variations. However, it can help keep the focus on the dying person's needs.[3]

[2]David Kuhl, *What Dying People Want: Practical Wisdom for the End of Life* (New York: Public Affairs, 2002), 8–10, 54.
[3]Hospice Foundation of America, *The Dying Process* (Washington, DC: Hospice Foundation of America, n.d.), 9 (www.hospicefoundation.org).

Needs of Dying Persons

Assurance that they will be cared for and not be abandoned: The dying need assurance that even if they are a lot of trouble or go through many difficult and unpleasant emotions or look awful or smell bad or whatever, they will not be left alone.

Assistance in developing and finalizing documents pertaining to terminal care: Advance directives are needed so that the patient's wishes will be carried out. Many include only a DNR (Do Not Resuscitate) directive and a living will. Unfortunately the living will is not very effective, is usually vague, cannot cover all the possible situations that may arise, and is often not given to the doctor. If you are going to choose one thing to do, it should in most cases be a health-care power of attorney. That document gives a person you select the legal right to make decisions for you if you no longer can. It is important to discuss your preferences with your proxy and with other family members so they will support the proxy's decisions. Another document for consideration is a durable power of attorney, which allows the designated proxy to make any and all legal decisions and transactions on behalf of the authorizing patient. (The health-care power of attorney is limited to decisions concerning medical care.)

Communication that is timely, honest, and open with family, friends, and caregivers: Patients need opportunity (if desired) to discuss their impending death with selected family and caregivers. If family members are unwilling to accept the approaching death, the patient may not feel like expressing his or her own feelings. The person may feel guilty about dying and put his or her limited energy into fighting to stay alive instead of moving to closure and connection with loved ones.

Excellence in the delivery of physical care, comfort, privacy, intimacy, sleep, and rest: These efforts communicate respect for the patient and help maintain his or her value and dignity.

Management of pain and other symptoms that are responsive to changing conditions: A significant part of end-of-life care, called palliative care (comfort care), is pain management. Many choose hospice care to help. Hospice can be medically ordered if the patient is believed to have less than six months to live. It specializes in pain management and patient comfort. A nurse will come to the home, assess the needs, arrange for any appropriate equipment (hospital bed, oxygen, etc.), consult with the doctor, administer appropriate medications, and set up a schedule for a hospice aid to be with the patient. Hospice personnel will also educate the family about the care of their loved one and the dying process. When someone is in hospice, treatment interventions stop, and the focus is only on comfort care. Insurance and Medicare typically pay some or all of the hospice charges. Because of the specialty of the care, hospice workers bring calmness to a distressing situation for both the patient and the family. It is not unusual for families to call hospice workers "angels from God."

Information that will be accurate, timely, and reliable: It is also helpful to write down any health or medication problems and questions to ask the doctor. Answers can be fast and forgotten, so an accompanying note taker can help collect the information and give the patient a greater sense of control.

Opportunity to explore the patient's finiteness and the spiritual dimensions of life: A chaplain, pastor, or other believers can be instrumental in assisting the patient with his questions about faith and God. Dying patients are looking for answers and want assurance about their future.

Occasion to discuss preferences about funeral arrangements as well as the impact of the patient's death on survivors: Giving information on specifics for the obituary, on the location for burial or scattering of ashes, and about the disposition of special possessions (to what persons or places) is helpful to the survivors and executor.

Permission to express feelings, both positive and negative: This includes permission to say "thank you," "I love you," "I forgive you," as well as to express dissatisfaction, anger, and resentment. This can be a time for long-awaited relational healing.

Time to reflect on the implications of the diagnosis and prognosis, and to identify and attend to thoughts, feelings, and needs: The patient needs time to tell his story, to reaffirm his identity, and to value his life, to reflect on and to grieve prior to, as well as during and after, the loss. The patient needs time with selected family and friends, time to attend to unfinished personal business, to plan for distribution of assets, and to address financial responsibilities. If he or she has small children, the patient will want time to make arrangements for their personal care and financial future. This can include writing letters to significant people, making a video for the children and grandchildren, writing a book of life lessons for a child's future birthday or wedding. The dying person wants enough time—a gift many do not get. Simply stated, dying persons need control, certainty, connection, and closure.

Control over as much as is possible and reasonable: This may be only over what to watch on TV or when to accept visitors. A sense of control counters the helpless feelings and affirms the person as an individual.

Certainty, needed to deal with anxiety: Encourage the person to verbalize the fear, to name it, and then to make a plan to handle the various fear-provoking situations. Rather than feeling out of control, fearful, and panicked, a person who has a plan can gain reassurance and a sense of certainty.

Connection, which creates closeness and love. This treats the patient as a person, not just a disease. Relationships with others gives emotional strength and comfort to cope with the ending of life.

Closure: This has many aspects that also depend on the time God allows. If only minutes are available before death, then closure includes loving good-byes. Or if death is seemingly weeks or months away, the focus can be on practical matters of business and work-related tasks, passing on helpful information to the company, spouse, or family (e.g., a location of documents, investments, professional contacts for maintenance and repairs, account passwords, addresses, special recipes, etc.). "Closing down" a life is difficult. The more matters of emotional and business closure are handled before death, the easier it is on the survivors to manage the ensuing process of grief.

When a family member is dying, the family's focus goes predominantly to the ill and dying member. Family members sacrifice their own needs, which in time can take an emotional and physical toll. Resentment, conflict, depression, or anger can build, and then guilt. Some may think, "Of course [the ill and dying person's] needs should come first! How can I be so selfish?" These feelings do not indicate an unloving person; just an exhausted person. It is called compassion fatigue. Caregivers need a break with time for themselves. Family members need some normalcy and fun, especially during a protracted illness. This is the time to utilize friends or nursing aids to manage the care so that the caregiver and perhaps family members can have a restorative break. Even brief outings will help. The dying person may feel guilty for consuming so much energy and time. Breaks for renewal can be helpful to both.

To ease the burden of updating family and friends on the patient's condition, a free Internet website such as CaringBridge.org or carepages.com can be used. One's story, along with photos, daily information, changes in treatment, prayer requests, answers to prayer, family needs, and so forth, can be posted. Friends can access the information and leave messages on the site. This informs people and spares the family from having to be on the phone, repeating the same information over and over. This is also the time to ask others to help with the various burdens that come with attending to the dying while trying to maintain household or family needs.

Grieving the Loss

Most grief specialists believe it is only after Kübler-Ross's stage 5 that one can truly begin grieving. Some have described tasks, steps, or additional stages that they believe mourners must go through to resolve their grief and continue on in life.

J. William Worden, in *Grief Counseling and Grief Therapy*, describes grieving as the need to accomplish the following four tasks:

Task 1: Accept the Reality of the Loss

When someone dies, even if the death is expected, there is always a sense that it has not happened. The first task of grieving is to come full face with the reality that the person is dead and will not return. Part of this acceptance is to come to understand that reunion is impossible, at least in this life.

The opposite of accepting the reality of the loss is denial. A person may keep possessions of the deceased, ready for use when he or she returns. Another way is to deny the meaning of the loss—to make it seem less important than it actually is. Statements like "We weren't close" or "I don't miss him" are examples of this.

Coming to accept the reality of the loss takes time, since it involves not only a mental acceptance, but also an emotional one. The grieving person may be mentally aware of the loss long before the emotions accept the information as true.

Task 2: Process the Pain of Grief

If pain is not acknowledged, it will show itself through dysfunctional behavior. Anything that allows the person to avoid or suppress this pain can be expected to lengthen the time spent grieving. Not everyone experiences pain in the same way, but it is impossible to lose someone to whom one has been deeply attached without experiencing some pain.

One way to fail at this second task is not to feel. Sometimes people use thought-stopping procedures to keep themselves from feeling the sadness of loss. But sooner or later, most of those who avoid it break down—usually with some form of depression. Those who do not break down carry the pain with them the rest of their lives.

Task 3: Adjust to a World without the Deceased

Losing someone important can lead to feeling helpless, inadequate, and incapable. First attempts to do for oneself things that the deceased person used to do may fail, and this can lead to a deeper sense of loss. However, over time grieving people must learn to do the things that used to be done for them and to learn new ways of dealing with the world.

Many resent having to develop new skills to take care of things formerly done by the one who is gone. Getting stuck here means not adapting to the loss. People work against themselves by excusing their own helplessness, by not developing the skills they need to cope, or by withdrawing from the world. The outcome of the grieving process depends on how the grieving person handles this step. The bereaved either recognizes and copes with the fact that things have changed or stays helpless and is continuously reminded that he cannot cope without the person who is gone.

Task 4: Find an Enduring Connection with the Deceased while Embarking on a New Life

A grieving person never altogether forgets the person who was highly valued. One can never erase those who have been close to him except by damaging himself. A grieving person's readiness to enter new relationships depends not on "giving up" those who are gone, but on finding a suitable place for them in his or her psychological life—a place that leaves room for others.

This fourth step is hindered by holding on to the past attachment rather than going on and forming new ones. Some people find loss so painful that they make a pact with themselves never to love again. Many get stuck at this point in their grieving and later realize that their life in some way stopped at the point when the loss occurred. But this too can be worked through. What many people come to realize, says Worden, is that "there are many other people to be loved. And it doesn't mean that I love the person who is gone less."[4]

Another grief specialist, Alan Wolfelt, describes the grief process in terms of needs. He listed "six central needs of mourning."

> (1) To experience and express outside of yourself the reality of death. (2) To tolerate the pain that comes with the work of grief while taking good care of yourself physically, emotionally, and spiritually. (3) To convert your relationship with the person who died from one of presence to memory. (4) To develop a new self-identity based on a life without the person in your life who died. (5) To relate the experience of your loss to a context of meaning. (6) To have an understanding support system available to you in the months and years ahead.[5]

The two previous lists show the commonality of emotions and perspectives that need to be worked through. The grief process may be summarized by the acronym TEAR.

---

[4] J. William Worden, *Grief Counseling and Grief Therapy: A Handbook for the Mental Health Practitioner* (New York: Springer, 2009), 39.
[5] Alan Wolfelt, *Understanding Grief: Helping Yourself Heal* (Bristol, PA: Accelerated Development, 1997), 104.

To accept the reality of the loss

Experience the pain of the loss

Adjust to the new environment without the lost object

Reinvest in the new reality

Individuality of Mourning

No person is exactly like another, and neither is one person's way of grieving exactly like another's. Differences in gender, age, culture, maturity level, life experience, and current responsibilities are just some of the factors influencing how a person will deal with the pain of death. Obviously the meaning of the loss will affect the intensity of pain, how grieving is done, and how long it will take to regain emotionally in order to reinvest in life and experience pleasure or joy again. Most mental-health professionals agree recovery takes one or two years or more, depending on the meaning of the relational loss.

Women are typically more verbal and expressive with sorrow. They take initiative to help others who need care. Most women are comfortable with expressing their pain openly and seeking out friends or family for support. The relief of their pain comes through connection and intimacy with others. Western culture allows and even expects women to respond these ways. Because of their more transparent expression of pain, they receive more comfort, understanding, and encouragement than men do. But men's emotions often differ from those of women.

Men are expected to be in control, confident, rational, analytical, assertive, and courageous. Men are encouraged to be competitive, accomplish tasks and achieve goals, endure stress without giving up or giving in, be knowledgeable about mechanical things, and be providers. Of course these expectations affect how they deal with their emotions.

Men use denial more than women do, and many men intellectualize their emotions. They often limit their show of grief, feeling that they need to be strong for their wives or children. Interestingly, their wives may view their stoicism not as strength, but as coldness and as evidence that they never really cared about the deceased person.

When men mourn, they tend to do so privately, to remain silent and engage in "secret" grief. To cope, some men try to block out grief, to refuse to think about the death, and to focus on practical and routine things. Activity is a natural way for men to escape pain or trauma; men might become obsessive about things such as work, sports, or a hobby. They may immerse themselves in activity, though this can also develop addictive behaviors. Linking their strength to action often helps men cope with this grief. This might take the form of gathering information on financial matters to help a young widowed mother or initiating a lawsuit for what might be negligence in a wrongful death, or walking fields looking for evidence in a murder. Action is their way of caring and managing grief.[6]

How Children Cope with Death

Attention is often not given to children who are grieving. If they are seen playing with favorite toys and not crying, adults may assume that they are not aware of what is happening and are fine. But children see, sense, and feel more than is apparent, especially in an emotionally charged loss. Do not assume that if children are not informed, they will be spared from feeling bad.

Infants and Toddlers

The youngest children have little understanding of death. They are more affected by a disrupted family routine and the emotional upset of those around them. Very young children may show their reaction through changes in sleeping, eating, and moods. For them it is important to keep routines and physical settings as familiar as possible. For reassurance they need constant nurturing. If the main parent is too distraught, then a safe, caring, and familiar adult substitute needs to be found.

Children Ages 3–6

Children ages 3–6 typically will not understand that death is permanent. They may think it is magically reversible or temporary, and so they may seem unaffected. They ask concrete questions such as, "Will she get cold and hungry?" "Does Grandpa have shoes on there?" or "Can we call him?" Children of this age may have frightening dreams, repeat questions about death, and revert to earlier behaviors. Because they take words so literally and have limited experiences, they may tend to connect events that do not relate. For example, knowing that Aunt Sally died after a headache and hearing Daddy say he has a headache may cause the child to think his daddy will die too.

How to Help
- Look into the child's eyes and touch the child gently when discussing a death.
- Shorten time away from the child. Be sure he knows where you are and how to reach you.

---

[6]Marilyn Gryte, *How to Lead Others through Complicated Grief* (Tucson: Carondelet Management Institute, 2001), 17.

- Avoid describing death as "sleeping," "resting," "loss," "passed away," and "taking a long trip."
- Talk in concrete terms about what it means to be dead, such as "Someone doesn't breathe, eat, go to the bathroom, or grow."
- Repeat simple, honest explanations as often as the child asks.
- Reassure the child of his own safety and your plan for continued presence. Share the fact that most people die when they are older.
- Allow expressions of feelings such as drawing pictures, reading and telling stories about death or the loved one, or reenacting the funeral service.

Children Ages 6–9

Children ages 6–9 may view death as something that comes and takes people away or can be caught like a cold. Some children may still think the dead person will return. Guilt may make a child feel responsible for the death through her own wishful thinking ("I wish he would die!"), harsh words spoken by the deceased adult ("You'll be the death of me yet"), or her not doing something ("I didn't help Grandpa mow the lawn. Now he died."). Fears related to death may arise. The child may feel distressed, confused, and sad, or show no signs at all. Fear of abandonment by other family members is common. They may be obsessed with the causes of death, as well as the physical processes to the body after death.

How to Help

- Be a good listener. Correct any confusing ideas the child may have.
- Provide play opportunities and routine.
- Reassure the child that the death was not his or her fault.
- Provide opportunities to open a discussion with a quiet child by reading stories related to death.
- A child who chooses not to talk about the death may be comfortable writing or drawing her thoughts in a journal.
- Reassure the child that God was not surprised by the death, but had prepared a place, was with that person when he died, and is with him now.

Children Ages 9–12

Those in the 9–12 age-group have a better understanding of the permanence of death. Some children in this age range may seem on the surface to be unaffected by death. They may see death as a punishment for bad deeds. The preteens' feelings may come out as anger directed at a variety of people, including themselves, their parents, others, the person who died, siblings. Feelings of responsibility and guilt may stem from anger.

How to Help
- Assure the child that the person did not die because he was "bad."
- Talk about the ways in which things are different and how they are the same.
- Reassure the child that he did not cause the death.

Teens
Young people have an adult-like understanding of the finality of death and the realization that everyone will die. They may inappropriately assume responsibility for adult concerns, such as family and financial well-being. Teens may assume the roles of the deceased person or deny feelings and express anger, which creates added pain.

How to Help
- Talk to the teen without criticizing or judging.
- Express your own feelings about the death.
- Guard against letting the teen assume adult responsibilities, and reassure him of his roles.
- Reassure the teen that he did not cause the death.
- Continue to support and listen to the teen's feelings, although he may seem to be handling it okay.
- Allow time for solitude and reflection. Be available to talk on the teen's time frame.

For all kids dealing with grief issues, adults can do several things to provide stability and healing. Have as much consistency of routine as possible. Give freedom to ask any questions or express any feelings. Show patience with regressive behavior. Be available and a good listener. Encourage open talking and reminiscing about the deceased. Assure kids of God's care for their loved one. And give the child many loving hugs and reassurances that everything is still in God's hands and the family will get through this together.

As previously stated, keeping children sheltered from seeing major illness, death, and funerals does not ensure their protection from emotional upsets. In fact such secrecy may intensify their anxiety. When a child senses change, problems, tensions, and sadness and no one talks about it, he projects his fears into silence. Children assume that the unspoken "it" is so bad it cannot be spoken about because it is a huge threat, something scary and apparently overwhelming. Openness communicates strength in the speaker, and confidence and trust in the child's ability to handle it. Explain the situation to the child and allow him to be part of the family's sadness. Assure the child that he will be loved and taken care of. Then the child does not have to try to figure out the secret "it." Openness reassures; it equips the child to manage and survive these feelings and to be better prepared for similar experiences in the future.

Include children but prepare them for what they will see and experience—who will be there, how people may be feeling, and what they will be doing. For young children, be specific in your descriptions of what the surroundings will look like. If visiting a parent or close relative in the hospital, describe the building, the many people, and how "they are giving medicines to make Grandpa feel comfortable, but the illness made him skinny so he will look different from when we last saw him." If going to a funeral home, for example, describe the casket and clothes and that the body will be lying still, not able to breathe or talk. Answer questions, and encourage the child to go with you. Bring along someone to care for the child if you are distraught. Funerals and memorial services provide needed rituals. But children of any age should not be forced to participate. Other rituals that may be more helpful, include remembering the loved one's birthday, reviewing photos and keepsakes of the loved one, and/or planting a rose or tree as a memorial.[7]

Care for Those in Mourning

The most supportive act a person can do when a friend has lost a loved one is simply to show up. The important thing will not be the words, the card, or the casserole, but rather that someone took the time and made the effort to be there. Some call this "supportive silent regard"; others call it "the ministry of presence"; but the mourner will call it evidence of love and care. All you need to say is, "I'm so sorry about your loss of [the person's name]." Open the door to communication, perhaps by saying, "How are you feeling?" or "I've been thinking about you." Sympathizers should not talk a lot; they should listen 80 percent of the time.

Other suggestions: Do not just say, "Call me if you need anything." Instead offer specific help and take the initiative to call the mourner. Do not say, "I know how you feel." Each griever's experience is unique, so invite the bereaved to share his or her feelings. Later talk about your own losses and how you coped with them. The self-disclosure then may be helpful. Do not say insensitive things like,

<hr />

[7]H. Danielson and K. Bushaw, *Talking to Children about Death*, rev. ed. (Fargo: North Dakota State University, 1995), 1–4.

"You need to get out and find another partner," or "God works in mysterious ways." This may inflict more hurt and show that you do not really understand. Do not try to cheer up the griever. That will reflect your unease with his pain. Let the shared silence or the hug do the speaking. Do not attempt to explain the loss in religious terms too early. Later he will be looking for those answers, and you may be helpful then. Do not hurry people through grief. Be patient and allow them time to share memories and stories. Use the name of the deceased. This recognizes the importance of the person and the connection to him or her.

Helping the Healing

Most people grieving a loss will not be part of an organized group. Their friends can be a great help. There is healing in the telling, so grievers should be encouraged to talk. They can be asked questions about their stories, such as, When did you hear the news? What was your first reaction? What was the most difficult? Who was (or was not) there for support? What memories are most special (or troubling)?

Explore the meaning of the loss by asking, What does it mean to you that this has happened? How is life different now? How are you different now? What beliefs or fears about life are you struggling with now?

Explore what feels unfinished by asking, What do you wish you could do? What do you wish you could say or could hear? Did you tell him good-bye? Did she tell you good-bye (literally or symbolically)?

Create ways to mark this ending by asking, Did you get to participate in any closing ritual or ceremony? What is your next step? What do you need or want to do now? And, most important, ask, What do you get to keep? What gift of the heart will you always keep from this person (or experience)? What message, gift, or symbolic object would this person give you now if she could? Stimulating the griever to talk will keep the wound clean and will aid healing.

Ministry of the Church

Many larger churches now have specific ministries to comfort people who are grieving a death. One program gaining in use is Grief Share (griefshare .org), a nondenominational program based on promises and comfort offered in Scripture. It is a thirteen-week class focusing on different topics introduced on a DVD. Workbook reflections are shared, and time is allowed for small-group discussions. These support groups are generally open to nonmembers also as a service to the community.

Churches can be a beautiful demonstration of the love of Christ. If a family is struggling with a chronic illness or with an impending or sudden death, the calls, visits, food, or availability to help is a godsend. I have talked with many people who were deeply hurt by their church's lack of response to their needs. Some have complained that when they were ill and did not attend church, no one noticed or called to check on them. Even people who were active for years in the church went uncalled when absent for several months. Many look to the church to be that "perfect parent" who will instruct them, be their safe refuge, watch over them, seek them out when they are in need, and take care of them. Yet it is unfair to place all that responsibility on the organization that is composed of fallible and busy people.

Most churches divide membership into smaller cell groups. In that context personal struggles can be shared and needs met. If a member chooses not to be part of a small group, he will less likely be noticed. When the church has a structure that organizes people into committees assigned to various needs, people will less likely be overlooked. The family in need or someone close to the family can help by informing the church of the need and not presume that their needs will be known. Those who request prayer should call or e-mail the church later to share the progress or outcome. Churches work best when members are interactive.

Summary

Death will painfully invade all of one's relationships. God's provision is himself, fleshed out through the people he indwells. Believers are the comforters and burden bearers for each other. Knowing more about the dynamics typically involved in loss, understanding ways people deal with pain and fear, and being aware of what actions and responses help those grieving will better prepare Christians to serve each other. "For us the death of a loved one is disquieting and distasteful, but for the Lord it is a delight because He has another trophy of His grace in His presence forever."[8] What a gift to be a part of a person's transition into glory and a support and encourager to those grieving and longing for that time of reunion when there will be no more good-byes.

---

[8]Roy B. Zuck, *Coping with Grief* (Garland, TX: American Tract Society, 2009) (www.atstracts.org). See this tract for nine suggestions on how to deal with bereavement.

PART FIVE

CONCLUSION

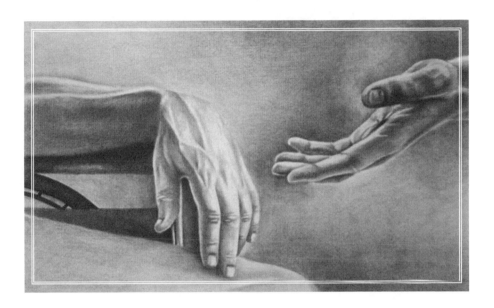

Reaching Out, by Dawn Waters Baker. In this drawing, a person waits in a wheelchair, perhaps one of many veterans who are rarely visited or thanked for all they have done for their country. Many other lonely people, disabled by disease or old age, wait for a visitor or help. A nail-scarred hand, that of Jesus, reaches out to the person in the wheelchair. Jesus was scarred in his earthly body on the cross, and yet he is whole, just as we too will be someday.

22

WHEELCHAIRS IN HEAVEN?

Joni Eareckson Tada

I am a quadriplegic. Forty-three years in this wheelchair is a long time. I just celebrated my sixtieth birthday, and I am a weak person. Do not think I am a veteran. I am no professional. I am no expert at disability. I need Jesus desperately every single day.

My husband, Ken, and I, and all of us at the ministry of Joni and Friends, have a real heart for people with disabilities. But I think Ken and I especially resonate with other quadriplegics. Let me tell you the story of Melissa.

A couple of summers ago Melissa and her husband were heading north to go camping along the edge of the eastern Sierras. Highway 395 is a long stretch, and they were clipping along at a good speed. Both were wearing seatbelts.

About two hours into the journey the boys in the backseat asked if they could have something to drink. Melissa unclipped her seatbelt and leaned over the front seat to rummage through the cooler to find drinks for the boys. It would only take a minute, and then she would be back in her seat and clip the seatbelt back on. In those few seconds of a seven-hour drive, as they were going north, a car coming south turned in front of them. Before her husband could brake, there was a head-on collision, which left Melissa a quadriplegic.

The next few months were very tough for her. I visited her when I was at Northridge Hospital on a routine checkup. I always go into occupational therapy or physical therapy to see who is new there. Melissa was not happy about being there, and the tears in her eyes showed it. Over the next year, there were many pressures—financial, emotional, physical, and marital. Her marriage did not survive, and right now she is in the middle of a custody battle for her children. She is emotionally worn down, physically a wreck, and extremely depressed. She has just about given up.

Life is difficult for Melissa as she struggles to be a mother to her two boys from a wheelchair. Melissa's situation is extremely urgent. Her experience shows that disability ministry is a life-and-death ministry, because this woman is contemplating whether her life is worth living. And I can identify with her. Forty-three years ago, when I broke my neck in a diving accident that left me a quadriplegic, at first I saw no reason to go on.

Back then, I remember when visiting hours were over and the nurses were off duty, I would wrench my head back and forth violently on the pillow hoping to break it up at some higher level, and thereby end my life that way. When I finally got a wheelchair and was learning how to power it down the long hallways, I toyed with the idea of even careening off a high curb and ending my life in that manner. But then I figured I would probably only become brain-injured, and that would make things worse. I was so depressed, I was suicidally despairing. And Melissa has begun to feel the same way.

Yet things are worse for her than they ever were for me over four decades ago. Forty years ago society was not so quick to agree that a person like Melissa or me could make perfectly rational choices if he or she decided to end his or her life. Forty years ago not many doctors bought into the premise that "you are better off dead than disabled." Forty years ago Dr. Jack Kevorkian was not standing in the wings, anxious to help people like me fulfill a death wish. Back then compassion was not three grams of phenobarbital in the veins.

A feeding tube for a quadriplegic like Melissa might be termed "futile care." In fact the hospital that served Melissa has futile-care policies in place. A futile-care policy is a directive that allows a doctor to overrule a family's wishes regarding their loved one's health-care treatment. Who would have ever thought care could be called "futile"? Today's society lacks heart, true heart. And that means that Melissa's life is at risk. People like Melissa—the infirm and the vulnerable—are exposed in a society that has lost its heart, its moral center.

The weak have never fared well in cultures that view life as dispensable. Roughly seventy years ago in Nazi Germany, the first ones to be carted away in the dark from institutions down long hallways in the middle of the night were the weakest of the disabled. Not just any disabled people. No, Nazi medical teams singled out disabled people who had no visitors, no family, no advocates, no friends. No one to dare contend for their lives. No Christians were there to say, "Stop! She bears the image of God, and we will be her spiritual community. We will keep her connected to reality. We will not let her suffer alone."

Seventy years later we are wrestling not simply against health-care reform or hospital ethics committees that wonder whether a person would be better off dead than disabled. No, we wrestle against powers and principalities of a powerful adversary, and our Savior calls that adversary a liar. Our adversary lies by telling people like Melissa that they really would be better off dead than living as a quadriplegic. And the Devil is an accuser. He tries to convince quadriplegics and others that they are a burden to their families and to society.

Jesus called him a murderer (John 8:44). And, in character, Satan seeks to encourage medical personnel to pull every hydration tube and push every three-gram injection of phenobarbital, every so-called "death-with-dignity" act in state assemblies across this nation. Disability ministry is a life-and-death ministry that ought not to be relegated to the bottom rung of some ministry-priority ladder in a church. And this problem exists not just here in America. When I served on the Disability Advisory Committee of the US State Department, I read one shocking report after another. Here is one:

> Disabled children are always at great risk of discrimination and are particularly vulnerable when there is a shortage of resources. An estimated 97% of disabled children in developing countries are denied even the most rudimentary rehabilitation services. . . . Disabled children suffer more violence and abuse than other children—they are imprisoned in institutions, cupboards and sheds and, all too often, starved to death.[1]

And this happens not only to children with disabilities.

Mr. and Mrs. Hill, an elderly couple, are dealing with the early stages of Alzheimer's disease. When they come to our church, sometimes Mrs. Hill has her gray wig a little askew, and Mr. Hill has his red sweater buttoned inside out. Every time I wheel up to them, they always say, "Oh, good morning, dear. And what's your name?" And for the fifteenth time, I say, "Well, Mr. and Mrs. Hill, it's a delight to meet you. My name is Joni."

I thought of the Hills recently when I read a newspaper article titled "The Toll of Alzheimer's Disease," by syndicated columnist Peter Gott.

---

[1] *Report of Rights for Disabled Children*, in *Seen and Heard*, International Disability and Development Consortium, October 1997, quoted in *Disability World*, July–August 2001, accessed http://www.disabilityworld.org/07-08_01/children/global.shtml.

Alzheimer's . . . ends in a catastrophe: extreme confusion, loss of judgment, the inability to recognize loved ones, belligerency, and the failure to be able to carry out everyday chores and activities of daily living (including bathing, dressing, and eating). In the truest sense of the word, the advanced Alzheimer's patient has lost all the qualities that make him or her human.

I wonder how many people read that article yet never noticed that last sentence? When my friend Stephanie Hubach read that last sentence, she observed that the author was saying, in essence, "If you can stay focused, have good judgment, connect with your family, be cooperative, complete your chores, and take care of yourself, then you are human."[2]

Stephanie noted that this statement rules out at least seventeen teenagers she knows. This erosion of human dignity began back in the 1970s with the Supreme Court decision on *Roe v. Wade*. Christian leaders back then warned that society would now change the very definition of what it means to be human. They predicted that eventually there would be such a slippery slope that it would jeopardize everyone's human dignity. And they were right.

The definition now of what it means to be human is being questioned because medical professionals now call infants who are born with multiple disabilities "pre-persons." And individuals in comas are now called "nonpersons." Perhaps a year or two from now someone like Mrs. Hill may be called a "post-person." This shows that little has been learned since the days of Nazi Germany.

Ironically, Germany now has the strongest laws against assisted suicide of people with severe medical conditions, as well as the toughest restrictions against stem-cell research that uses human embryos to kill and then harvest their stem cells. Perhaps this is because Germany experienced firsthand what happens to a society when human dignity is stripped away. Perhaps that country knows all too well what happens when a society loses its moral bearings, when a culture loses its heart.

With no moral compass, society does not know what to do with affliction, pain, and suffering. No biblical gyroscope exists to give balance to someone like Melissa, who is struggling with what it means to be human and to live with severe suffering. Disability in a society that has lost its moral center is viewed as an intrusion to one's comfort and convenience.

Now society has downright contempt for suffering. People do everything to eradicate it, to exorcise it surgically, institutionalize it, give it ibuprofen, divorce it—everything but live with it. And it is only a short philosophical hop,

[2]Stephanie O. Hubach, "The Dignity of Every Human," *By Faith*, December 2006, accessed http://byfaithonline.com/page/in-the-world/the-dignity-of-every-human.

skip, and jump to the point where society also has contempt for people who suffer. Society seems to have no room for Alzheimer's survivors who drain the grandkids' college fund. Society does not seem to have room for people who contribute nothing to it except medical costs.

What is at the root of that thinking? Psalm 10:2 states,

> In his arrogance the wicked man hunts down the weak,
>   who are caught in the schemes he devises. (NIV)

And it becomes a society of survival of the fittest, a society that lacks not just a moral center, but any kind of heart at all. If culture cannot fix it, escape it, sidestep it, avoid it, or institutionalize it, then attempts are made to clone it, cure it, or kill it. And not just the profoundly disabled are at risk. Every person's life is at risk when life can be altered, aborted, or euthanized.

Sometime ago a friend in a wheelchair said, "This is not a slide down the slippery slope. The way to stop it is to draw the line right now, not just because that line is right, but because the very notion of drawing lines is at stake." I think that was the thinking behind the recent Manhattan Declaration.[3] This is a declaration of conscience where that line is now drawn in the sand, which the signers agreed not to cross. This is why disability ministry is critical, for only in the Bible and in the public ministry of Jesus Christ is high value ascribed to people with disabilities.

Jesus often associated with people with handicaps. He reserved his most gentle touch for the blind. He always reached out to the deaf. He stopped to talk to the fathers of little boys with seizures. When Jesus and his disciples were leaving Jericho, a large crowd was following him (Mark 10:46). On the side of the road was a blind man named Bartimaeus, screaming, "Jesus, Son of David, have mercy on me!" (v. 47).

The man was creating a scene. And many rebuked him. Then Jesus stopped. How amazing that the Lord of the universe stopped for the cry of a blind beggar! The disciples called to Bartimaeus, "Cheer up! On your feet! He is calling you" (v. 49, NIV). This is strange, because their usual response was "Shut up!" And now it is "Cheer up!" What accounts for that 180-degree reversal of attitude? The disciples saw this incredibly high value their Master placed on the lives of people with disabilities. And no doubt those disciples never looked at another blind beggar the same way again. When people ask, Why have a disability ministry? the answer is to view the life of Jesus. He modeled it. He is the one

---

[3]See www.manhattandeclaration.org for more information.

who commanded, "When you give a feast, invite the poor, the crippled, the lame, the blind" (Luke 14:13). And later in that same chapter he said, "Compel people to come in, that my house may be filled" (v. 23).

Jesus said that if someone gives a banquet, he should not invite only his rich friends, neighbors, and relatives (v. 12), people he can relate to. No, he should get beyond his comfort zone and go into the streets and the alleys, the highways and the byways, and find the disabled and bring them in (v. 21). The world of disability is not the Devil's domain, though he likes to think it is. The Devil takes things like multiple sclerosis, osteogenesis imperfecta, spinal-cord injury, and muscular dystrophy, and he likes to think those terms are his own. He uses the world of disability to try to defame God's good name, to smear his reputation.

Many people ask, How can God be good if he allows something like this to happen? God is in control of everything from paralyzing accidents to autism, and he permits what he hates in order to accomplish what he loves. He loves showcasing his power from the platform of a person's weakness. Disability ministry may not be a life-and-death ministry for the disabled person, but in a sense it is a life-and-death ministry for the sake of the church. The church does not function as God intended until it is involved in ministry to those with disability. Jesus longs to be gracious, to show compassion on the weak and the needy.

God has a special affection for people with disabilities. He hears the cry of the afflicted (Ps. 10:17). He raises up the poor from the dust (113:7). He lifts the needy like Melissa up from the ash heap of their emotions. He seeks to alleviate the suffering and rescue the fragile, to console the dying and comfort the despairing, to be a friend to and speak up for those who are sometimes too weak or perhaps too infinitesimally small, to speak up for themselves.

God, however, uses the hands and hearts of people like you, because you are the ones who can speak up on behalf of those who are too weak or too vulnerable to speak up for themselves. Believers should not despise suffering. Instead they should see it fitting into the grand scheme of things from God's perspective. Believers should not despise the cross of Christ or the ridicule that it brings. And they should speak up for the destitute, for those who cannot speak for themselves (Prov. 31:8).

Some people may complain about the triumphs of evil, or whine about secular humanism, but believers know that good will ultimately triumph. So we showcase what that good should look like by helping people like Mr. and Mrs. Hill.

Crossroads Community Church in West Covina, California, now provides daycare for the elderly. The women at Monte Vista Presbyterian Church in

Newbury Park, California, are now serving as Melissa's attendants, helping her get up, get bathed and dressed, and face the day with hope. And if a child with autism goes ballistic in Sunday school, then the college and career kids at Pasadena Nazarene Church in Pasadena rotate as that child's buddy. The Evangelical Free Church of Fullerton, California, has a Friday evening class called "Save Our Sanity," in which parents can leave their children with Down syndrome or other disabilities, and trained church volunteers can provide activities for those children while Mom and Dad have a date.

When churches practice this kind of Christianity, people sit up and take notice. Grace Community Church in Sun Valley, California, has received numerous awards from the local United Cerebral Palsy Association for their program called Grace, in which parents can bring their disabled children to church. In the gymnasium, trained volunteers do tumbling and arts and crafts activities with the children while the parents in the Fireside Room hear a lecture from the local Social Security Administration on the benefits for their children. Or a lawyer talks about setting up a trust fund for their children when they get older. Or someone from Shepherd's Home speaks about long-term-care placement opportunities for their children when they get older. Many parents, including unbelievers, come back to church. And many have come to Christ because they see that here is a church that cares about them.

During my tenure on the National Council on Disability under Presidents Reagan and Bush, we authored the first draft of the Americans with Disabilities Act. About a year or two later Congress passed that civil rights legislation. I will never forget when our entire council—all fifteen members—and our executive director, Paul Hearn, were on the south lawn of the White House to witness President Bush sign the Americans with Disabilities Act.

All of us were so excited. We had labored hard to get this law passed. After the signing ceremony there was a reception at the hotel for the council. But at the reception I noticed that Paul was very quiet, sitting off to himself thinking. And then suddenly he said, "I want to propose a toast." He then said, "This is a great law, and it will remove many discriminatory policies in hiring people with disabilities into jobs. And this law will mean that there will be more ramps and widened doorways in restaurants and public accommodations such as theaters and museums. And this law will mean that there will be ramps into restaurants. And it will mean that eventually there will be mechanical lifts on city buses." Then he added, "But this law will not change the hearts of employers. This law will not change the hearts of maitre d's in restaurants, or theater owners. The law will not change the hearts of the bus drivers. So here's a toast to changed hearts."

At that point I could hardly keep from crying. Even now I get tears just talking about it. Christians have the means and the methods by which to change the hearts of people, and it is at that level that a nation's heart is changed. People's hearts will not be changed by the Americans with Disabilities Act, or by health-care reform. People's hearts will not be changed by new legislation, city proclamations, or state declarations. Only the gospel of Jesus Christ can change people's hearts, and the laws and public policies that undergird those laws rest on the hearts of the people. People's hearts need to be changed by the marvelous gospel that showcases the love of Jesus Christ for the weakest and most needy among us.

I have been talking about those with disabilities, but I am actually talking about all of us. When I hear my girlfriend in the kitchen running water for coffee, and I know she will come into the bedroom to give me a bed bath, get me dressed, and sit me up in my wheelchair, I'm thinking, "Oh, God, I'm so tired! I don't think I can face one more day of quadriplegia. I'm already thinking about how wonderful it will feel when my head is back on this pillow tonight. But, Lord, I need to give a smile to this girl who is ready to get me up. So, Lord Jesus, please give me your smile. I cannot 'do' quadriplegia, but I can do all things through you who strengthens me."

If God's grace can send a smile straight from heaven at 7:35 in the morning, before I have even gotten out of bed, then we all ought to be boasting in our affliction. We all ought to be delighting in our infirmities. We all ought to be glorying in our weaknesses, for then we too can be convinced that God's power can show up best in our lives also. And is that not what people with disabilities can teach the church? Sometimes I think people with disabilities are God's best audiovisual aid for other believers to understand that weakness is something for which we can be thankful. For then we know Christ's power rests on us, and God always seems bigger to those who need him most.

Believers often forget that. That is why God has people like me, and the child with Down syndrome, and the woman with multiple sclerosis. That is why he has us packing the pews with our wheelchairs, our white canes, and our walkers. We are the best audiovisual aid for the Lord Jesus. So disability ministry is not just a life-and-death ministry for people like Melissa; it is, as I've said, a life-and-death ministry for the church. Churches need to view people with disabilities as truly indispensable, because through them the church learns how to serve sacrificially.

I know Melissa lies broken and bruised; her heart-wrenching circumstances are not getting easier. She is a very weak woman, who has yet to realize how indispensable she is in a culture that has yet to realize its heartlessness. Recently I wrote her this letter:

> Dear Melissa, I can appreciate the fact that you just do not want to go on; really, I can. When Jesus said that in this world we will have trouble, you know what? He was right. Life is full of trouble, and there are days when I wake up, even now after all these years, and I think, "Jesus, I don't have the strength." But Melissa, the weaker I am physically, the harder I have to lean on the Lord. And the harder I lean on Him, the stronger I discover Him to be. God always seems bigger to those who need Him most. He is drawn to people like you and me. He has a special heart for the weak.
>
> You are not better off dead than disabled, and I will tell you flat out, I would rather be in this chair knowing Him than on my feet without Him. I will be praying for you over the next few weeks, asking God to aid and comfort you, that the Lord Jesus—the Bread of Life, the Resurrection and the Life, He who has the words of life, and who is the Way, the Truth, and the Life—will help you to want to live.

That is the message that will change Melissa's heart, and it is the message that with prayer and with your helping hands and heart will change the soul of society and the heart of this nation.

I am looking forward to going to heaven. I long for heaven with such eagerness and anticipation. When I occasionally look at home movies of me on my feet, I never think, "Oh, I wish it were like that!" No. There are too many years between me and that. There are far fewer years between me and my new glorified body, so it is kind of exciting. All of my memories of what it was like to be on my feet are very hopeful memories, because they inspire hope for the future, which is so exciting.

I cannot wait for that day when the Lord comes back. In his first advent he dealt with people with disabilities by healing the lame, touching the sick, opening the eyes of the blind. And all those miracles were proofs, as it were, of his messiahship during his first advent. Perhaps he may do the same during his second advent, when he comes back as King of kings and Lord of lords. I have a feeling that he will showcase himself around the disabled then too.

> Then the eyes of the blind shall be opened,
>   and the ears of the deaf unstopped;
> then shall the lame man leap like a deer,
>   and the tongue of the mute sing for joy. (Isa. 35:5–6)

The lame will leap like a deer. Wild and tame animals will be together, "and a little child will lead them" (Isa. 11:6). This child may well be a child now with Down syndrome. When I receive my new glorified body, I will have such fun jumping, dancing, kicking, and doing aerobics!

I hope in some way I can take my wheelchair to heaven. With my new glorified body I will stand up on resurrected legs, and I will be next to the Lord Jesus. And I will feel those nail prints in his hands, and I will say, "Thank you, Jesus!" He will know I mean it, because he will recognize me from the inner sanctum of sharing in the fellowship of his sufferings. He will see that I was one who identified with him in the sharing of his sufferings, so my gratitude will not be hollow.

And then I will say, "Lord Jesus, do you see that wheelchair over there? Well, you were right. When you put me in it, it was a lot of trouble. But the weaker I was in that thing, the harder I leaned on you. And the harder I leaned on you, the stronger I discovered you to be. I do not think I would ever have known the glory of your grace were it not for the weakness of that wheelchair. So thank you, Lord Jesus, for that. Now, if you like, you can send that thing off to hell."

General Index

Scripture Index